Best Rail Trails
CALIFORNIA

Praise for the previous edition

"There's no better guide for these multipurpose trails. Like the Rails-to-Trails system, this series is a service that's long overdue."

—Sarah Parsons, Associate Editor, *Sports Afield*

"Recreation trails are one of America's great outdoor secrets, but probably won't be for much longer thanks to the [Best Rail Trails] Series. Now adventurers of all abilities have an excellent guide to help them enjoy all that the paths have to offer."

—Stephen Madden, Editor in Chief, *Outdoor Explorer*

Help Us Keep This Guide Up to Date

Every effort has been made by the author and editors to make this guide as accurate and useful as possible. However, many things can change after a guide is published—hiking trails are rerouted, establishments close, phone numbers change, facilities come under new management, and so on.

We would love to hear from you concerning your experiences with this guide and how you feel it could be improved and kept up to date. While we may not be able to respond to all comments and suggestions, we'll take them to heart and we'll also make certain to share them with the author. Please send your comments and suggestions to the following address:

The Globe Pequot Press
Reader Response/Editorial Department
P.O. Box 480
Guilford, CT 06437

Or you may e-mail us at:

editorial@GlobePequot.com

Thanks for your input, and happy trails!

Best Rail Trails
CALIFORNIA

More Than 70 Rail Trails Throughout the State

TRACY SALCEDO-CHOURRÉ

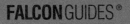

FALCONGUIDES®

GUILFORD, CONNECTICUT
HELENA, MONTANA
AN IMPRINT OF THE GLOBE PEQUOT PRESS

FOR MY PARENTS

FALCONGUIDES®

Copyright © 2001, 2008 by Morris Book Publishing, LLC

Portions of this book were previously published as *Rail-to-Trails California*.

Text design: Lesley Weissman-Cook
Maps: Tim Kissel/Trailhead Graphics, Inc.; © The Globe Pequot Press.
The map on page 148 was adapted from a map in *Explore the Forest of Nisene Marks,*
written by Jeff Thomson, and published by Walkabout Publications.

Photo credits: All photos are by Tracy Salcedo-Chourré. The photo on page 15 depicts the Hammond Coastal Trail; page 73, the Sir Francis Drake Bike Path; page 161, the Truckee River Trail; page 195, the Ojai Valley Trail; and page 219, the Hermosa Valley Greenbelt.

Library of Congress Cataloging-in-Publication Data
Salcedo-Chourré, Tracy.
    Best rail trails California : more than 70 rail trails throughout the state /
Tracy Salcedo-Chourré. — 1st ed.
            p. cm.
    ISBN 978-0–7627–4677-4
    1. Rail-trails—California—Guidebooks. 2. Hiking—California—Guidebooks. I.
Title.
    GV199.42.C2S25 2008
    917.94—dc22
                                            2008027729
Printed in the United States of America
10 9 8 7 6 5 4 3 2 1

The Globe Pequot Press and the author assume no liability for accidents happening to or injuries sustained by readers who engage in the activities described in this book.

CONTENTS

ACKNOWLEDGMENTS

As you peruse this book, you will see that a trail manager is mentioned for each hike. These managers and their staffs, as well as the historians and other experts to whom they referred me, were critical to the compilation of this guidebook. They are too numerous to name here, but my heartfelt thanks go out to each and every one of them.

The first edition of this guide was compiled with information provided by the Rails-to-Trails Conservancy staff. My thanks for their help, as well as for the thoughtful comments of the readers of the first edition who took the time to correct or augment trail descriptions and historical information.

Thanks also to Jesse Chourré for his steady assistance negotiating the traffic and trails of the mazelike Los Angeles region, and to Cruz Chourré for his help in gathering details about the trail through the Sonoma Regional Park. Mark Keppler, who provided thoughtful additions to the trail description for the Fresno Sugar Pine and Clovis Old Town Trails also has earned my gratitude.

Thanks also to Jeff Serena and the editors at The Globe Pequot Press, especially Shelley Wolf, for their infinite patience and for thinking of me when this project was proposed.

Finally, I would like to acknowledge my debt to my husband, Martin, and my sons, Jesse, Cruz, and Penn, who were real troupers as we crisscrossed California hiking and cycling these trails. Without their love and support, this book would not have been possible.

INTRODUCTION

In a state as large and diverse as California, it should come as no surprise that its rail trails run the gamut. Trails in the mountains, trails along the beach. Trails in the boondocks, trails in the city. Trails that stretch for miles and miles, trails little more than a block in length. Trails steeped in the history of the railroads that once ran on the grades, trails that run alongside active railroad lines. They all are here, and they all are intriguing.

California can be divided into distinct regions that vary greatly not only in topography but also culturally. The rail trails in each region show-

The Merced River Trail is one of the most challenging and beautiful rail trails in California.

case the landscape and offer insight into the temperaments of the people who live there.

In northern California, the land is rugged and densely forested, from the high country surrounding Paradise and Lassen Volcanic National Park all the way west to the beaches at Fort Bragg and Eureka. The railroads punched through these woodlands were primarily used for logging, so the trails that now run along them thread through thick stands of timber and snake through spectacular river canyons.

In the San Francisco Bay Area, city and country struggle to find balance. The beauty of the landscape—oak woodlands, rolling hills, and redwood forests that stretch toward the ocean—is integral to the draw of the region, and Bay Area residents grapple daily with the issue of preservation versus development. Their dedication to preserving quality of life shows in the number and quality of the rail trails that have been established here. From the relative seclusion of the Sir Francis Drake Bikeway and the Loma Prieta Grade to the more urban but equally appealing Ohlone Greenway and Tiburon Linear Park, the trails in the area are superlative.

Eastward, in the Sierra Nevada, the terrain folds sharply upward from the flats of the Central Valley toward high snowy peaks. Most of the rail trails in this region lie in the foothills—Gold Country—again following the grades of railroads that served either logging or mining interests. These are perhaps the most challenging of all California's rail trails, for they have been shaped by the steepness of the mountains through which they run. Some, like the Truckee River Bike Trail, are extremely popular and often crowded; others, like the West Side Rails from Hull Creek to Clavey River, venture into remote areas, where you will be lucky to find another soul on the trail.

The trails of Central California, a diverse region that, for the purposes of this guide, stretches from Monterey down the coast to Ventura and inland to Fresno and Bakersfield, are an eclectic bunch. The Monterey Peninsula Recreational Trail is a well-established regional attraction, the Ventura River Trail takes travelers from the sea to the fancy boutiques and eateries of Ojai, and trails in the Central Valley burg of Fresno do double duty as recreational outlets and commuter routes.

Southern California, in spite of its notorious love affair with the automobile, has established an intriguing system of rail trails. Often the focal point of linear parks, like the charming Electric Avenue Median Park, these trails are urban or suburban in nature and serve primarily as commuter or neighborhood paths. There are two stunning exceptions to this general rule: the Mount Lowe Railway Trail, which climbs into the steep San Gabriel Mountains, offering unsurpassed views of the Los Angeles basin; and the Bayshore Bikeway, a breathtaking stretch of trail that traces the narrow strip of land separating San Diego Bay from the Pacific Ocean.

A Slice of California's Railroad History

California fostered a love affair with the railways that blossomed around the turn of the twentieth century and lasted until the automobile began its ascendance in the 1930s. The Golden State's railroads served a number of industries in California, but those that have been converted to rail trails came primarily from two classes: railroads that moved timber and railroads that moved people.

The gold that drew men by the thousands to California played out relatively quickly, but the forests held another, seemingly limitless source of wealth: trees. Vast forests carpeted the Sierra Nevada, the Coast Ranges, and much of northern California, and the American philosophy of manifest

The Depot Historical Museum on the Sonoma Bike Path preserves Sonoma's railroading past.

destiny that drove settlers westward demanded, for better or worse, that these resources be utilized. A number of railroads in the state were established to serve logging industries, including the Hammond/Little River Railroad in Eureka, the Fernley and Lassen Branch of the Southern Pacific, and the Loma Prieta Lumber Company Railroad, all of which are now spectacular rail trails.

Transporting passengers from city to city, and from place to place within large urban areas, also proved a lucrative endeavor for California railroads. Some of the rail lines established for this purpose blossomed into mini empires, like the Pacific Electric Railway system, which ran its famous Red Cars throughout the Los Angeles area during the early 1900s. Many of the rail trails now in place in the Los Angeles basin have been built on former Pacific Electric grades.

The lines of smaller interurban railroads, many of which were electric, also have made significant contributions to California's rail trail system. Two of these systems—the Sacramento Northern Railway system, which ran north from Sacramento to Chico and east into the San Francisco Bay Area, and the Northwestern Pacific Railroad complex, which served the North Bay—enjoyed great success and popularity in the early part of the twentieth century. They both suffered increasing losses beginning in the 1930s that were attributed to the Great Depression and the increasing popularity of the automobile. The systems were gradually abandoned, and some of their tracks scrapped during World War II, but their legacy lives on in wonderful trails like the Sonoma Bike Path and the Lafayette–Moraga Trail in the Bay Area, and the Sacramento Northern Bike Trail in Sacramento.

The History of the Rails-to-Trails Conservancy

As road construction and increased reliance on cars forced railroads to the sidelines, the question arose: What to do with all the abandoned tracks that crisscrossed the state?

Enter the Rails-to-Trails Conservancy, an environmental group that since 1986 has campaigned to convert the railroad tracks to nature paths.

The beauty of the Rails-to-Trails Conservancy (RTC) is that by converting the railroad rights-of-way to public use, it has not only preserved a part of our nation's history, but has provided a variety of outdoor enthusiasts with miles of paths and trails to enjoy. Bicyclists, in-line skaters, nature lovers, hikers, equestrians, and cross-country skiers enjoy California's rail trails, as do railroad history buffs. There is truly something for everyone on these trails, many of which are wheelchair accessible.

In California, there are more than seventy-four rail trails in place, and more are slated to come online each year. Some are so secluded you can imagine yourself a pioneer arriving with the first iron horses, others are meshed completely in the urban landscape, and many combine aspects of both, offering users a diverse experience.

The concept of preserving these valuable corridors and converting them into multiuse public trails began in the Midwest, where railroad abandonments were most widespread. Once the tracks came out, people started using the corridors for walking, hiking, and exploring the railroad relics that were left along the rail beds, including train stations, mills, trestles, bridges, and tunnels.

Although it was easy to convince people that the rails-to-trails concept was worthwhile, the reality of converting abandoned railroad corridors into public trails proved a great challenge. From the late 1960s until

A family enjoys the Larkspur–Corte Madera Path.

the early 1980s, many rail trail efforts failed as corridors were lost to development, sold to the highest bidder, or broken into many pieces.

In 1983, Congress enacted an amendment to the National Trails System Act directing the Interstate Commerce Commission to allow about-to-be abandoned railroad lines to be "railbanked," or set aside for future transportation use while being used as trails in the interim. In essence, this law preempts rail corridor abandonment, keeping the corridors intact as trails or for other transportation uses into the future.

This powerful new piece of legislation made it easier for public and private agencies and organizations to acquire rail corridors for trails, but many projects still failed because of short deadlines, lack of information, and local opposition.

In 1986, the Rails-to-Trails Conservancy was formed to provide a national voice for the creation of rail trails. The RTC quickly developed a strategy that was designed to preserve the largest amount of rail corridor in the shortest period of time. A national advocacy program was formed to defend the new railbanking law in the courts and in Congress; this was coupled with a direct project-assistance program to help public agencies and local rail trail groups overcome the challenges of converting a rail into a trail.

The strategy works well. In 1986, the Rails-to-Trails Conservancy knew of only seventy-five rail trails in the United States, and there were ninety projects in the works. As of summer 2007, according to the RTC Web site, more than 1,400 trails were on the ground, spanning over 13,500 miles; another 1,200 (or so) rail trail projects were identified that would more than double the existing miles of trail. The RTC vision of creating an interconnected network of trails across the country has become a reality.

Benefits of Rail Trails

Rail trails are flat or have gentle grades, making them perfect for multiple users, from walkers and bicyclists to in-line skaters and people with disabilities. In snowy climates, people enjoy cross-country skiing, snowmobiling, and other snow activities on the trails.

In urban areas, rail trails act as linear greenways through developed areas, efficiently providing much-needed recreation space while serving

Cyclists stop to check out the sights along the Tiburon Linear Park rail trail.

as utilitarian transportation corridors. They link neighborhoods and workplaces and connect congested areas to open spaces. In many cities and suburbs, rail trails are used for commuting to work and provide students with safe routes to school.

Rail trails, along with other recreational amenities, have proven to be a significant stimulus to local businesses. People who use trails spend money on food, beverages, camping, hotels, bed-and-breakfasts, bicycle rentals, souvenirs, and other local products and services. The financial benefits bolster town coffers and even boost property values.

Rail trails allow for the preservation of historic structures, such as train stations, bridges, tunnels, mills, factories, and canals. These structures shelter an important piece of history and enhance the trail experience.

Wildlife enthusiasts also enjoy the benefits of rail trails, which provide habitats for birds, plants, wetland species, and a variety of small and large mammals. Many rail trails serve as plant and animal conservation corridors; in some cases, endangered species can be found in habitats located along the routes.

Recreation, transportation, historic preservation, economic revitalization, open space conservation, and wildlife preservation—these are just some of the many benefits of rail trails and the reasons people love them.

The strongest argument for the rails-to-trails movement, however, is ultimately about the human spirit. It's about the dedication of individuals who have a dream and follow that vision so that other people can enjoy the fruits of their labor.

How to Get Involved

If you really enjoy rail trails, join the movement to save abandoned rail corridors and create more routes. Donating even a small amount of your time can help get more trails on the ground. Here are some ways you can help the effort:

- Write a letter to your city, county, or state elected official in favor of pro-trail legislation. You can also write a letter to the editor of your local newspaper highlighting a trail or trail project.

- Attend a public hearing to voice support for a local trail.

- Volunteer to plant flowers or trees along an existing trail or to spend time helping a cleanup crew on a rail trail project.

- Lead a hike along an abandoned corridor with your friends or a community group.

- Become an active member of a trail effort in your area. Many groups host trail events, undertake fund-raising campaigns, publish brochures and newsletters, and carry out other activities to promote a trail or project. Virtually all of these efforts are organized and staffed by volunteers, and there is always room for another helping hand.

California is part of the Rails-to-Trails Conservancy's Western Region; the regional office is located at 26 O'Farrell Street, Suite 400, San Francisco, CA 94108; the phone number is (415) 397–2220. Follow the links on the RTC Web site, www.railstotrails.org, to contact the office via e-mail.

The RTC Web site is a rich source of information on everything to do with rail trails, from how to find a trail to how to build a trail. If rail trails are your passion, this is the site to visit and the organization to join. The address is 1100 17th Street NW, 10th Floor, Washington, D.C., 20036; the phone number is (202) 331–9696.

When available, contact information for each of the rail trails in this guide has been included with the trail listing. You can support rail trail development—and other kinds of trail and open-space development— by contacting these organizations as well.

Whatever your time and pocketbook allows, get involved. The success of a community's trail system, including its rail trails, depends on the dedication and energy of its citizens. It's time and money well spent.

Some Notes on Rail trails in this Guide

Rail trails in California are proliferating like proverbial rabbits, some with the help of the Rails-to-Trails Conservancy, and some outside the RTC's purview. As this guide went to press, I had heard about more than twenty rail trail projects in various stages of development, from those in the final stages of construction to those that are still dreams in the minds of cyclists and trail advocates. I've kept notes on all these projects, and hope to explore and describe each over time.

Given the rapid and ongoing evolution of California's rail trail system, this guide cannot be comprehensive. In addition to those that will come online after this guide's publication, there may be rail trails on the ground, such as the Sonoma Regional Park Path in my own backyard, that utilize former railroad rights-of-way but are so obscure that even local governing agencies aren't aware of them. Regional cycling coalitions are excellent resources for identifying trails on railroad grades. If you hear of any trails that deserve exploration in future editions of this guide, please contact The Globe Pequot Press; the information will be forwarded to me.

A final observation: Some of the trails in this guide are rail trails by virtue of the fact that they are built on abandoned railroad grades; others are technically rails-with-trails, running alongside or in the rights-of-way of active railroad lines. Some are a combination of the two. Trail descriptions make clear the category into which each route falls.

How to Use Rail Trails

By design, rail trails accommodate a variety of trail users. While this is generally one of the many benefits of rail trails, it also can lead to occasional conflicts. Everyone should take responsibility to ensure trail safety by following a few simple trail etiquette guidelines.

One of the most basic etiquette rules is "Wheels yield to heels." The figure below indicates the correct protocol for yielding right-of-way. Bicyclists (and in-line skaters) yield to other users; pedestrians yield to equestrians.

Generally, this means that you need to warn the users to whom you are yielding of your presence. If, as a bicyclist, you fail to warn a walker that you are about to pass, the walker could step in front of you, causing an accident that easily could have been prevented. Similarly, it is best to slow down and warn an equestrian of your presence. A horse can be startled by a bicycle, so make verbal contact with the rider and be sure it is safe to pass.

Here are some other guidelines you should follow to promote trail safety:

- Obey all trail rules posted at trailheads.

- Stay to the right except when passing.

- Pass slower traffic on the left; yield to oncoming traffic when passing.

- Give a clear warning signal when passing.

- Always look ahead and behind when passing.

- Travel at a responsible speed.

- Keep pets on a leash.

- Do not trespass on private property.

- Move off the trail surface when stopped to allow other users to pass.

- Yield to other trail users when entering and crossing the trail.

- Do not disturb wildlife.

- Do not swim in areas not designated for swimming.

- Watch out for traffic when crossing the street.

- Obey all traffic signals.

How to Use This Book

At the beginning of each chapter, you will find a map showing the location of the rail trails within that region. The main rail trails featured in this book include basic maps for your convenience. It is recommended, however, that street maps, topographic maps such as USGS quads, or a state atlas be used to supplement the maps in this guide. The text description of every trail begins with the following information:

Trail name: The official name of the rail trail.

Activities: A list of icons tells you what kinds of activities are appropriate for each trail.

Location: The towns and counties through which the trail passes.

Length: The length of the trail, including how many miles are currently open and, for those trails that are built on partially abandoned corridors, the number of miles actually on the rail line.

Surface: The materials that make up a rail trail vary from trail to trail. This section describes each trail's surface. Materials range from asphalt and crushed stone to the significantly more rugged original railroad ballast.

Wheelchair access: Some of the rail trails are wheelchair accessible. This allows physically challenged individuals the opportunity to explore the rail trails with family and friends.

Difficulty: The rail trails range from very easy to hard, depending on the grade of the trail and the general condition of the trail. The difficulty ratings assigned—easy, moderate, and hard—have been derived with all possible users in mind and are relative to one another. Some may think it absurd that San Diego's scenic Bayshore Bikeway has been rated "hard," given that it's a perfectly flat, easy bike ride, but for a hiker or in-line skater, the length of the route alone moves it out of the "easy" category. Additionally, it must be scored relative to other rail trails in the state. To place the Bayshore Bikeway, at 18 miles round-trip, in the same "easy" category as the Sonoma Bike Path, at 2 miles round-trip, wouldn't make sense.

Food: The book indicates the names of towns near the rail trails in which restaurants, grocery stores, and fast-food shops are located.

Restrooms: If a restroom is available near the trail, the book provides you with its location.

Seasons: Most of these trails are open year-round, but special circumstances, such as severe winter rains or localized flooding, may preclude the use of certain routes during some seasons.

Access and parking: The book provides you with directions to the rail trails and describes parking availability.

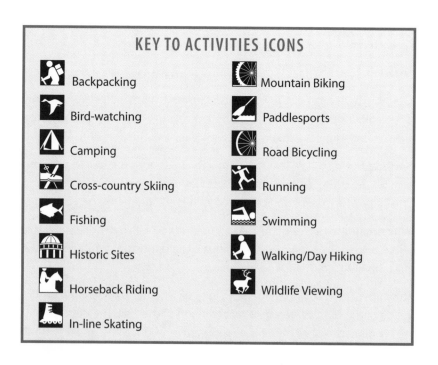

KEY TO ACTIVITIES ICONS

Backpacking

Bird-watching

Camping

Cross-country Skiing

Fishing

Historic Sites

Horseback Riding

In-line Skating

Mountain Biking

Paddlesports

Road Bicycling

Running

Swimming

Walking/Day Hiking

Wildlife Viewing

Transportation: Contact information for public transit in each area is provided, including phone numbers and Web sites when available.

Rentals: Some of the rail trails have bicycle shops and skating stores nearby. This will help you locate bike or skate rentals, or a shop in which you can have repairs made if you have problems with your equipment.

Contact: The name and contact information for each trail manager is listed. The selected contacts are generally responsible for managing the trail and can provide additional information about the trail and its condition.

Following these categories is a narrative trail description that provides an overview and historical facts, and traces the trail, giving mile-by-mile highlights.

Legend

Local Roads	4N01
State Roads	151
U.S. Highway	101
Interstate	5
Main Route	
Other Trail	
Railroad	
State Line	
County Line	
Creeks	
Rivers	
Park/Open Space	
Gate	
Dam	
Picnic	
Rentals	R
Parking	P
Camping	
Restrooms	
Point of Interest	
Start/End	START END
North Arrow	N
Scale	0 1 2

Best Rail Trails
NORTHERN CALIFORNIA

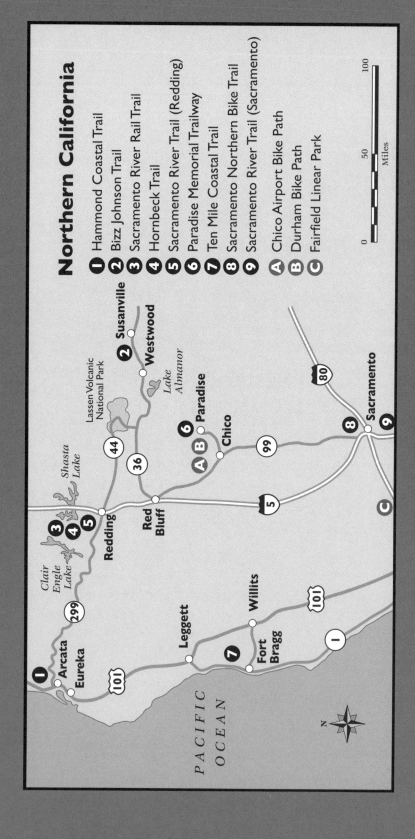

Northern California

1. Hammond Coastal Trail
2. Bizz Johnson Trail
3. Sacramento River Rail Trail
4. Hornbeck Trail
5. Sacramento River Trail (Redding)
6. Paradise Memorial Trailway
7. Ten Mile Coastal Trail
8. Sacramento Northern Bike Trail
9. Sacramento River Trail (Sacramento)

A. Chico Airport Bike Path
B. Durham Bike Path
C. Fairfield Linear Park

Northern California's
Top Rail Trails

1 HAMMOND COASTAL TRAIL

Although the north coast of California usually brings to mind towering old-growth redwood forests, the Hammond Coastal Trail showcases the spectacular beaches that stretch along the coastline.

Activities:

Location: McKinleyville, Humboldt County

Length: 5 miles one way. Three miles of the trail extend from the Mad River Bridge north to Widow White Creek; an additional 2 miles stretch north from Widow White to Clam Beach County Park.

Surface: Asphalt and crushed stone.

Wheelchair access: The 3 miles of trail between the Mad River Bridge and Widow White Creek are suitable for wheelchair users; the section from Clam Beach south to the vista point is also wheelchair accessible.

Difficulty: Moderate. The path is exposed, and the southernmost portion includes some short but steep hills.

Food: You can pick up a snack at Roger's Market, which is near the southern end of the trail at the intersection of Fischer Avenue and School Road. This is also the only place along the route where you will find water, so bring what you need.

Restrooms: There are public restrooms at Hiller Park, which is at about the halfway point of the paved portion of the trail.

Seasons: The trail can be traveled year-round.

Access and parking: To reach the southern end point at Mad River Bridge, from U.S. Highway 101 in McKinleyville, take the Janes Road/Giuntoli Lane exit. Go west on Janes Road for 1.4 miles to Upper Bay Road and turn right (west). Follow Upper Bay Road for 0.7 mile to Mad River Road and turn right (north). The trailhead is at the bridge 2.4 miles north on Mad River Road. There is limited but adequate parking at this trailhead.

To reach the north end of the 3-mile stretch at Widow White Creek, take the Murray Road exit off US 101 and go 0.3 mile west to where Murray Road ends; the trailhead is west of the end of the road. There is ample streetside parking here.

To reach the northern end point of the trail at Clam Beach County Park, continue north on US 101 to the Clam Beach County Park exit. The trail-head is adjacent to the west side of the freeway, tucked in the dunes. There is a large parking lot at the park.

Transportation: Humboldt Transit Authority's Redwood Transit System serves McKinleyville. The address is 133 V Street, Eureka, CA; call (707) 443–0826. The Web sites are www.hta.org and www.redwoodtransit.org.

Rentals: There are no rentals along the trail.

Contact: Parks Department, Humboldt County Department of Public Works, 1106 Second Street, Eureka, CA 95501-0531; (707) 839–2086. You can also contact Jennifer Rice, interim co-director with the Natural Resources Services division of the Redwood Community Action Agency, at (707) 269–2060; www.nrsrcaa.org.

|||||||||||||||||||||||||||||||||||||||||||||||||||||||||||||||||||||||||||||||||||||||||||||||||

The Mad River Bridge is a dramatic launching pad for the Hammond Coastal Trail. The old railroad trestle carries the rail trail through several separate coastal environments, including the pastoral expanses of the Arcata Bottoms, the pleasant neighborhoods on the west side of McKinleyville, shady arbors formed by gnarled shore pines, and the spectacular estuary at the mouth of the Mad River. A tangled riparian zone hugs the shores of Widow White Creek at the end of the southern section of the route. Beyond Widow White Creek, once the site of a gap in the route called the "Hole in the Hammond," the trail arcs west around a vista point to

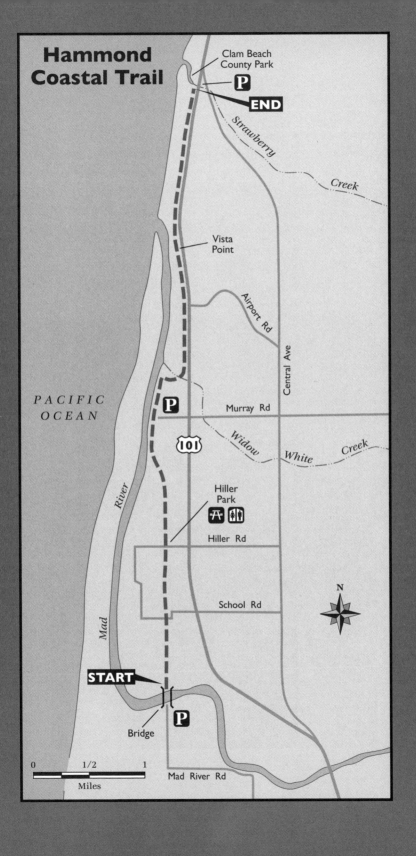

Hammond Coastal Trail

Clam Beach
County Park

P

END

Strawberry

Creek

Vista
Point

Airport Rd

Central Ave

*PACIFIC
OCEAN*

P

Murray Rd

101

Widow

White

Creek

River

Hiller
Park

Hiller Rd

Mad

School Rd

N

START

P

Bridge

0   1/2   1

Miles

Mad River Rd

skirt the beach fronting the Pacific Ocean, passing through rolling dunes to Clam Beach County Park.

Beginning at the turn of the twentieth century, the Hammond/Little River Railroad used the oceanside route to link logging operations in Crannell, east of Clam Beach County Park, with the Hammond Lumber Mill of Eureka. The railroad system was badly damaged in a forest fire in 1945, and, rather than rebuilding the tracks, many of the grades were converted to roadways. The line was abandoned in the late 1950s, and development of the trail, which has been built in segments, began in 1979.

Information about the diverse natural and cultural history of the trail's surroundings, including a discussion of the indigenous Wiyot tribe,

A picnic bench overlooks the Pacific Ocean on the Hammond Coastal Trail.

which thrived in the Humboldt Bay region until the 1850s, when disease and battles with invading settlers resulted in their near extinction, can be found on interpretive signs along the route and on a pedestrian side trail at Widow White Creek.

The trail is described here from the Mad River trestle to Widow White Creek. Another section of the trail has been paved heading south through the dunes near Clam Beach, but the pavement ends before you reach the vista point near Letz Road.

Climb a relatively steep hill from the signed trailhead onto the Mad River Bridge, which affords a wonderful overlook of the tidal river and the verdant bottomlands that surround it. Beyond the bridge, the trail merges with a narrow county road and traverses pastureland to a steep hill at 0.5 mile. Once atop the hill, the trail, which is basically a country lane, runs north through a small community to the intersection of the lane (Fischer Avenue) with School Road at 0.8 mile. Roger's Market sits on the northwest corner of the intersection.

Continue north on Fischer Avenue to the end of the road at 1.1 miles, where the Hammond Trail, which is part of the California Coastal Trail, enters a tree- and blackberry-lined greenbelt that runs between homes. At 1.4 miles, you will cross Hiller Road and enter Hiller Park, which boasts a playground, ball fields, and restrooms. The trail skirts the east side of the park, then passes a gate and again is contained within a lush greenbelt lined with ferns and overhung with evergreens.

At about the 2.4-mile mark, the rail trail crosses Kelly Street amid a cluster of elaborate homes that resemble castles. Pass a picnic bench that offers wonderful views of the Pacific Ocean and the narrow line of dunes that separate it from the placid Mad River. The paved path is etched into the bluff overlooking the ocean until it arcs sharply east at 2.7 miles and ends on Murray Road.

Follow the obvious railroad grade for another third of a mile to the north to Widow White Creek. An interpretive pedestrian trail explores the creek; the rail trail continues north, across Letz Road and past a lovely vista point. Beyond the viewpoint, the route traces US 101 and the scenic beachfront to Clam Beach County Park at the 5-mile mark.

2 BIZZ JOHNSON TRAIL

The Bizz Johnson Trail is one of California's longest rail trails and arguably the most scenic. The wonderful route leads through the dense woodlands of the high country into the spectacular Susan River canyon, and incorporates numerous historic sites, including trestles and tunnels.

Activities:

Location: From Westwood to Susanville in Lassen County

Length: 25 miles one way

Surface: Gravel and original ballast

Wheelchair access: There is limited wheelchair access at the Susanville end point.

Difficulty: Hard

Food: There is no food or water available along the trail, so be sure to pack what you need. Restaurants and grocery stores can be found in Susanville.

Restrooms: There are restrooms at the Susanville Depot, at Devils Corral, and in Goumaz.

Seasons: This trail can be used year-round, although it can be difficult to use when it is muddy. The Westwood end of the trail generally has snow on it from December to March.

Access and parking: There is abundant parking available at both Mason Station Depot in Westwood and the Susanville Depot in Susanville, and at the trailheads at Goumaz and Devils Corral. All trailheads can be reached from California 36, which runs between Chester and Susanville.

To reach the Mason Station trailhead, turn north off of CA 36 onto Lassen County Road A–21. Follow CR A–21 north for 3 miles to the intersection with Lassen County Road 101, which breaks off to the right (northeast) and is signed for the Bizz Johnson Trail. Follow CR 101 for about a quarter of a mile to the trailhead, which is on the left (northwest) side of the dirt road.

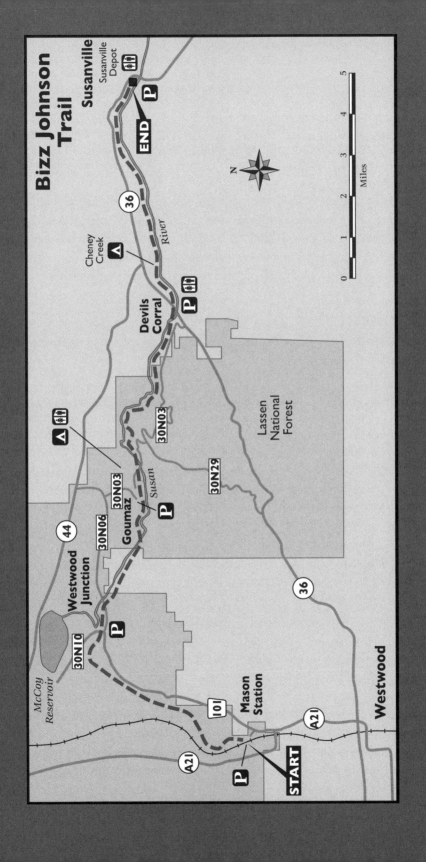

To reach the Goumaz trailhead, continue east on CA 36 from Westwood to the summit of Fredonyer Pass and turn left (north) onto Lassen Forest Road 30N29. Follow this road north for 6 miles to the Goumaz trailhead. The Devils Corral trailhead, which is well signed, is on the south side of CA 36 just east of where the highway crosses the Susan River at the base of the pass.

To reach the Susanville Depot and the eastern end point, follow Main Street to its intersection with Weatherlow Street. Turn south on Weatherlow Street; this becomes Richmond Road. Richmond Road continues south to the depot, which is on the left (southeast) side of the road; more parking and a formal trailhead are located across the street by the caboose.

Transportation: The Lassen Rural Bus provides transportation for those who want to shuttle between Susanville and Devils Corral, Fredonyer Pass, or Westwood. Bus schedules are available from the Lassen Rural Bus service (530–252–7433).

Rentals: You can rent bicycles at The Bike Depot, which is located at 702 Main Street in Susanville. Call (530) 257–2525 for more information or to reserve a bike.

Contact: Stanley Bales, Bureau of Land Management, Eagle Lake Field Office, 2950 Riverside Drive, Susanville, CA 96130; (530) 257–0456; www.blm .gov/ca/st/en/fo/eaglelake/bizztrail.html. Lisa Sedlacek, Recreation Officer, USFS Eagle Lake Ranger District, 477–050 County Road A1 (Eagle Lake Road), Susanville, CA 96130; (530) 252–5861. Lassen Land & Trails Trust, Susanville Depot, 601 Richmond Road, Susanville; (530) 257–3252; www .bizzjohnsontrail.com. Lassen County Chamber of Commerce, P.O. Box 338, Susanville, CA 96130; (530) 257–4323; www.visitlassen.com. Lassen County Visitor Center at the replica of the Westwood Railroad Depot, 462–885 Birch Street, Westwood, CA 96137; (530) 256–2456.

|||||||||||||||||||||||||||||||||||||||||||||||||||||||||||||||||||||||||||||||||||||||||

Of all the jewels in the rail trail system of California, the Bizz Johnson Trail is among the brightest and most beautiful.

Like any quality gem, the Bizz Johnson Trail has many facets. Up high, near Westwood, it is a meditative track that cuts a straight line through the thick woodlands east of Lassen Volcanic National Park. The route passes stations that once bustled with the loggers and millers who supplied the business of the railroad; these stations are now lonely outposts marked by white signs.

The trail picks up speed, much as the trains used to, after it meets the Susan River near Westwood Junction. The river dives into a canyon and out of sight as the descent steepens, and the trail whistles past spills of black talus and cliffs of orange rock. Beyond the Goumaz station, at about the midpoint of the trail, the pitch mellows and the trail slips out of the forest into a broad valley, then down to meet the river again at Devils Corral.

A sign announces Westwood Junction on the Bizz Johnson Trail.

On its easternmost leg, the rail trail runs alongside the Susan River, a broad waterway that has sliced a lovely canyon through the foothills of the mountains. The railroad carved a parallel path, plunging through rock outcrops that barred its passage, necessitating the construction of long, dark tunnels that add mystery and history to the journey.

The trail rides atop the former Fernley and Lassen branch of the Southern Pacific Railroad. This line, and a number of spurs in the high country, served the thriving lumbering community that worked the dense forests of Lassen County in the early part of the twentieth century. Established in 1914, the railroad operated for more than forty years, transporting logs, milled lumber, and people from Westwood to Fernley, Nevada, and to points in between.

The last train ran on the line in 1956, and Southern Pacific abandoned the line in 1978. That was when the Rails-to-Trails Conservancy, along with Congressman Harold "Bizz" Johnson (for whom the trail is named), the Bureau of Land Management, the U.S. Forest Service, and a number of community groups set to work converting the old line into a trail. Their hard work paid off in a big way, resulting in one of the best long-distance trails in the state.

The entire trail can be ridden one-way via mountain bike or horseback comfortably in a single day. If you are on a bike, you can take advantage of the Lassen Rural Bus or make other arrangements for a shuttle back to the original trailhead. You can also enjoy the trail in segments on foot, wheels, or hooves. The most popular short route heads west out of Susanville into the Susan River canyon, where you will find the railroad tunnels and a number of swimming holes that are especially inviting in late summer when the weather is warm and the river is placid.

The trail is described in its entirety as a downhill run from Mason Station in Westwood to the Susanville Depot. A short connector trail leads from the parking area and informational billboard to the trail proper, which lies adjacent to the existing tracks of the Burlington Northern Santa Fe Railroad. This is Mason Station, marked with an interpretive sign. Indeed, you will find that this section of the Bizz Johnson Trail is very well signed and interpreted, with posts at regular intervals as well as mile markers designating the distance of the remote stations from Southern Pacific's base station in the San Francisco Bay Area.

The Susanville Depot

Located at the eastern end point of the Bizz Johnson Trail, the Susanville Depot is a great place to learn more about the history of the rail line that served the area. Built in 1913, the depot was destroyed by fire in 1989, but an addition built in 1927 survived the blaze and now serves as both depot and visitor center. Inside, you'll find educational displays and an abundance of information about the area, as well as souvenirs and a friendly and knowledgeable staff. The depot is open year-round, Monday to Friday, from 9 A.M. to 5 P.M., and on weekends from May to October, and can be reached by calling (530) 257–3252.

The Lassen Land & Trails Trust (LLTT), a nonprofit organization that helps preserve land and restore historic sites throughout Lassen County, operates out of the depot. The LLTT and the city of Susanville, along with the Bureau of Land Management and the U.S. Forest Service, have invested a lot of energy in the development and promotion of the Bizz Johnson Trail, and celebrate annually with a Rails-to-Trails Festival. This popular autumn event features great food, railroad handcar racing, arts and crafts, and, of course, hiking and cycling activities on the rail trail. The festival is a fund-raiser for the land trust. Call the Susanville Depot at (530) 257–3252 for information.

Head east along the open swath through the forest, passing Facht Station and Lasco Station, and crossing a couple of Forest Service roads. The trail climbs almost imperceptibly as it follows long straightaways and sweeping turns through the forest, arriving at Westwood Junction at the 7.3-mile mark. Southern Pacific had a maintenance station at this junction from 1923 to 1930. Not quite a half mile beyond this marking, you will pass the Westwood Junction trailhead. A broad meadow stretches to the north, in the direction of McCoy Reservoir.

Pass Blair Station at about the 8-mile mark. A large red sign that directs snowmobilers playing on the maze of roads in winter points left (north) down a forest service road at this point. The Bizz Johnson Trail continues straight (east) on the flat, fairly obvious railroad grade.

The rail trail continues into the seemingly endless forest, blazing a marginally monotonous line until it reaches a bridge over the fledgling Susan River at about the 10-mile mark. Cross the bridge and pass through the gate. This is a turning point; the trail's aspect goes from predictable to enlivening beyond.

The river is placid in its willow-lined bed on the right (south) side of the trail, then dives into a canyon. The route is bordered by cliffs and black talus, dropping to pass an old shack, "Frank's House," at 11 miles. Pass another gate, then arrive at the Goumaz station at 12.3 miles.

At Goumaz you will find restrooms, a parking area, and a billboard upon which is posted trail information and a description of the history of the Goumaz station. Lying about halfway between Westwood and Susanville, this is a great place to rest and picnic.

On the east side of Goumaz, pass another gate and cross a bridge, then begin a steep downhill run that is cut into a mountainside, exposing the crumbly orange rock underlying the forest. Another gate, at 17 miles, marks the trail's passage through private property, where you must remain on the railroad grade to avoid trespassing. The broad river valley opens to the left (north) as you descend, and the ranch buildings of the lucky souls who work this high-country paradise are visible across the grassy valley floor.

The forest and its undergrowth pick up a more desertlike quality as you pass through the ranch, via another gate at 18.1 miles. Continue down and across a spectacular and thrilling bridge at 18.7 miles; the Susan River lies far below. An old bridge spans the river on the north side; the highway, on a sturdy and modern bridge, lies to the south.

Beyond the span, the trail veers sharply down to the right (south), and plunges under the highway bridge, then climbs just as steeply to the gate at the Devils Corral at 19.3 miles. Remember to close the gate behind you.

Devils Corral, like Goumaz, is host to parking, an information kiosk, and restrooms. The trail skirts the corral on its south side, slips through another gate, and proceeds eastward into the Susan River canyon, with the river a tempting companion.

The primitive Cheney Creek camping area (check with the BLM for permits/restrictions) lies riverside at about the 21-mile mark; beyond it you will encounter the first tunnel. It's dark and creepy inside, and reflective posts keep you safely away from the tunnel walls. A bridge lies on the east side of the tunnel. Another bridge and tunnel follow, the tunnel again a cool and intriguing addition to the experience. As you continue down the canyon, you will pass a waterfall that runs into late summer, and several swimming holes.

You near the end of the trail at the signs for Hobo Camp. A gate admits you onto a fire lane, then the rail trail continues for about 0.3 mile to a last informational billboard, which indicates that the Susanville Depot lies a quarter mile to the east.

To reach the depot, drop down paved Miller Road to Lassen Street, and turn right (south). Cross the bridge to the trail sign and climb up alongside the railroad tracks, where you again pick up the rail trail. Follow the tracks east past the caboose; cross Richmond Road to the quaint depot.

3 SACRAMENTO RIVER RAIL TRAIL

This amazing route, which will one day be part of a greater trail system that will circumnavigate Shasta County's scenic Keswick Reservoir, stretches along the wide, green Sacramento River to the foot of Shasta Dam.

Activities:

Location: North of Redding, Shasta County

Length: 18 miles round-trip

Surface: Crushed gravel and ballast

Wheelchair access: The trail is not wheelchair accessible.

Difficulty: Hard

Food: There is no food or water along the route. This is a long, hot ride or hike in summer, so be sure to pack plenty of water. Do not drink from the reservoir or river without treating the water first.

Restrooms: You'll find restrooms at the Keswick Reservoir boat ramp trailhead and at the Chappie-Shasta Off-Highway Vehicle trailhead.

Seasons: Year-round, though heavy rains or snow may make the trail impassable.

Access and parking: To reach the Rock Creek trailhead from Interstate 5 in Redding, head west on California 299 (Eureka Way in the town of Redding) for about 3.7 miles to Iron Mountain Road. Turn right (north) on Iron Mountain Road and head north 2.2 miles to the Rock Creek trailhead on the right (east). There is parking for four or five cars at this trailhead.

There is ample parking at the Keswick Reservoir boat ramp trailhead, which is about 1 mile north of the Rock Creek trailhead on Iron Mountain Road. Drop to the right down the paved access road for 0.3 mile to the large parking area.

The Chappie-Shasta Off-Highway Vehicle (OHV) trailhead and campground, at the north end of the trail, are accessible via Lake Boulevard and Shasta Dam Boulevard, which head west from I–5 and run along the east

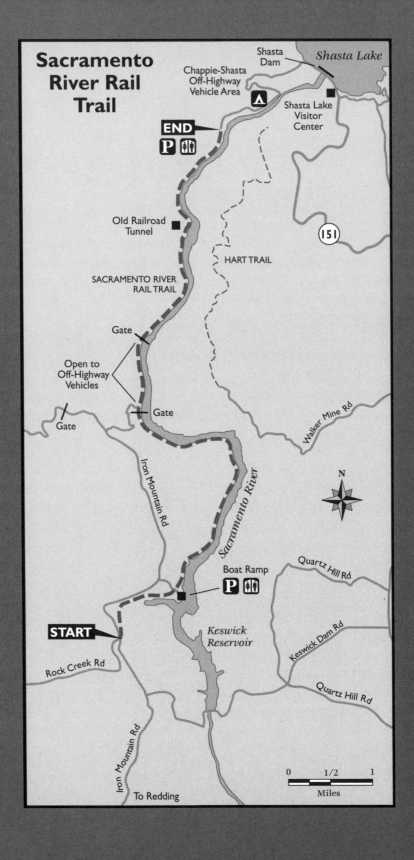

Sacramento River Rail Trail

Shasta Lake

Shasta Dam

Chappie-Shasta Off-Highway Vehicle Area

Shasta Lake Visitor Center

END

151

Old Railroad Tunnel

HART TRAIL

SACRAMENTO RIVER RAIL TRAIL

Gate

Open to Off-Highway Vehicles

Gate

Gate

Walker Mine Rd

Iron Mountain Rd

Sacramento River

N

Boat Ramp

Quartz Hill Rd

START

Keswick Reservoir

Keswick Dam Rd

Rock Creek Rd

Quartz Hill Rd

Iron Mountain Rd

To Redding

0   1/2   1

Miles

side of the Sacramento River. However, this trailhead can only be reached by driving across the Shasta Dam, and you must have a permit to accomplish this. Permits take a minimum of seven days to process; applications can be downloaded at www.usbr.gov/mp/ncao/shasta/access_permits_complete.pdf. You can also contact the Shasta Dam Bureau of Reclamation at 16349 Shasta Dam Boulevard, Shasta Lake, CA 96019; (530) 275–1554 (area manager's office). The Web site is www.usbr.gov/mp/ncao/shasta/index.html.

There is ample parking at the Chappie-Shasta trailhead, as well as camping facilities. No permit is required if you choose to ride a bike or hike across the dam and down to the trailhead.

Transportation: There is no public transportation to the trailheads.

Rentals: There are no rental outlets along the trail.

Contact: Bill Kuntz, Supervisory Outdoor Recreation Planner for the Bureau of Land Management, (530) 224–2157. The BLM Redding Field Office is at 355 Hemsted Drive, Redding, CA 96002. The Web page is www.ca.blm .gov-redding.

|||||||||||||||||||||||||||||||||||||||||||||||||||||||||||||||||||||||||||||||||||||||||||||

In the battle for primacy of north country rail trails, the Sacramento River Rail Trail and the nearby Bizz Johnson Trail would be leading contenders. The Sacramento River route, relatively new to the system, is home to the best that wilderness rail trails have to offer: superb views, river frontage, a railroad tunnel, an easy grade, and enough length to get travelers "out there."

The trail stretches along the shores of Keswick Reservoir and the swirling Sacramento River to the river's headwaters at massive Shasta Dam. An 18-mile out-and-back endeavor, it requires strength and perseverance, rewarding those who exhibit both with a sense of accomplishment and a new appreciation for Shasta's spectacular woodlands.

It took strength and perseverance to build the rail bed upon which the trail lies. Constructed in the heyday of the iron horse, the line first belonged to the Central Pacific Railroad, which also built the west-to-east

Shasta Dam rises above the northern end point of the Sacramento River Rail Trail.

leg of the fabled transcontinental railroad. Later the rails fell under the purview of the Southern Pacific Railroad, which ran express trains from Oregon to California through the Sacramento River Canyon on the Shasta Route, dubbed the "Road of a Thousand Wonders." The line was rerouted for construction of Shasta Dam; the original rails lie beneath the blue waters of Shasta Lake.

After the line was abandoned in the 1980s, and the rails and ties salvaged, the Bureau of Land Management, the city of Redding, and other private and public partners set about converting the line into a trail system. That system has since been designated a National Recreation Trail.

Beginning at the Rock Creek trailhead, which offers no amenities other than an information kiosk, head north through a gate on the wide gravel trail. Cross a levee at 0.3 mile: Above and to the left (west) is the Spring Creek Dam, and below and to the right (east) is a narrow arm of Keswick Reservoir. The trail rides the slope above the sparkling waters of the lake, curving east through sparse evergreens and mountain manzanita to the gate at the Keswick Reservoir boat ramp trailhead at 1.1 miles. You'll find restrooms, an information kiosk with maps, a shaded bench, trash receptacles, and lots of parking at this point.

A New Loop

Bureau of Land Management plans call for the Sacramento River Rail Trail, the Sacramento River Trail in Redding, and the Hornbeck Trail to be incorporated into a single 20-plus-mile loop trail. As of summer 2007, a 2.5-mile link between the Sacramento River Trail, which terminates near the base of Keswick Dam, and the Sacramento River Rail Trail, which begins above the dam, was in the final stages of development; other links, including hitching the Hornbeck section to the Sacramento River Rail Trail, were expected to be completed in 2008. Check out the Bureau of Land Management Redding office Web site at www.ca.blm.gov/redding for more information.

Another gate bars the trail from motorized vehicles as you head north from the boat ramp. The route continues to shadow the mountain-green reservoir, but is more exposed, with fewer trees proffering shade. The grade passes through cuts and over filled ravines, with chaparral growing close on its edges. In the stillness of a hot autumn morning, the reservoir is a mirror, inviting travelers to crash through its smooth surface to cool off.

At about 3.5 miles, as the reservoir narrows to river and bends westward, the brush alongside the trail grows a little more riparian in nature, with more evergreens and berry brambles. You can also see the volcanic rock that makes up the base of the rail bed at the trail's edges; the path has been paved in blue stone, but the darker, more elemental rock is still visible.

At 4.6 miles, pass another gate; for the next mile you might find yourself sharing the trail with OHVs. The trail surface is a bit rougher, too. An access road meets the route; a sign indicates this is part of the Chappie-Shasta OHV area; the Shasta Dam staging area is up and to the left (west).

Continue north on the obvious rail trail. There's another trail intersection at 4.7 miles; pass through the gate and the trail is OHV-free. Traverse a drainage and press on.

At 6.7 miles, the route leaves the railroad grade to drop through a little creek that's dry by late summer; a narrow bridge spans the waterway if it's running. At 7.3 miles, you'll reach the railroad tunnel: It's just long enough to get spookily dark at the middle, its roof arching high and cathedral-like overhead.

Side trails interrupt the route at 8.3 miles; stay straight on the railroad grade. The river swirls around little islands of dark rock, some capped with hearty vegetation; the currents and eddies trace intricate patterns in the water's surface, hinting at the dangerous power of the flow.

At 8.8 miles, reach the Chappie-Shasta trailhead for the Sacramento River Rail Trail. Shasta Dam looms to the northeast. There is ample parking, an information kiosk, and restrooms at the trailhead. The turnout for the trailhead is 0.2 mile farther north, at the intersection with the paved access road.

Travel 0.1 mile down the pavement to the Chappie-Shasta OHV area proper, with a day-use area, camping, more restrooms, additional parking, and shaded benches and picnic tables.

Unless you've acquired a permit and made arrangements to be picked up here, return as you came.

4 HORNBECK TRAIL

On the Hornbeck Trail, narrow gauge has evolved perfectly into single-track. The route zips through narrow cuts and along exposed hillsides, with views across Keswick Reservoir and the Sacramento River drainage to the high green peaks of the Trinity Mountains.

Activities:

Location: Shasta Lake, Shasta County

Length: 8 miles round-trip

Surface: Dirt

Wheelchair access: The trail is not wheelchair accessible.

Difficulty: Hard. It's not long, but the route is winding and features more ups and downs than a typical rail trail.

Food: There is no food or water available on or near the trail.

Restrooms: No restrooms are available.

Seasons: Year-round, though snow or heavy rain may make the trail impassable.

Access and parking: To reach the Quartz Hill parking area from Interstate 5 in Redding, head west on California 299 (Eureka Way in the town of Redding) for about 3.7 miles to Iron Mountain Road. Turn right on Iron Mountain Road and head north for 1.9 miles to Keswick Dam Road. Go east for 2.2 miles on Keswick Dam Road, across Keswick Dam, to Quartz Hill Road, and turn left (north). The trailhead is 1.7 miles up Quartz Hill Road on the left (north) side of the road. A small parking lot is available.

To reach the Walker Mine Road trailhead, continue east on Quartz Hill Road for 1 mile to Lake Boulevard. Turn left (north) on Lake Boulevard and go about 2 miles to Walker Mine Road. Go left (west) on Walker Mine Road and follow it to the trailhead and parking area at the end of the road.

Transportation: Public transportation to the trailheads is not available.

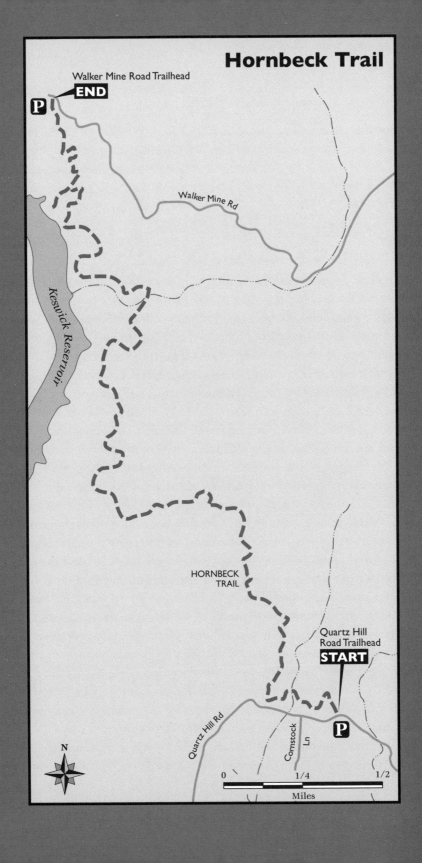

Hornbeck Trail

Walker Mine Road Trailhead

END

Walker Mine Rd

Keswick Reservoir

HORNBECK
TRAIL

Quartz Hill
Road Trailhead
START

Quartz Hill Rd

Comstock Ln

N

0   1/4   1/2

Miles

Rentals: There are no rentals on or near the trail.

Contact: Bill Kuntz, Supervisory Outdoor Recreation Planner for the Bureau of Land Management, (530) 224–2157. The BLM Redding Field Office is at 355 Hemsted Drive, Redding, CA 96002. The Web page is www.ca.blm.gov-redding.

|||||||||||||||||||||||||||||||||||||||||||||||||||||||||||||||||||||||||||||||||||||||||||||||||||||

N arrow-gauge rail bed to superb single-track: The Hornbeck Trail exemplifies this logical evolution. The route doesn't stay true to the former rail line in its entirety, sometimes curling through manzanita and oak woodlands before rejoining the bed to hurtle through steep-sided cuts and hug hillsides with sublime views of Keswick Reservoir. Hikers and equestrians will enjoy the route, but mountain bikers will love it.

The trail climbs on and off of the former Quartz Hill narrow-gauge line, which supplied quartz to nearby copper smelting operations, according to the Bureau of Land Management. You can find remnants of that quartz, sparkling white amid the reds and deep browns of the surrounding soil, along the route. The trail was named in honor of engineer Chuck Hornbeck, a volunteer who was active in development of the route.

The Hornbeck Trail is considered part of the Sacramento River Rail Trail and is slated to be integrated into a 20-mile loop trail in the Sacramento River basin below Shasta Dam. Take note: This is not your typical rail trail, as it involves some steep pitches and switchbacks. If you are on a mountain bike, make sure you are well versed in gearing up and down.

The route is described heading north from the signed Quartz Hill Road trailhead, which is under a large power line. A gate blocks the service road for the power line corridor; the trail is on the left (west) side of the parking area, where you'll also find an information signboard (with maps) and a distinctive trail mile marker. The marker, about 2 feet high and fashioned of stamped metal, is one of several along the route; the Hornbeck, which is intersected by drainages and other paths upon which you may go astray, is also identified by slender metal posts topped with painted green metal knobs.

The initial section of the trail lies off the grade and winds vaguely uphill through a forest of manzanita, the blood-colored branches provid-

The single-track Hornbeck Trail is great fun on a mountain bike.

ing spindly shade. The surface is dirt, and the path is narrow. Cross over a culvert and continue through the brush; at 0.3 mile, pass a neighborhood trail access and stay right on the Hornbeck Trail.

At about 0.5 mile, the trail curls onto what appears to be the former railroad grade, a straight swath through the oak woodland. At 0.7 mile, reach a trail intersection; a green-topped trail marker directs you straight on the grade. White posts at this junction forbid the use of off-road vehicles. Follow the green-topped markers around a switchback at the 1-mile mark (passing one of the low stamped-metal markers as well).

The route levels after a nice quarter-mile downhill run; the railroad grade proper is visible through the brush to the right. Regain the grade at 1.3 miles, where you can also spy what appear to be leftover railroad ties. Mountain views open at about 1.6 miles as you follow the contour of the hillside. Reach a bench in the shade of oak and manzanita at 1.8 miles; the quartz for which the hill was named is scattered about the trail at this point.

The 2-mile marker is beyond a cut in the hillside. Stay on track at 2.3 miles by following the green-topped trail markers; stay left through the railroad-grade cut. You will enjoy reservoir views by the 2.5-mile mark, where a bench is set against the hillside in the shade. A marker here commemorates the Quartz Hill narrow-gauge railroad.

The route veers away from the reservoir, and a series of trail markers directs you through a winding section until you rejoin the railroad grade at about 2.8 miles. Reach the 3-mile marker and again enjoy views of the reservoir from a bench in the shade of oak and manzanita; from here you can see the blue gravel of the Sacramento River Rail Trail winding through the scrub on the western shore of the lake.

At 3.5 miles, pass the 0.1-mile-long side trail to the Freitas Overlook, which is on the left (west). The rail trail climbs gently through the woods to the Walker Mine Road trailhead at 4 miles. You'll find parking and a trail information sign here, as well as the gated trailhead for the Hart Trail, which continues north toward Shasta Dam.

Unless you have a ride waiting at Walker Mine, return as you came.

5 SACRAMENTO RIVER TRAIL (REDDING)

This trail follows the broad Sacramento River up a beautiful canyon to a striking "stress ribbon" bridge, then arcs back along the river's opposite bank to the trailhead. It also links to a 3-mile loop through the stunning arboretum and all the amenities of Turtle Bay Exploration Park, as well as the Sacramento River Rail Trail.

Activities:

Location: Redding, Shasta County

Length: 5.5 miles round-trip, plus an optional lollipop loop through the arboretum

Surface: Asphalt and concrete

Wheelchair access: The entire trail is wheelchair accessible.

Difficulty: Hard. Although the portion of the trail that is on the railroad grade is easy, the portion that isn't features several steep hills. The length of the route also precludes an easier rating.

Food: There is no food available along the trail, but there are many restaurants and markets nearby in Redding. Water fountains are few and far between on the path, and Redding is notorious for its summertime heat, so bring plenty to drink with you.

Restrooms: There are no restrooms on the upper part of the trail, but several are located downstream from the trailhead, in Lake Redding Park and at Turtle Bay Exploration Park.

Seasons: The trail can be used year-round, but when the Sacramento River is high, portions may be flooded.

Access and parking: To reach the trailhead from Interstate 5 in Redding, take the exit for California 299/California 44. Head left (west) on CA 299 toward Eureka. The highway leads into downtown Redding, where the freeway ends. Signs mark the passage of CA 299 as it winds through town, first heading west on Shasta Street, then right (north) on Pine Street, then left (west) on Eureka Way. Follow Eureka Way/CA 299 to Court Street. Turn right (north) on Court Street and follow it for a half mile to the parking lot on Middle Creek. The lot is on the left (west) side of Court Street just before it crosses the bridge over the Sacramento River. You can also reach the trail from Turtle Bay Exploration Park at 840 Auditorium Drive in Redding. From I–5, take the CA 299 exit and head west on CA 299 to the Auditorium Drive exit in about 0.5 mile. The exploration park is to the north along the river.

Transportation: There is no public transportation serving the trail.

Rentals: There are no rentals on the trail.

Contact: Terry Hanson, Manager of Community Projects, City of Redding, 777 Cypress Avenue, Redding, CA 96001; (530) 225–4009; thanson@ci.redding.ca.us.

|||||||||||||||||||||||||||||||||||||||||||||||||||||||||||||||||||||||||||||||||

The broad Sacramento River and the incredible "stress ribbon" bridge that spans it just below Keswick Dam are the centerpieces of this wonderful rail trail.

The Diestelhorst Bridge is at the east end of the Sacramento River Trail loop.

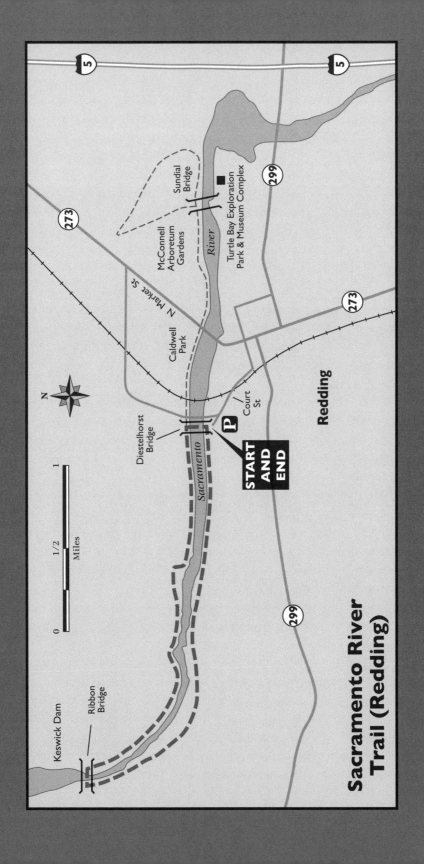

Sacramento River Trail (Redding)

5

5

299

273

273

299

Redding

Turtle Bay Exploration Park & Museum Complex

McConnell Arboretum Gardens

Sundial Bridge

River

N Market St

Caldwell Park

Court St

P

START AND END

Diestelhorst Bridge

Sacramento

N

0   1/2   1

Miles

Keswick Dam

Ribbon Bridge

The river, milky green and swift, has carved a gentle canyon that curls through the center of Redding. It waters a strip of riparian habitat on either shore, through which the riverside path meanders. The Sacramento River Trail Bridge, a simple, graceful arc of concrete more than 400 feet long, links the trail over the river at the western edge of the route. At the eastern end, the historic and more traditional Diestelhorst Bridge ties the trail into a pleasing, 5.5-mile loop. The Diestelhorst is mirrored by the Court Street bridge, which runs alongside and is overshadowed by the high trestle that supports an active Southern Pacific line. Watching a train pass over this trestle will thrill more than railroad buffs.

Interpretive signs along the route describe the natural and man-made history of the area and add to the trail's charm. Views westward are of the Trinity Mountains; if you head east on the north side of the river, you will be treated to vistas of Lassen Peak, one of two Cascade volcanoes that dominate Redding's skyline. The other, Mount Shasta, can't be seen from the river valley.

But that's not all. Follow the river east of the Diestelhorst Bridge, and you will reach the Turtle Bay Exploration Park and the McConnell Arboretum & Gardens, home to an oak savanna of unrivaled beauty and rich with artifacts left by the Wintu tribe, which lived in the area prior to the arrival of Europeans.

Only a mile of the trail is on a former railroad grade, with the rest of the route on historic roads that served mining operations along the river. That mile of former railway, which was installed with the rest of a line in the 1880s as part of the Southern Pacific system in the area, was incorporated into the portion of the trail on the south side of the river when the path was built in 1986.

The trail begins at the western end of the parking area. Pass the Court Street water fountain and the initial trail sign; restrooms lie 0.2 mile up the route.

The path overlooks the turquoise river and is overhung with trees and bushes that bloom pink and white in spring and are alive with darting hummingbirds and butterflies. Benches and mile markers line the route. At 1.2 miles, pass a riverside bench dedicated to the memory of Christine Munro. At 1.5 miles, the trail breaks out from under the cover of the trees, and views open to the western mountains. Climb a short hill onto the railroad grade, which runs above the exposed and rocky shoreline. An

Turtle Bay Exploration Park

Redding takes great pride in its Sacramento River frontage, and that pride has found perfect expression in both its lovely riverside trailways and in Turtle Bay Exploration Park.

The park's centerpiece is the Sundial pedestrian bridge, a spectacular structure that spans the river between the McConnell Arboretum & Gardens and the Turtle Bay Exploration Park's museum complex. Its sail-like pylon soars 220 feet into the sky, the frosted green glass that paves its deck mirrors the color of the water below, and its railings offer bird's-eye views of the Sacramento's whorls and swirls.

Though the railroad portion of the trail doesn't extend into this neck of the woods, it's worth exploring. From the Diestelhorst Bridge, continue east on the concrete path, which leads first through Lake Redding Park, with its playground, restrooms, and picnic facilities. Beyond, you will pass the Redding Museum of Art and History, then the rolling lawns and picnic grounds of Caldwell Park.

The path drops under the Market Street bridge. About a mile east of the Diestelhorst Bridge, you will reach the 200-acre McConnell Arboretum & Gardens. The gardens are planted with species from Mediterranean climates around the world, including South Africa, Chile, and Australia. Within the arboretum you can explore a fantastic oak savanna dotted with archaeological sites left by the native Wintu tribe; the savanna rings with birdsong and dances with shadows at sunset. A 3-mile paved loop winds through the arboretum and links to the Sundial Bridge.

On the south side of the bridge, you'll find more to explore in the Turtle Bay museum complex, including a river aquarium, a butterfly exhibit, a historic railroad exhibit, and Paul Bunyon's Forest Camp, which showcases the area's rich forestry and logging history.

More information on Turtle Bay Exploration Park is at www.turtlebay.org; call (800) 877-TurtleBay (887-8532) or (530) 243-8850.

interpretive sign explains how the area was damaged by hydraulic mining in the early 1900s.

Cross a bridge over a small creek, beyond which the railroad grade is elevated, running alongside the trail on its south side. Pass a private home, then cross the bridge spanning Middle Creek, which also has an interpretive marker.

At 2.5 miles, the gray ramparts of Keswick Dam and the silver strand of the Sacramento River Trail Ribbon Bridge come into view. The formal trail bears right (east) across the bridge, but a trail extension will continue on the railroad grade past the Keswick Dam and link to the Sacramento River Rail Trail, traveling approximately 10 miles north to the Shasta Dam.

On the north shore of the river, the trail bends east and mimics a roller coaster as it undulates past trail signs, a restroom, and an interpretive marker that identifies the Copley Greenstone/Quartz Mine at the 3-mile mark.

Lassen Peak, often snow-covered into late spring and early summer, dominates the eastern horizon as you continue downstream. Climb a rather steep hill, arcing through a drainage in the midst of a cluster of madrone and oak. At 4 miles, the trail loops past a couple more interpretive markers and over a small bridge to a quiet residential street. Go about 400 yards down the street to the continuation of the trail, which heads for the river through a small meadow on the right (south) side of the road.

The trail is now more suburban, passing the yards of lovely riverfront homes. At 5.4 miles, you will enter the elaborate memorial to Leisha Montel Graves, with its stone bench and green arches. The train trestle and Diestelhorst Bridge are 0.1 mile south of the memorial. To return to the trailhead, head left (north), away from the concrete riverside path and onto the bridge approach, and turn right (south) to cross the bridge.

For a longer excursion, stay on the riverside path, which continues downstream, passing under the triad of bridges, to Turtle Bay Exploration Park and the Sundial Bridge.

6 PARADISE MEMORIAL TRAILWAY

The thick woodlands that insulate and decorate the charming town of Paradise are the setting for this delightful rail trail.

Activities:

Location: Paradise, Butte County

Length: 5.2 miles one way

Surface: Asphalt, with a short section of dirt that can be avoided by using on-street bike lanes

Wheelchair access: The trail is wheelchair accessible.

Difficulty: Hard, due to the trail's length and relatively steep incline. The difficulty can be whittled down if the trail is taken in sections, or if you plan a shuttle.

Food: There is no food available along the route, other than quick access from the trail to a fast-food joint at about the midway point. You are never far from the commercial strip that lines the Skyway through Paradise, however, where you will find restaurants and markets. There is no water available along the route, so bring what you need.

Restrooms: There are no public facilities along the rail trail or at either end point. You will find restrooms in the Paradise Community Park near the route's south end.

Seasons: The trail is passable year-round.

Access and parking: To reach the southern trailhead, follow the Skyway, the main route through Paradise, to its intersection with Neal Road, which is at the southernmost end of town. There is a small parking lot at this location. To reach the upper, northernmost trailhead, follow the Skyway through town to its intersection with Pentz Road. The trail heads off to the right (south) from this intersection. There is limited parking off the roadway at this end point, with more on-street parking available on Pentz Road.

Transportation: Butte County Transit provides some bus service to the area, but doesn't run regularly from trailhead to trailhead. Call (530) 342–0221 for schedule information.

Rentals: There are no rentals along the trail in Paradise.

Contact: Craig Baker, Assistant Community Development Director, Town of Paradise, 5555 Skyway, Paradise, CA 95969-4931; (530) 872–6291. The Web site is www.townofparadise.com.

||||||||||||||||||||||||||||||||||||||||||||||||||||||||||||||||||||||||||||||||||||||

With a name like Paradise, it had better be good. Fortunately, like the town through which it runs, the Paradise Memorial Trailway lives up to its billing. Climbing into the pine-shrouded foothills that buckle up where California's great Central Valley meets the Sierra Nevada, the trail is gentle but rugged, on the safe side of untamed. It is mostly wooded, with evergreens dominating the landscape higher up, and more diverse oak woodland flourishing down low. Insulated for the most part by the curtain of the forest, the trail offers easy access to the Skyway, Paradise's main drag, and all the amenities of the town.

The Diamond Match Company was the primary user of the Southern Pacific rail line upon which the trail now lies. The company, like many other enterprises in the mountains of California, ran logging and milling operations that used railroads for hauling logs and lumber. The company's logging town was located north of Paradise in Stirling City, and the line ran through Butte Canyon down into Chico. Southern Pacific eventually abandoned it, and the opportunity to transform the corridor into a rail trail opened. Five miles of trail are in place, and there are "tentative" plans to extend the trail both up toward Stirling City and down toward Chico.

The grade of the Paradise Memorial Trailway averages 3 percent, making for an easy downhill run, especially on a bicycle, and a more strenuous uphill trek. The trail is described here heading downhill from the Pentz Road end point, but if you don't plan to shuttle, you might want to reverse the direction so you aren't laboring uphill at the end of your adventure.

The trail is set a bit below the grade of the Skyway as it heads south from Pentz Road, sheltered from the road by a row of evergreens—you can almost imagine that the hum of the thoroughfare is the wind in the trees. Private homes and cabins are on the left (southeast) side of the paved path. Small mile markers measure the route.

At 0.7 mile, the trail rises to meet the Skyway, then the two are separated again by a thin wedge of trees and broom. Beginning at the 1-mile

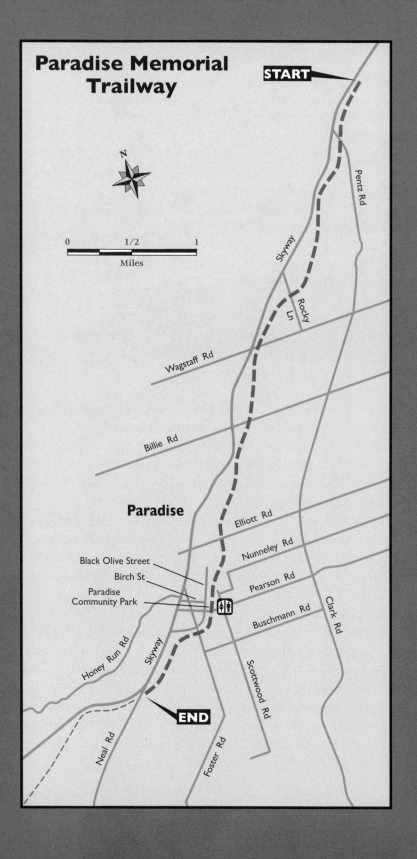

Lovely forests caress the Paradise Memorial Trailway.

mark, the trail stretches uninterrupted through the woodlands until it reaches a bench and its intersection with Rocky Lane at 1.7 miles.

Plunge back into the woods beyond Rocky Lane, reemerging to cross Wagstaff Road at 2.2 miles. Between Wagstaff Road and Billie Road, at 2.9 miles, the woodlands open, allowing more sun through the canopy and exposing patches of red earth.

South of Billie Road, the trail becomes more of a town path, which is easily shared by hikers, cyclists, dog walkers, strollers, and squirrels. At 3 miles, you pass Paradise's skate park and a fast-food restaurant on the right (northwest) side of the trail. A ballpark is on the left (southeast) side of the route at 3.5 miles.

The paved path makes a sharp right-hand (west) turn and climbs to Black Olive Street at about the 4-mile mark; a memorial plaque marks the spot. From Cedar Street to Pearson Road, the route passes through Paradise Community Park, with restrooms, a pavilion, a tot lot, and the renovated railroad depot.

The final section of the trail passes through oak woodlands, with only a scattering of pines to remind you that you are in the foothills. Birdsong and wildflowers accompany you to the trail's end at Neal Road. Unless you have arranged a shuttle, return as you came.

7 TEN MILE COASTAL TRAIL

Magical beaches on the Pacific Ocean lend enchantment to the Ten Mile Coastal Trail (a.k.a. the Logging or Haul Road), a spectacular rail trail that runs the length of a state park.

Activities:

Location: MacKerricher State Park, Fort Bragg, Mendocino County

Length: 7 miles one way

Surface: Asphalt, except where the trail is washed out in the Ten Mile Dunes

Wheelchair access: The trail is wheelchair accessible from Pudding Creek through the main part of MacKerricher State Park, but wheelchairs—or any other kind of wheeled machine, for that matter—cannot negotiate the section of trail that has been washed out in the Ten Mile Dunes.

Difficulty: Hard, due to the trail's length and the stretch of beach-walking at the Ten Mile Dunes

Food: There is no food along the route, but you can find water in the campgrounds within the state park. The park also has areas for picnicking. Restaurants and a market can be found in Fort Bragg to the south of the park.

Restrooms: There are public restrooms in the campgrounds of the state park.

Seasons: The trail is passable year-round, although high tides and inclement weather may render the route impassable at times.

Access and parking: To reach the southern end point at Pudding Creek from California 1 in Fort Bragg, head north from town to the bridge that spans Pudding Creek. Access to the Logging Road and Pudding Creek Beach is just north of the bridge, on the left (west) side of the highway.

The Ten Mile Coastal Trail can also be reached via the main entrance of MacKerricher State Park, which is about 3 miles north of Fort Bragg on CA

1. Turn left (west) into the park, following Mill Creek Road past the entrance station and the access road to the East and West Pinewood campgrounds. Mill Creek Road arcs south around the west shore of Lake Cleone and forks. Take the right (west) fork into the parking area for the main beach and Laguna Point. The left fork leads south into the Surfwood campground.

Transportation: There is no public transportation serving the trail.

Rentals: There are no rentals available along the trail.

Contact: California State Parks Department, Mendocino Office, P.O. Box 440, Mendocino, CA 95460; (707) 937–5804. The Ten Mile Coastal Trail Foundation maintains a Web site on the trail at www.mcn.org/1/10milecoastaltrail. You can contact the foundation by mail at P.O. Box 1534, Fort Bragg, CA 95437-1534; by phone at (707) 964–9430; or by e-mail at tenmictf@mcn.org.

From end to end, the views from the Ten Mile Coastal Trail are mesmerizing. The uncrowded beaches are washed with rhythmic insistence by the waves, which in some locations have created tidal pools that grow warm and inviting under the summer sun, and in others have shaped dunes that offer refuge to seabirds and trail travelers alike.

The trail's local nickname, the Logging Road, reflects the route's previous incarnation as a road used to haul lumber from woodlands in the Ten Mile River watershed to the Union Lumber Company mill in Fort Bragg. The railroad that originally occupied the route was established in 1916 by the lumber company, which operated the line until 1949. The tracks were ripped up in a single day, according to historian Gene Lewis of Fort Bragg, so that the lumber company could build a private "high speed" logging road that could accommodate special logging trucks.

The lumber company used the Logging Road until 1983, when rainwater spilling out of the dunes in MacKerricher State Park washed out nearly 7,000 feet of the route. The state parks department, which had acquired most of the land surrounding the road, didn't permit the road to be rebuilt. It was subsequently abandoned and transformed into a lovely rail trail.

The trail runs through the sensitive habitat of three endangered species, including the snowy plover, a lovely little bird whose numbers have

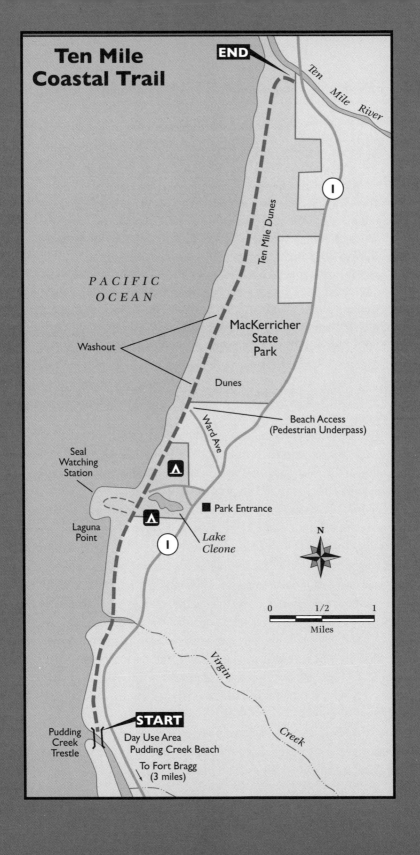

Take a Ride on the Skunk Train

In addition to the Ten Mile Coastal Trail and lovely MacKer-richer State Park, Fort Bragg is also home to the western terminus of the famous California Western Railroad Skunk Train. This historic train travels 40 scenic miles through the redwoods and oak woodlands of the Coast Ranges to the town of Willits, climbing to an elevation of 1,700 feet and tracing the path of the Noyo River as it spills to the sea.

Trains depart from the Fort Bragg Depot, located on Laurel Street 1 block west of California 1. The trip is extremely popular with families and railroad buffs, so it is recommended that you make reservations for your journey. For information and reservations, call (800) 866–1690 or visit www.skunktrain.com.

been in decline due to increased use of beaches by people. There is some controversy about access to the trail north of Ward Avenue, where it enters the dunes at the washout. If you venture into this spectacular but sensitive territory, tread with care, and obey all signs.

The trail begins at Pudding Creek, near an old trestle that is slated to be open to trail traffic in 2008. Once open, walkers and cyclists will be able to connect the trail to Fort Bragg via Glass Beach Drive, a city street that dead ends at the trestle. The rail trail heads north, passing between the backyard lawns of motels on the east side and the narrow beach on the west. At about the 1.5-mile mark, the rail trail crosses the bridge at Virgin Creek, then passes northward into the core of MacKerricher State Park.

At about 2.5 miles, the paved roadway breaks away from the ocean as it skirts the east side of Laguna Point. The point, a highlight of MacKer-richer State Park, juts out into the ocean, and boardwalks lead past the woodlands on the promontory to the open areas surrounding the seal-watching station.

North of the point, the elevated trail passes the main beach at the park, and side trails lead through the driftwood onto the soft sand. The Surfwood campground and Lake Cleone are on the right (east) side of the road.

The path is arrow-straight and abundantly scenic as it continues northward over the pedestrian tunnel that allows folks camping in the Pinewood campgrounds to reach the beach. At about the 3.5-mile mark, pass the beach access at Ward Avenue and head into the dunes. There is a small parking lot at this access point.

The washout is about a quarter mile north of Ward Avenue. Leave the railroad grade and walk down onto the beach via a small trail, then follow the beach northward. The dunes along this stretch are off-limits: They are part of the Inglenook Fen–Ten Mile Dunes Natural Preserve. You can hop back onto the paved trail or remain on the beach once you've passed the washout. It's all dune and ocean from this point north to the trail's end at the Ten Mile River. There is no public access at this point, so you will have to retrace your steps to the trailhead.

Joggers pad along the Ten Mile Coastal Trail in MacKerricher State Park.

8 SACRAMENTO NORTHERN BIKE TRAIL

The Sacramento Northern Railroad slices through a cross section of California's capital city, leading from the old neighborhoods of Sacramento through the suburbs north of town, then out into scenic farmland.

Activities:

Location: From Sacramento to Rio Linda in Sacramento County

Length: 10 miles one way

Surface: Asphalt

Wheelchair access: The entire trail is accessible to wheelchair users.

Difficulty: Hard, given the trail's length. If taken in short enough sections, the rail trail's difficulty can be reduced to easy.

Food: The trail passes a grocery store in Del Paso Heights, which is the nearest food outlet along the route, and there is a small market across the street from the trailhead in Rio Linda. Other restaurants and stores are located in Sacramento and neighborhoods along the route. There are picnic facilities at Rio Linda's Sacramento Northern Depot Visitor Center. You can picnic in Discovery Park or in one of the gazebos along the route, as well as at Rio Linda.

Restrooms: The only public facilities along the trail are at the Rio Linda–Elverta Community Center at the Rio Linda trailhead.

Seasons: The trail can be used year-round, but in spring, when the American River runs high, the portion from California 160 to the intersection with the Jedediah Smith Memorial Trail may be flooded.

Access and parking: To reach the Sacramento end point from the west-bound lanes of Interstate 80 (Capital City Freeway), take the 15th Street (CA 160) exit (the 16th Street exit if you are headed eastbound). Go north on 16th Street, which is a one-way road, to D Street. Go right (east) on D Street to 20th Street and turn left (north) on 20th Street to C Street. The trail, which is obvious, is located between 19th and 20th Streets, on the north side of the road. There is plentiful streetside parking.

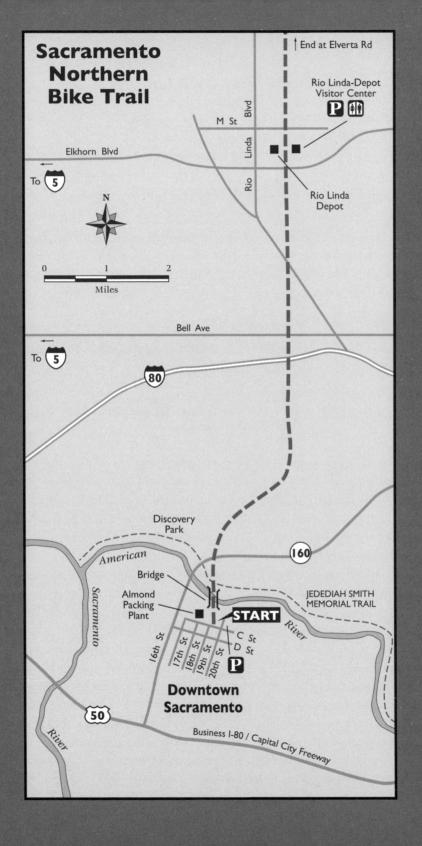

Sacramento Northern Bike Trail

↑ End at Elverta Rd

Rio Linda-Depot Visitor Center

M St

Linda Blvd

Rio Linda Depot

Elkhorn Blvd

To 5

N

0   1   2
Miles

Bell Ave

To 5

80

Discovery Park

160

American

Bridge

JEDEDIAH SMITH MEMORIAL TRAIL

Almond Packing Plant

Sacramento

START

C St
D St

16th St
17th St
18th St
19th St
20th St

River

P

Downtown Sacramento

50

River

Business I-80 / Capital City Freeway

To reach the Rio Linda trailhead from Interstate 5 in Sacramento, head north on I–5 to its junction with California 99. Go right (north) on CA 99 to the Elkhorn Boulevard exit. Follow Elkhorn Boulevard east to Rio Linda Boulevard. Turn left (north) on Rio Linda Boulevard and follow it to M Street. Turn right (east) on M Street and follow it to Front Street; the entrance to the park, the Rio Linda Depot, and the trailhead are on the right (south) side of M Street.

Transportation: Sacramento Regional Transit District, which operates public transportation throughout the Sacramento area, can be reached by writing P.O. Box 2110, Sacramento, CA 95812-2110. Call (916) 321–BUSS; the Web site is www.sacrt.com.

Rentals: There are no rentals along the trail.

Contact: Ed Cox, Bicycle Coordinator, City of Sacramento, 915 I Street, Room 2000, Sacramento, CA 95814; (916) 808–8434.

|||||||||||||||||||||||||||||||||||||||||||||||||||||||||||||||||||||||||||||||||||||||||||||

Four facets of Sacramento are in evidence along this rail trail. You will pass grand Victorian homes in the old town area, industrial complexes that thrive along most railroad corridors, unremarkable but pleasant suburban neighborhoods north of the American River, and rural farm communities in Rio Linda. These 10 miles offer a snapshot of life in the heartland of northern California.

The trail runs along the former Sacramento Northern Interurban Electric Rail line, which ran from downtown Sacramento to Chico, carrying passengers between these two bustling agricultural communities. The trains stopped running in the mid-1940s, and the rail line was eventually abandoned. Construction on the trail, which has been upgraded through the years, began in 1980.

The trail begins on C Street between 19th and 20th Streets, at the edge of a charming old neighborhood of classic homes and sycamore-lined streets. There are no signs, but the trail is obvious, beginning adjacent to the railroad tracks on the east side of the Blue Diamond almond factory.

Head north on the paved trail, passing under the bridge of the active Union Pacific Railroad tracks, and meander through industrial complexes for a half mile to a trail intersection. Stay right (north) on the Sacramento Northern trail, which passes across the American River on a spectacular metal trestle, then drops into the riparian greenery on the north shore of the river.

At 1 mile, pass under CA 160 and merge briefly with the Jedediah Smith Memorial Trail, which runs east to west along the American River. Follow the merged trails east for 0.3 mile to the next trail intersection and head left (north) across Del Paso Boulevard into Discovery Park. This section of the trail, along with the trails that border the ponds in this area of the park, may be flooded in spring.

The westbound continuation of the Jedediah Smith trail branches off to the left (northwest), circling the shady ponds that ring with birdsong. The Sacramento Northern trail takes the high road, climbing right onto the raised bed, from which you can look down upon the ponds.

At about 1.5 miles, the trail leaves the raised bed and drops down across railroad tracks, then continues north. Industry gives way to homes as you cross a small bridge, then pass under the arch that marks the border of Noralto. Paths break from the trail to both right and left, giving access to neighborhood streets, and kids from these neighborhoods share the trail with more serious recreationalists. You will cross a series of residential streets, most of which are quiet but require caution.

Homes border the trail to about the 3-mile mark, where the trail enters a narrow greenbelt lined with garbage cans. The greenbelt is brief, and after a quarter mile you are once again traveling among backyard fences.

At 3.9 miles, pass over a creek and its twin levees, then leave Noralto for Del Paso Heights, with the border again marked by a green arch. This is another quiet residential neighborhood, but the trail is broader here, with gazebos that offer shade, benches, trash cans, and a water fountain.

At about the 5-mile mark, just beyond the last gazebo on this stretch of trail, you reach Harris Avenue. Turn right (east) on Harris Avenue for 25 yards to the crosswalk, and cross busy Rio Linda Boulevard. The trail continues north on the east side of Rio Linda Boulevard. Cross a couple of side streets, then pass under the arch designating the border of Robla, and the I–80 overpass. A second arch for Robla is at 5.2 miles.

Yet another gazebo offers respite and shade in the broad, exposed greenbelt at the intersection of Bell Avenue and Rio Linda Boulevard. Cruise through a section of trail that hints at country, with widely spaced homes on large pieces of property bordered by rustic fences. Then you reenter suburbia, and a dirt footpath borders the paved rail trail.

Cross Marysville Boulevard at 6.7 miles; a last gazebo marks the spot. The trail now enters country proper, stretching between pastures that are richly green and dotted with wildflowers in spring, and bleached blond after the long, hot summer. Pass under another arch, then cross a series of levees and a creek at 7 miles.

The canopies of broad-leaved trees shade the trail and insulate it from the airport that borders the trail on the right (east) side. At 7.6 miles, cross a stream and pass the memorial for Jeromy Shinault; beyond, the oaks form a substantial and welcome bower of shade over the lovely path. The waterway runs alongside the trail, adding its coolness to that of the trees.

Pass a ball field on the right (east) side of the path, then cross a rather busy roadway to a series of bridges spanning a braided creek or ditch that has cut ragged channels into raw-looking earth.

Trees again crowd the trail as you head into the park complex surrounding the Rio Linda Depot, which is near the 8-mile mark. The community center grounds include a tot lot, broad lawns, picnic facilities, and the depot itself, now a visitor center. You can get cool drinks and snacks at the small market across M Street from the park.

The trail was extended northward from M Street to Elverta Road in 2006, offering recreationalists an additional 1.8 miles of paved path. The additional mileage offers access to local schools and neighborhoods and includes amenities such as arches that identify communities, benches for rest and contemplation, three drinking fountains, and more than 700 shade trees, including a number of native oaks. At the Elverta end point, you'll find a shelter with benches, water, and a parking area.

Unless you've arranged a shuttle, return as you came.

9 SACRAMENTO RIVER TRAIL (SACRAMENTO)

The city center that was home to the first railroad in the state of California serves as a fitting setting for this rail trail. Saturated in history and culture, wedged between the Sacramento River and a working rail line, the Sacramento River Trail is a pleasure to walk or ride.

Activities:

Location: Downtown Sacramento, Sacramento County

Length: 1.5 miles one way

Surface: Wooden boardwalk, concrete, asphalt

Wheelchair access: The entire route is wheelchair accessible.

Difficulty: Easy

Food: A plethora of eateries crowds the trail in Old Sacramento. From candy to crab, take your pick.

Restrooms: There are facilities at the trail's northern end point in Old Town Sacramento and at Miller Park at the southern end point.

Seasons: The trail may be used year-round.

Access and parking: The northern end point of the trail is located along the Sacramento River behind the California State Railroad Museum in Old Sacramento. To reach Old Sacramento, take the J Street exit from Interstate 5 and follow the signs. Both on-street parking and parking garages are available in the area; fees are charged. The closest garage is across the street from the railroad museum, which is at 111 I Street in downtown Sacramento.

Miller Park, at the south end point, is adjacent to the mazelike confluence of the Capital City's freeways. From Old Sacramento, head south on Second Street to Front Street, which is south of Capitol Mall, and continue south on Front Street to Broadway. Turn right (west) on Broadway; this

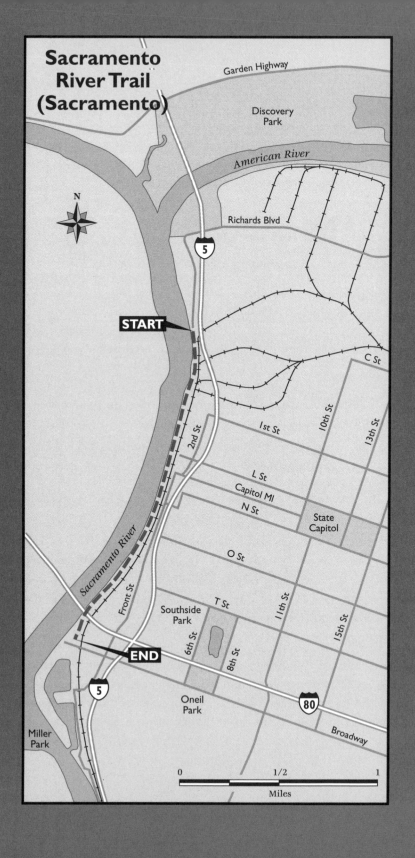

Sacramento
River Trail
(Sacramento)

Garden Highway

Discovery
Park

American River

Richards Blvd

N

5

START

C St

1st St

10th St

13th St

2nd St

L St

Capitol Ml

N St

State
Capitol

O St

Sacramento River

Front St

Southside
Park

T St

6th St

8th St

11th St

15th St

END

5

Oneil
Park

80

Broadway

Miller
Park

0   1/2   1
Miles

becomes Marina View Drive and leads into the large parking areas for the park and the Sacramento Marina.

Transportation: Sacramento Regional Transit offers transportation services in the area. Call (916) 321–BUSS (2877); write P.O. Box 2110, Sacramento, CA 95812-2110; or visit the Web site at www.sacrt.com.

Rentals: There are no rental outlets on the trail proper, but rentals are available in the greater Sacramento metropolitan area. Check the local telephone directory for options.

Contact: Ed Cox, Bicycle Coordinator, City of Sacramento, 915 I Street, Room 2000, Sacramento, CA 95814; (916) 808–8434.

Culture and history envelop this short route. Sandwiched between the Sacramento River and a working rail line in the heart of California's capital city, it begins in the busy historic district behind the California State Railroad Museum, skirts the preserved historic buildings of Old Sacramento, then cruises the banks of the broad river that flows from gold country to San Francisco Bay.

The trail lacks nothing: It serves up eateries, riverboat rides, tattoo parlors, candy shops, a broad promenade, a mile-long stretch of pavement upon which to stretch your legs, a riverfront park in which to picnic, and the chance to see an old-time locomotive unleash a backlog of steam on the pillars of a modern freeway bridge.

The trail runs adjacent to the tracks of the working Sacramento Southern Railroad, upon which the railroad museum runs excursion trains from April to September. The railroad dates back to the turn of the twentieth century, when the Southern Pacific built the line to facilitate transportation of the bounty of the Central Valley's fields and orchards to port cities in the Bay Area. Both freight and passenger trains operated on the branch line, which ran south for 24 miles to Walnut Grove and beyond until the late 1970s, when floods destroyed miles of track. The Southern Pacific ceased operations on the rail line by the early 1980s; the state railroad museum began running its summertime excursion trains at the Sacramento end of the route beginning in 1984. According to railroad museum literature, more than 60,000 passengers board Sacramento Southern cars annually; you can wave at some of them from the trail as they pass.

The Sacramento River Trail heads through historic Old Sacramento.

Begin in Old Sacramento, behind the railroad museum and near the freight yard and Central Pacific Railroad Depot, on the narrow paved path that runs atop the river levee. The levee gives way shortly to a boardwalk bordered by touristy shops and restaurants; the working tracks are on the left, and riverboats are docked along the waterfront to the right.

At 0.25 mile reach the Capitol Mall intersection, with the yellow pylons of Tower Bridge rising on the right (west), and the capitol building gracing the end of the mall on the left (east). Carefully cross the mall and continue south along the wide, lighted promenade, lined with flower-filled planters on pedestals bearing plaques that describe the colorful history of Old Sacramento. Benches overlook the river, where pleasure boats ply the deep green water. This is a big, dangerous river; no swimming is permitted.

The formal promenade ends at 0.5 mile, but the trail, with the tracks on the left and the levee wall and river on the right, proceed south. At 0.6 mile, the trail is pinched between the levee wall and the track; a bike lane takes you onto the adjacent roadway, which is followed south for about 100 feet until the paved rail trail resumes.

The bikeway narrows at 0.8 mile. The focus is now on the river, which teems with recreational boaters and wildlife, including flocks of waterfowl that perch on timber structures along the riverbank. The urban/wildland interface is stark here, with the Capital City Freeway, a manmade span of concrete and metal, arcing over the powerful waterway that preceded it and will no doubt long outlast it.

At 1.4 miles, pass a field of oil tanks, and reach the trail's end at the intersection of Broadway at 1.5 miles. Turn right and head down toward the river into Miller Park, a linear stretch of lawn dotted with trees and picnic tables.

Amenities of Old Sacramento

Old Sacramento and the capitol district are rich with cultural and historical amenities. Here's a short list of activities you can enjoy before or after your promenade on the Sacramento River Trail.

- Explore the historic district, where cobblestone streets and boardwalks front elaborate old buildings that house candy shops, ice cream parlors, cafes and restaurants, clothing boutiques and souvenir shops, toy stores and purveyors of antiques and jewelry, photographers, tobacconists, and fortune tellers. It's a feast for the eye, stomach, and pocketbook.

- Visit the many museums around downtown Sacramento, including the California State Railroad Museum, the California Military Museum, the Discovery Museum, the California State Indian Museum, and Sutter's Fort.

- Visit the capitol, seat of the Golden State's government.

- Take a trip on the excursion train or a riverboat—or both.

More information is available online at www.old sacramento.com; you can also call the Old Sacramento Visitor Center at (916) 442-7644. For information on tours of the state capitol, a California State Park, visit www.parks .ca.gov/?page_id=495, or call (800) 777-0369 (916-653-6995 local). The e-mail address is info@parks.ca.gov.

You can travel the length of the park to where it dead-ends at the mouth of the Sacramento Marina if you choose. Otherwise, return as you came.

You can see the railroad grade extending south on the far side of the marina; plans call for the rail-with-trail to extend down the line toward Walnut Grove.

More Rail Trails

A CHICO AIRPORT BIKE PATH

The grassy expanses surrounding the Chico Airport are surprisingly scenic, hosting a variety of songbirds that raise a pleasant ruckus in spring. This rail trail runs from the airport, south into downtown Chico, where it offers residents a shady alternative to walking or cycling on the streets.

Activities:

Location: Chico, Butte County

Length: 3.5 miles one way

Surface: Asphalt

Wheelchair access: The trail is entirely wheelchair accessible.

Difficulty: Easy

Food: There are no stores or restaurants at the airport end of the trail, but the path ends on Esplanade, which runs through the heart of town and provides access to a variety of eateries and markets. No water is available along the route, so pack all you will need.

Restrooms: No restrooms are available along the trail.

Seasons: The trail can be used year-round.

Access and parking: To reach the Chico Airport trailhead from California 99 in Chico, take the Cohasset Highway/Mangrove Avenue exit. Head north on Cohasset Road for about 3 miles to Boeing Avenue and turn left (west). Follow Boeing for 0.2 mile to Fortress Street and turn left (south). Sikorsky Avenue intersects Fortress Street at about 0.1 mile; the rail trail is on the left (east) side of Fortress Street.

The southern end of the rail trail is at the intersection of Esplanade and Eleventh Avenue. To reach this from CA 99, take the Cohasset Highway/Mangrove Avenue exit and head west on Cohasset Road. Follow Cohasset Road for 0.5 mile to its intersection with Esplanade and turn left (south). Follow Esplanade for 0.3 mile to Tenth Avenue and turn left. The rail trail is located just north of this junction. There is no public parking in the convenient lots of the Chico Nut Company; the nearest parking is along the residential streets south and east of the trailhead.

Transportation: For transit information, contact Butte Regional Transit; (530) 342–0221 or (800) 822–8145; www.blinetransit.com or www.bcag .org/%5F%5Ftransit.

Rentals: There are no rentals available along the trail, but Chico is a biking town; it was rated the Most Bike Friendly City by *Bicycling* magazine in 1997. It should come as no surprise, then, that the town boasts a number of shops offering bike rentals and repairs. For more information about rental shops, and for brochures about the various trails, contact the Chico Chamber of Commerce, 300 Salem Street, Chico, CA 95928; (530) 891–5556; www.chicochamber.com.

Contact: Chico Parks Department; (530) 896–7800. City of Chico, P.O. Box 3420, Chico, CA 95927; (530) 895–4800; www.chico.ca.us.

B DURHAM BIKE PATH

Orchards—brilliant with pink and white blooms in spring, laden with fruit in summer and autumn, and naked in winter—line this rural bike path, which borders the Midway road in southern Chico. Popular with cyclists and in-line skaters, it links with other bike routes in this bike-friendly college town.

Activities:

Location: Chico, Butte County

Length: 2.5 miles one way

Surface: Asphalt

Wheelchair access: The trail is entirely accessible to wheelchair users.

Difficulty: Easy

Food: There is no food or water available along the trail. Eateries and markets abound, however, just a few miles north in central Chico.

Restrooms: There are no public restrooms along the trail.

Seasons: The trail can be used year-round.

Access and parking: To reach the northern end point of the Durham Bike Path from California 99 in Chico, take the Paradise/Park Avenue exit. Go east on East Park Avenue to Midway and turn south. Follow Midway south to Hegan Lane, where you will find limited parking.

To reach the southern end point at Jones Avenue and Midway, continue south on Midway for 2.3 miles to its intersection with Jones Avenue. There is perhaps room for a single car alongside the road at this end point.

Transportation: For transit information, contact Butte Regional Transit; (530) 342–0221 or (800) 822–8145; www.blinetransit.com or www.bcag .org/%5F%5transit.

Rentals: There are no rentals available along the trail. As noted in the Chico Airport Bike Path description, Chico is a biking town, and there are a number of shops that offer bike repairs and rentals. For more information about rental shops, and brochures about the various trails, contact the Chico Chamber of Commerce, 300 Salem Street, Chico, CA 95928; (530) 891–5556; www.chicochamber.com.

Contact: Chico Parks Department; (530) 896–7800. City of Chico, P.O. Box 3420, Chico, CA 95927; (530) 895–4800; www.chico.ca.us.

C FAIRFIELD LINEAR PARK

This is primarily a commuter route that leads from the Solano Mall and the subdivisions of urban Fairfield to Solano Community College. A portion of the trail runs through a nicely landscaped greenbelt featuring small playgrounds and benches; another portion is separated from busy Interstate 80 by little more than a hedge of flowering oleander.

Activities:

Location: Fairfield, Solano County

Length: 4 miles one way

Surface: Asphalt and concrete

A small bridge connects portions of the Fairfield Linear Park Trail.

Wheelchair access: The route is entirely wheelchair accessible.

Difficulty: Moderate

Food: Fast-food outlets are located in the Solano Mall at the trail's east end. Other restaurants are available throughout Fairfield.

Restrooms: Portable toilets are available at the ball fields on the Solano Community College campus at the trail's western terminus. Restrooms also can be found in the Solano Mall.

Seasons: The trail can be used year-round.

Access and parking: To reach the western end point from I-80, take the Abernathy Road exit. Go north on Abernathy Road for 0.5 mile to Rockville Road. Turn left (west) on Rockville Road and go 1.7 miles to Suisun Valley Road. Turn left (south) on Suisun Valley Road and go 0.3 mile to Solano Community College. Circle the college to the baseball diamond, which is in the southeast section of the campus. The trail begins across the bridge on the southwest side of the field, behind the backstop and home base. There is ample parking at this location.

To reach the eastern end point from I-80 in Fairfield, take the Travis Boulevard exit. Follow Travis Boulevard east to Solano Mall and park in the mall parking lots fronting Travis Boulevard. The trail is located opposite the mall, on the south side of Travis Boulevard between Second Street and Pennsylvania Avenue.

Transportation: Fairfield/Suisun Transit System operates in this area. Contact the Public Works Department of the City of Fairfield at 1000 Webster Street, Fairfield, CA 94533-4883; (707) 422–BUSS.

Rentals: There are no rentals available along the trail.

Contact: Fred S. Beiner, Park Planner, Community Services Department, City of Fairfield, 1000 Webster Street, Fairfield, CA 94533-4883; (707) 428–7431, www.ci.fairfield.ca.us/6169.htm.

Best Rail Trails
SAN FRANCISCO BAY AREA

San Francisco Bay Area

10 West County Trail – (Joe Rodota Trail)
11 Sonoma Bike Path
12 Sir Francis Drake Bikeway/Cross Marin Bike Trail
13 Old Railroad Grade
14 Tiburon Linear Park
15 Mill Valley–Sausalito Path
16 Lands End Trail
17 Barbary Coast Trail
18 Black Diamond Mines Regional Preserve Railroad Bed Trail
19 Ohlone Greenway
20 Iron Horse Regional Trail
21 Lafayette–Moraga Trail
22 Creek Trail
23 Loma Prieta Grade

D Sonoma Regional Park Path
E Larkspur–Corte Madera Path
F Richmond Greenway
G Bol Park Bike Path
H Shepherd Canyon Trail
I Los Gatos Creek Trail

PACIFIC
OCEAN

Point Reyes
National
Seashore

San Francisco

Oakland

Napa

Santa
Rosa

Danville

San Jose

Santa
Cruz

S. F.
Bay

N

0   50   100
Miles

San Francisco Bay Area's
Top Rail Trails

10 WEST COUNTY TRAIL (JOE RODOTA TRAIL)

The springtime green and summertime gold of the oak wood-lands that border sections of the West County Trail and the linked Joe Rodota Trail hint at what the landscape of Sonoma County looked like prior to development.

Activities:

Location: Santa Rosa, Sebastopol, Graton, and Forestville in Sonoma County

Length: 13 miles one way

Surface: Asphalt

Wheelchair access: The trail is wheelchair accessible.

Difficulty: Hard, due to the trail's length

Food: The town of Sebastopol, through which the trail passes, boasts a number of restaurants and grocery stores. There are other outlets along the trail to the north.

Restrooms: There are no public restrooms along the trail.

Seasons: The trail can be used year-round.

Access and parking: A small parking lot is available at the Sebastopol Road trailhead, but parking is limited at other trailheads. To reach the Sebastopol Road trailhead from U.S. Highway 101 in Santa Rosa, take the California 12 exit. Follow CA 12 west for 3 miles to the stoplight at Wright Road. Turn left (south) on Wright Road and go 0.2 mile to Sebastopol Road. Turn right (west) on Sebastopol Road for 0.2 mile to the road's end in the trail's parking area.

In Sebastopol, trailhead parking is along the road fronting Analy High School. To reach this trailhead, follow CA 12 to its intersection with California 116 in Sebastopol. Turn right (north) on CA 116, and follow it to its intersection with North Main Street. Go 0.1 mile north on North Main Street to the trailhead, which is on the left (west) side of the road opposite the high school. There is no parking at either access point on CA 116. There is a parking lot with restrooms and trail information at the Graton Road trailhead. Parking in Forestville is streetside.

Transportation: Sonoma County Transit provides service to the Santa Rosa and Sebastopol areas. Bus schedules can be obtained by calling (707) 576–7433. The Web site is www.sctransit.com.

Rentals: While there are a number of rental outfits in Santa Rosa and Sebastopol, none are located on the trail.

Contact: Ken Tam, Planner, Sonoma County Regional Parks Department, 2300 County Center Drive, Suite 120A, Santa Rosa, CA 95403; (707) 565–2041. The Web sites for the trails are www.sonoma-county.org/parks/pk_rodta.htm and www.sonoma-county.org/parks/pk_westc.htm. A trail brochure can be downloaded at www.sonoma-county.org/parks/pdf/brochures/wct_millenium.pdf.

|||||||||||||||||||||||||||||||||||||||||||||||||||||||||||||||||||||||||||||||||||

Sonoma County is synonymous with the Wine Country, but this trail passes through a landscape that harkens back to the county's ranching roots. For a couple of miles, the route is adjacent to expanses of oak woodland and grassland, vistas similar to those that were once predominant. This pastoral terrain, however, is under enormous threat of development by homes and businesses, and by the vineyards that have supplanted dairies and apple orchards as the mainstay of Sonoma County agriculture.

The trail follows the bed of the Petaluma and Santa Rosa Railroad, an electric line that carried passengers between Santa Rosa and Forestville. The first part of the trail, from downtown Santa Rosa to Petaluma Avenue in Sebastopol, is named for Joe Rodota, the first director of the Sonoma County Regional Parks Department.

The route as described here can be done as a single trail or separated

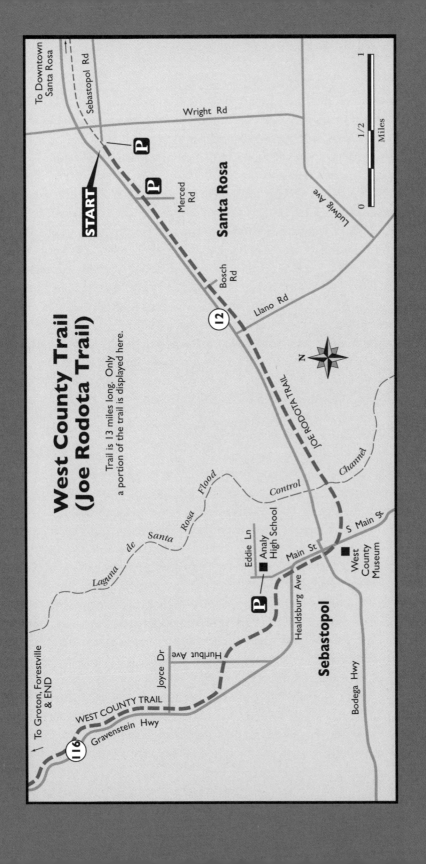

West County Trail (Joe Rodota Trail)

Trail is 13 miles long. Only a portion of the trail is displayed here.

To Downtown Santa Rosa

Sebastopol Rd

Wright Rd

START

P

P

Merced Rd

Santa Rosa

Ludwig Ave

Bosch Rd

Llano Rd

12

N

JOE RODOTA TRAIL

Laguna de Santa Rosa Flood Control Channel

Eddie Ln

Analy High School

Main St

S Main St

West County Museum

P

Healdsburg Ave

Sebastopol

Bodega Hwy

Joyce Dr

Hurlbut Ave

WEST COUNTY TRAIL

Gravenstein Hwy

116

To Groton, Forestville & END

1

1/2

0

Miles

into sections. The first section, from Santa Rosa to downtown Sebastopol, is friendlier for in-line skaters and cyclists looking for a workout; the section that heads west out of Sebastopol is more neighborly, lending itself nicely to hiking and walking. The trail becomes rural and agricultural as it heads north from Sebastopol to Forestville.

The trail begins in busy downtown Santa Rosa, just south of the Railroad Square shopping district, where it links to the Santa Rosa Creek Trail. Parking here will cost you a small fee. The route crosses to the south side of CA 12, then heads west, with the freeway and busy roads constant companions. The setting is distinctly urban/industrial, bursting with strip malls. Cross Dutton Avenue at about 0.3 mile, then Stony Point Road (with an informational kiosk about the Petaluma and Santa Rosa rail line) at about 1.2 miles.

Continue for about 1.5 miles to the trailhead parking area at Sebastopol and Wright Roads, where the route changes temperament, taking on a more agricultural demeanor. From the parking area the trail heads west, paralleling the highway and shaded by oaks and eucalyptus. Go for 0.4 mile, crossing several residential streets, to the Merced Avenue trailhead, where limited parking is available.

Beyond Merced Avenue, the trail is separated from the road by oak trees and shoulder-high cow parsnip, and the land to the south is open pastureland dotted with the occasional oak. Blackberry brambles border the path; look for the tasty berries in late summer and early fall.

Cross Bosch Road at 3.7 miles, and Llano Road at 4 miles. The trail veers south, away from the highway. An industrial yard is on the right (north), emphasizing the trail's location on the urban/rural interface.

Beyond the road, cattails line a ditch that runs adjacent to the trail on the south side. Blackberry bushes climb the fences that separate the path from neighboring businesses. The trail continues to arc south, away from the highway, until distance and a buffer of earth and trees muffle the road noise. At 6.2 miles, cross a small bridge; at 6.5 miles, a larger bridge spans the Santa Rosa Flood Control Channel.

Homes border the trail as you near Sebastopol, the western terminus of this trail section, which ends on CA 116 in town, opposite the West County Museum and an old railroad car on a disembodied section of track.

To reach the second section of the path, you must travel bike lanes along Sebastopol's quiet city streets. Head north along Morris Street for almost 0.4 mile to Eddie Lane, which travels for about 0.3 mile, passing behind the ball fields of Analy High School, to High School Road. The trail resumes about 0.1 mile south (left) of the Eddie Lane outlet.

Now you'll head west from Analy via a tree-shrouded corridor between lovely homes. The summer scents of blackberry, eucalyptus, and ripening apples alternate as you cross two quiet residential streets. About 0.5 mile from the Analy trailhead, the rail trail crosses East Hurlbut Avenue and enters a small apple orchard. This section ends after about 1 mile at CA 116.

CA 116 marks the end of the Joe Rodota Trail; from here on out to Forestville, it's known as the West County Trail. Follow the paved path north along the east side of the two-lane highway for about 0.9 mile, passing several side streets and a produce stand, to Occidental Road. The trail leaves the railroad grade at this point, bearing left (west) along the shoulder of Occidental Road for nearly 0.9 mile. Turn right (north) on the signed paved path at the gate, heading north into the vineyards. You have traveled about 9 miles from Santa Rosa at this point.

As the trail nears the quaint little town of Graton, at about 9.7 miles, it parallels a shady street called Railroad. Turn right on Grey Street, then hook quickly left onto Bowen Street and follow it for 0.2 mile to Graton Road. Cross the main thoroughfare through town and go a bit left (west) of the fire station; you'll find a large parking lot with restrooms and an informational sign behind the station at the Graton trailhead.

The path rejoins the railroad grade north of Graton Road, tracing rural Ross Road for 0.7 mile north to a junction at Green Valley Road. Travel west (left) along the shoulder of Green Valley Road for about 0.3 mile to where the route picks up again, heading right (north). The path crosses boardwalks and unpaved sections as it passes through the Atascadero Creek Marsh Ecological Preserve.

The next major street crossing, at Ross Station Road, is 1 mile north of Green Valley Road. Travel east on Green Valley a short distance to Ross Station Road; the trail continues from here. It's not quite another mile north to the trail's end near Forestville. There was no formal trailhead at the Forestville end point as of 2007, but plans call for one to be installed. By the time you reach this end point, you will have traveled about 13 miles. Unless you've made other arrangements, return as you came.

11 SONOMA BIKE PATH

The scenic splendor of the Wine Country surrounds this short rail trail, which passes several historic sites, including the lovely home of General Mariano Vallejo, as it winds through downtown Sonoma. The trail also passes the Depot Park Museum, where you can peruse exhibits that focus on both railroad and other aspects of local history.

Activities:

Location: City of Sonoma, Sonoma County

Length: 3 miles round-trip

Surface: Asphalt

Wheelchair access: The trail is entirely wheelchair accessible.

Difficulty: Easy

Food: The trail is located only blocks from Sonoma's famous Plaza, where fine dining establishments abound. A grocery store is located within easy walking distance of the trail's end at Maxwell Farms. There are picnic tables at the park.

Restrooms: There are restrooms at Depot Park, near the midpoint of the trail, and at the western end point in Maxwell Farms Regional Park.

Seasons: The trail can be used year-round.

Access and parking: To reach the eastern end point from California 12 and Napa Street, which intersect on the south side of the Plaza, go right (east) on Napa Street for less than a half mile to Fourth Street East. Turn left (north) and follow Fourth Street East for about a half mile to Lovall Valley Road. There is limited parking along the street. You also may park in the lot for the Sebastiani Winery.

To reach the western end point from CA 12 at the Plaza, follow Napa Street/CA 12 west to where CA 12 veers north near Petaluma Avenue (follow the signs). Follow CA 12 north about 1 mile to Verano Avenue, and turn left (west). The entrance to Maxwell Farms Regional Park is on the left (south) side of Verano Avenue. Abundant parking is available at Maxwell Farms; a parking fee is levied.

Transportation: Sonoma County Transit provides service to the Plaza and other points along the trail. Call (707) 576–7433 for more information. The Web site is www.sctransit.com.

Rentals: Sonoma Valley Cyclery is at 20093 Broadway in Sonoma; (707) 935–3377.

Contact: Wendy Atkins, Assistant Planner, City of Sonoma, No. 1, The Plaza, Sonoma, CA 95476; (707) 938–3794; www.sonomacity.org.

|||||||||||||||||||||||||||||||||||||||||||||||||||||||||||||||||||||||||||||||||||||||||

A ah, the fabled Wine Country. Bunches of fragrant grapes, both red and bright green, weighing down orderly vines. The smells of gourmet cheeses and other delicacies wafting from restaurants with doors flung open to the warm summer breezes. Hills shaded by stately oaks rolling up to a sky painted a perfect California blue.

The Sonoma Bike Path captures all this in a neat, easy package. The paved path begins adjacent to a vineyard, passes through quaint Depot Park, where the old depot serves as a historical museum, then rolls through the former estate of Spanish landowner General Mariano Vallejo, now part of the Sonoma State Historic Park. Wander south from the trail down a quiet neighborhood street, and you'll find yourself on the Plaza, where you can shop, eat, take in a bit of California history at the Sonoma Barracks or Mission San Francisco Solano (Sonoma Mission), then relax and unwind in the Plaza's rose garden.

The Sonoma Valley Railroad Company, organized in 1879, operated the passenger and freight trains that ran on what was initially a narrow-gauge line through the valley. The line ran from Vineburg to the Sonoma Plaza, and was later extended north to Glen Ellen. Later, after the track was changed to standard gauge, the SVRR became part of the Northwestern Pacific Railroad complex, which in turn was purchased by Southern Pacific.

The railroad began its decline in the early 1940s, when passenger service north to Kenwood was discontinued and the tracks torn up. Trains had stopped running on the main line by 1960. Historical information about the Sonoma Valley Railroad, and other railroads in the region, can be explored at the Depot Park Museum, which lies alongside the route.

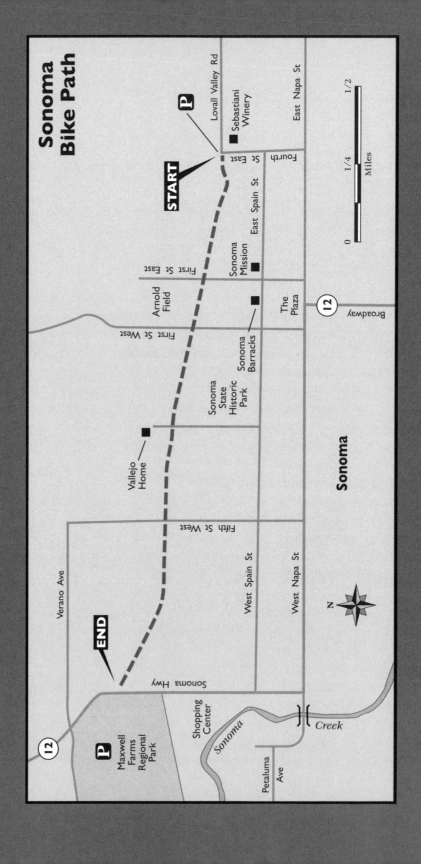

A walker passes by the historic General Vallejo Home.

The trail begins opposite the Sebastiani Winery at the intersection of Fourth Street East and Lovall Valley Road. The path rolls through grapevines, then is bordered on either side by well-kept community gardens. A series of residential streets intersect the path, and at Second Street East, a parcourse begins.

At First Street East, you will enter Depot Park. Here you'll find picnic sites and ball fields busy with baseball games in spring and soccer games in autumn. The Depot Park Museum, complete with a Southern Pacific Railroad car on a salvaged strip of track, is the centerpiece of the park. The museum is open Wednesday through Sunday from 1:00 to 4:30 P.M., and can be reached by calling (707) 938–1762. First Street East also offers great access to the Plaza.

At about the half-mile mark, cross First Street West, pass the Depot Hotel and more ball fields, then enter the near-pristine meadow serving as a buffer to the Vallejo Home. The home was known as Lachryma Montis, which is Latin for "mountain tears," although it's difficult to imagine being sad amid all the beauty surrounding the place. After crossing the paved driveway serving the historic site, the trail enters a residential area and appears to split. Stay right on the bike path.

Cross the busiest street intersection at Fifth Street West at about 1 mile; beyond, the trail passes petite Olsen Park and becomes distinctly residential in nature. A series of street intersections follows. Most are quiet neighborhood drives, but cross with care. Beyond the intersection with Robinson Road, the trail splits again. As before, stay right (north) on the bike path.

At the 1.5-mile mark, you reach CA 12. The trail ends here, but Maxwell Farms Regional Park, with a series of paved paths, frontage on Sonoma Creek, a playground, and manicured lawns, as well as a skateboard park and other amenities, lies just across the street. This is a busy crossing: It's best and safest to head south along the sidewalk to the signal and cross-walk at Maxwell Village Shopping Center, then backtrack north to the park. Return as you came.

12 SIR FRANCIS DRAKE BIKEWAY/CROSS MARIN BIKE TRAIL

This spectacular rail trail in western Marin County parallels the course of scenic Lagunitas Creek. Sunny meadows and rolling hills overlook the waterway, and dark, cool redwood groves lie along the path. Samuel P. Taylor State Park is at the midpoint, offering picnic facilities and other amenities.

Activities:

Location: From Tocaloma to Shafter's Bridge in Marin County

Length: 4.5 miles one way

Surface: Asphalt for 3 miles, to the Irving Group Picnic Area; dirt and ballast for the last 1.5 miles, from the picnic area to Shafter's Bridge

Wheelchair access: Yes, on the paved section of the trail. Hardy wheelchair users may attempt the dirt section to Shafter's Bridge, but this is generally fairly rough and can be muddy in wet weather.

Difficulty: Moderate, due only to the trail's length

Food: None is available along the trail, so bring a picnic. If you plan to eat before or after visiting the rail trail, a deli and a restaurant are available in Olema, which is 2 miles west of Tocaloma at the intersection of Sir Francis Drake Boulevard and California 1. Point Reyes Station, which offers a variety of restaurants as well as a market, is located 2.3 miles north of Olema on CA 1.

Restrooms: Restrooms, including those accessible to persons with disabilities, are available in Samuel P. Taylor State Park.

Seasons: The trail can be used year-round. The dirt/ballast section of the trail may be muddy in winter and early spring.

Access and parking: There is limited roadside parking at both ends of the Sir Francis Drake Bikeway. To reach either trailhead from U.S. Highway 101 in Larkspur/Corte Madera, take the Sir Francis Drake Boulevard exit and head west on Sir Francis Drake Boulevard through the towns of Kentfield, San Anselmo, and Fairfax, and then through the pastoral San Geronimo Valley. Shafter's Bridge is 15.5 miles from US 101; the Tocaloma parking area at Platform Bridge Road is 20 miles.

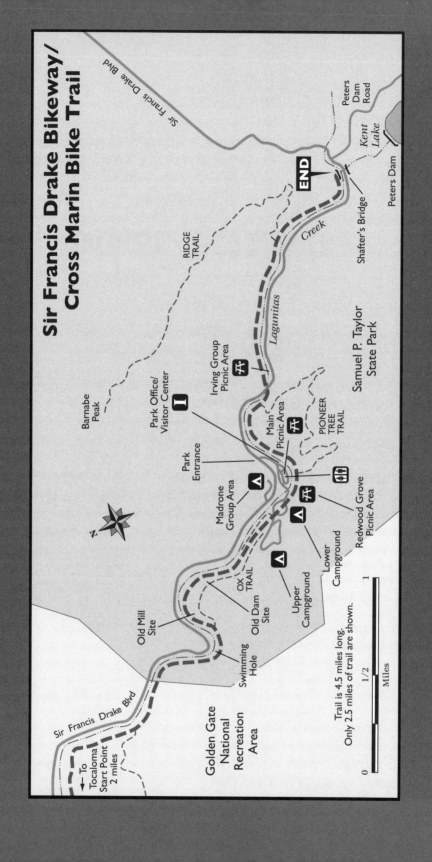

The best parking and access can be found at the Tocaloma end point. At the intersection of Sir Francis Drake Boulevard and Platform Bridge Road, turn right (north) and park in the pullout on the left (west) side of Platform Bridge Road, at the east end of the old bridge (about 100 yards from Sir Francis Drake Boulevard). A few additional spots are available 0.1 mile west of Platform Bridge Road on Sir Francis Drake along the right (north) side of the road.

Parking at Shafter's Bridge is extremely limited and located just beyond the bridge along the north side of the highway. Additional parking is available in the small lot on the south side of Sir Francis Drake Boulevard, which is open for a few months in the winter when steelhead make spawning runs up the creeks.

You may also reach the rail trail through Samuel P. Taylor State Park. The park entrance is midway between Shafter's Bridge and Tocaloma. Pay the fee and follow the park road to parking adjacent to the trail.

Transportation: Golden Gate Transit buses provide public access from the more populated areas of Marin (such as San Rafael and Mill Valley) to Lagunitas. Contact the transit service by calling 511 (toll free in the Bay Area) or (415) 455–2000 outside the Bay Area, or visit the GGT Web site at www .goldengate.org.

The West Marin Stagecoach provides bus service to Samuel P. Taylor Park, Point Reyes National Seashore, Point Reyes Station, and points in central Marin. Contact the stage service at (415) 499–6099; the Web site is www .marintransit.org.

Rentals: There are no rental facilities available near the trail.

Contact: The ranger's office at Samuel P. Taylor State Park, P.O. Box 251, Lagunitas, CA 94938-0251; (415) 488–9897; can provide information on the trail within the park. For the trail section in the Golden Gate National Recreation Area, contact the visitor center at Point Reyes National Seashore at (415) 464–5100 ext. 2.

||||||||||||||||||||||||||||||||||||||||||||||||||||||||||||||||||||||||||||||||||||||

If you simply must have it all now, you can find it along the Sir Francis Drake Bikeway. A gentle, inviting creek with a swimming hole; a sun-drenched meadow with views onto rolling pastureland dotted with black-

and-white dairy cows; cool, dark redwood groves; a lovely picnic area with all the amenities; a scenic cascade filling rock basins with clear water . . . this easy, mostly paved trail is a Marin County dream come true.

The soul of the trail is Lagunitas Creek, also known as Papermill Creek. The creek played an important role in the history of western Marin County: In the mid-nineteenth century, Samuel Penfield Taylor, for whom the state park is named, used the proceeds of a gold-mining operation to purchase property along the creek. Instead of logging the land, a logical endeavor for entrepreneurs of the period as building boomed in San Francisco, Taylor established two mills along the creek, one manufacturing paper and the other black powder.

Trees overhang the Sir Francis Drake Bikeway.

The powder mill was short-lived: It blew up in 1874. The paper mill, however, thrived, especially after a narrow-gauge railroad through the canyon made shipment of Taylor's goods easier. Taylorville, a small town that grew up around the mill and railroad, with its resort hotel and camp, was a popular destination in the 1870s and 1880s.

The 4.5-mile route follows the abandoned bed of the Northwest Pacific Railroad, which began in Larkspur and continued up the coast to Tomales and beyond. The rail trail is also called the Cross Marin Bike Trail and is a portion of the Bay Area Ridge Trail.

Beginning at the Platform Bridge Road parking area, cross the lovely old bridge that spans Lagunitas Creek and turn left (south) onto the trail at the sign that reads CROSS MARIN TRAIL. The path dives under the bridge supporting Sir Francis Drake Boulevard, then cruises through thick bays and scattered redwood groves to a long, open meadow. Towering eucalyptus trees guard the southern reach of the meadow; just beyond, at 1.4 miles, you'll reach the Jewell Trail intersection. From here you can climb steeply onto the Bolinas Ridge Trail, a popular mountain-bike ride.

At about 2 miles, you'll pass a gate that marks the boundary of the state park, and the trail follows a park road through lovely stands of redwoods. Stay straight on the park road, ignoring roads that branch left and right to housing and other park service facilities. On the north (creekside) border of the trail, in a tiny clearing, a historic marker commemorates the Pioneer Paper Mill, built by the park's namesake, Samuel Taylor, in 1856. The Ox Trail takes off to the east opposite the marker.

Pass another creekside marker at the 2.5-mile mark (post 7), which makes note of the first fish ladder on the creek. At 3 miles another gate marks a park boundary; now you are in the park proper, ,passing campsites, picnic areas, and restrooms. Stay straight on the park road, again ignoring any roads that depart right or left, passing the Redwood Grove Picnic Area and then through yet another gate. The Pioneer Tree Trail takes off to the south just past the gate.

The rail trail's surface changes from asphalt to gravel as it heads south across a bridge that spans the highway and creek at 3.5 miles. The Irving Group Picnic Area is on the east side of the bridge. Now a dirt road with a wilder feel, the trail is separated from the highway by the creek and dense walls of redwood and bay. The Ridge Trail, which leads to the summit of

Barnabe Peak, leaves from the north side of the railroad grade a half mile beyond the picnic grounds.

A gate and the Kent Lake trailhead mark the end of the route at 4.5 miles. Take the narrow trail on the south side of the grade down to the creek and head upstream about 100 yards to the cascades that fill swimming holes beneath Shafter's Bridge. This ideal picnic spot is also a great place to watch steelhead spawn in winter.

Follow the trail in the opposite direction to return to the Tocaloma trailhead.

13 OLD RAILROAD GRADE

Climbing nearly 2,000 feet to the summit of Mount Tamalpais, the Old Railroad Grade boasts some of the best views in the San Francisco Bay Area. The steady grade of the winding dirt track, now frequented by mountain bikers in shiny Lycra, once was a weekend destination of upper-class ladies and gentlemen, who would travel by ferry from San Francisco to spend a day in the country.

Activities:

Location: Mill Valley to Mount Tamalpais State Park, Marin County

Length: 9 miles one way

Surface: Ballast and dirt

Wheelchair access: The trail is not wheelchair accessible.

Difficulty: Hard. As railroad grades go, this one is long and steep, but wonderfully rewarding.

Food: There is no food available along the trail; pack a picnic lunch to eat at the inn or at the summit. Grocery stores are available in Mill Valley, along with a great variety of fine restaurants.

Restrooms: There are restrooms at the West Point Inn and at the summit of Mount Tamalpais, but no facilities at the trailhead in Blithedale Park.

Seasons: The trail can be used year-round, but may be muddy or impassable when it rains. Also, the mountain may be swathed in cool—sometimes Minnesotan—fog, even in summer, so be prepared for changing weather conditions.

Access and parking: To reach the Blithedale Park end point from U.S. Highway 101 in Mill Valley, take the East Blithedale Avenue exit and follow East Blithedale Avenue into downtown Mill Valley, where it ends at the intersection of Throckmorton and West Blithedale Avenue. Turn right (north) on West Blithedale Avenue and follow the narrow road up through neighborhoods into Blithedale Park. The trailhead is on the right (east) side of the road at a green gate.

To reach the summit of Mount Tamalpais from US 101 in Mill Valley, take the California 1/Stinson Beach exit and head west on CA 1 (a.k.a. the Shoreline Highway) to the intersection with the Panoramic Highway. Turn right (north) on the Panoramic Highway and climb the slopes of Mount Tamalpais to Pantoll Road. Turn right (north) on Pantoll Road and keep climbing to its end at the Rock Spring picnic area on Ridgecrest Boulevard. Turn right (east) on East Ridgecrest Boulevard and follow this to its end in the East Peak parking lot.

Adequate parking is available at both end points, but lots may be packed on weekends or during the summer.

Transportation: Golden Gate Transit buses serve Mill Valley. Contact the transit service by calling 511 (toll free in the Bay Area) or (415) 455–2000 outside the Bay Area, or visit the GGT Web site at www.goldengate.org.

Rentals: No rentals are available along the trail.

Contact: For trail status, contact the Marin Municipal Water District, 220 Nellen Avenue, Corte Madera, CA 94925; (415) 945–1195. The Web site is www.marinwater.org; click on the watershed link.

|||||||||||||||||||||||||||||||||||||||||||||||||||||||||||||||||||||||||||||||||||||||||||

Like a benevolent but temperamental goddess, the Pacific Ocean lords over Mount Tamalpais. On clear days, when the ocean pulls back its blanket of fog, views from the mountain sweep in every direction for miles—north up the ragged, emerald California coast; east to the snow-capped Sierra Nevada; south over San Francisco Bay and across its glittering city; and west to the ocean itself, past the shadowy Farallon Islands to the endless horizon. Sun bathes the forested slopes of the peak, and the Old Railroad Grade offers the perfect opportunity to bask in these gifts.

But when the goddess shows her temper, allowing the fog to envelop the mountain in cold mists and brisk winds, other gifts become apparent. For despite the peak's location in the midst of a sprawling urban area, a traveler caught on a fog-shrouded ridge may suddenly find him or herself alone in a viewless wilderness, transported back to a wilder time, before the mountain became an escape for busy city dwellers and recreationalists.

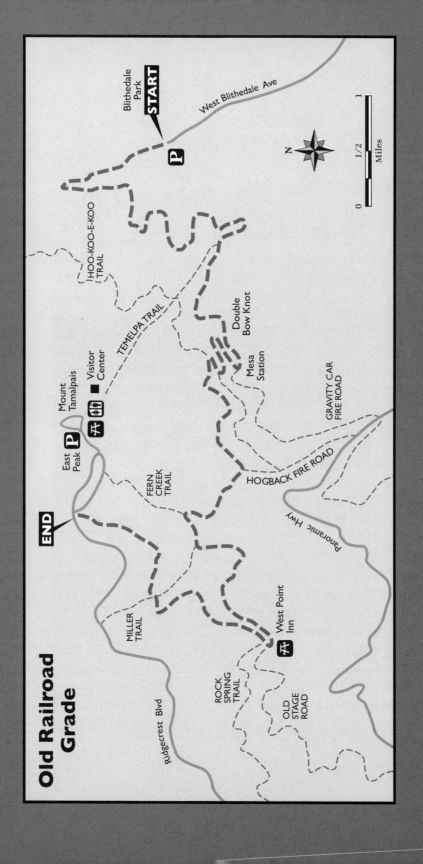

Old Railroad Grade

Blithedale Park

START

West Blithedale Ave

P

N

0 — 1/2 — 1 Miles

HOO-KOO-E-KOO TRAIL

Double Bow Knot

TEMELPA TRAIL

Mesa Station

GRAVITY CAR FIRE ROAD

Mount Tamalpais

Visitor Center

East Peak

P

FERN CREEK TRAIL

HOGBACK FIRE ROAD

Panoramic Hwy

END

MILLER TRAIL

Ridgecrest Blvd

ROCK SPRING TRAIL

West Point Inn

OLD STAGE ROAD

Around the turn of the twentieth century, the Mill Valley & Mount Tamalpais Scenic Railway Company operated "The Crookedest Railroad in the World" on the mountain. Passengers rode the winding line—more than 280 curves—to the summit, savored the views, and perhaps took a hike along the rolling crest, then rode the rails back down to Mill Valley. The line was abandoned in 1930, and the former grade is now a popular hiking and mountain biking route.

The trailhead is at Blithedale Park on the gated Blithedale Summit/ Northridge Fire Road. Green posts line the route, which begins by following the course of heavily wooded Arroyo Creek northward. It climbs steadily for the duration, so set your pace, and prepare yourself for the long haul.

Remnants of track are visible atop the Old Railroad Grade on Mount Tamalpais.

Exploring Mount Tamalpais

The Olmsted Bros. Map Company has produced a very nice map of trails on Mount Tamalpais. The map, "A Rambler's Guide to the Trails of Mount Tamalpais and the Marin Headland," is available at local outdoor-equipment retailers and bookstores, or can be acquired by contacting the company at P.O. Box 5351, Berkeley, CA 94705; (510) 658–6534.

The historic West Point Inn offers accommodations for hikers and cyclists wishing to spend the night on the mountain. Contact the inn by writing 1000 Panoramic Highway, Mill Valley, CA 94941, or by calling (415) 388–9955. Reservations can be made by calling (415) 646–0702. The Web site is www.westpointinn.com.

Camping is also available within Mount Tamalpais State Park on a first-come, first-served basis. For more information, contact the park headquarters at Pantoll, 801 Panoramic Highway, Mill Valley, CA 94941; (415) 388–2070. The Web site is www.parks.ca.gov/?page_id=471. Campground reservation information can be obtained at (800) 444-7275.

At the first trail intersection, another fire road switchbacks up and to the right (northeast); stay left on the railroad grade. At the next intersection, go left (southwest), down and over the creek, then continue climbing through a forest of bay, oak, madrone, and manzanita that opens a bit as you ascend.

At about 1.5 miles, the trail passes a gate and merges with paved Summit Avenue. Go right (north) on Fern Canyon, enjoying lovely views of San Francisco and the bay, and pass the Temelpa Trail, which breaks off the pavement to the right (north). The pavement ends at a gate posted with watershed signs. Pass the gate to the right (the left road is a driveway) and continue upward on the Old Railroad Grade.

At about the 3-mile mark, near the site of Mesa Station and the start of the Gravity Car Fire Road, the road reaches a T intersection. Go right (east) and up on the switchbacking rail trail, which negotiates the Double Bow

Knot, where the grade gains an incredible 600 feet in elevation. Less than a half mile beyond, pass the Hoo-Koo-E-Koo Trail, which breaks off to the right (northeast); stay left (west) on the obvious railroad grade.

As you climb, the forest gives way to low-growing coastal scrub, thick with the blooms of sticky monkey flower and Scotch broom in the spring, dry and silvery in summer and fall. At the Hogback Road intersection, at about the 4-mile mark, stay right (west); above, as you cruise through moist draws that boast waterfalls in winter and spring, pass the Fern Canyon Trail, a water tank, and the Miller Trail, all on the right (north) side of the grade.

At about 6 miles, the trail switches back around the West Point Inn. The inn has offered hospitality to mountain visitors since it was built in 1904, and provides the perfect setting for hikers or cyclists to stop, rest, enjoy the spectacular views, and perhaps, if you are done climbing, to picnic before returning down the same route. A number of other trails also depart from this spot, including the Matt Davis Trail and the Old Stage Road. With a good map and some time, you can explore these other routes.

To continue on the Old Railroad Grade, round the broad switchback, passing behind the West Point Inn's cabins, and head east, climbing above the wooded canyons that stretch down toward Mill Valley. Another couple of miles of easy climbing, during which you pass the Miller and Tavern trail junctions, lead to the end of the grade on East Ridgecrest Boulevard. Go right (east) on the paved highway, which climbs steeply in spots, to the summit area parking lot. A fragment of the railroad is on the west side of the East Peak; in the barn on East Peak you can also check out a replica of a gravity car. Cap your journey with an ascent to the summit and bask in vistas and a profound feeling of accomplishment.

Unless you've arranged for a shuttle, you must return the way you came, or you can choose one of many alternative trails for the descent.

14 TIBURON LINEAR PARK

Scanning the western and southern horizons from this shoreline rail trail, hikers, cyclists, and skaters will be treated to views of Mount Tamalpais, the wooded hills of Sausalito, and the shimmering skyline of San Francisco.

Activities:

Location: Tiburon, Marin County

Length: 2.1 miles of the 2.7-mile one-way trail are on the abandoned railroad grade.

Surface: Asphalt with a walkway of crushed stone alongside

Wheelchair access: The trail is entirely wheelchair accessible.

Difficulty: Easy

Food: There is no food available along the trail itself, but once you arrive in Tiburon, restaurants, delis, and markets offer a variety of gastronomic temptations.

Restrooms: There are restrooms available at the Blackies Pasture trailhead and at South of the Knoll Park. Public restrooms are also available in the ferry terminal for the Blue and Gold Fleet in Tiburon.

Seasons: The trail is wonderful year-round.

Access and parking: To reach either trailhead from U.S. Highway 101 in Mill Valley, take the Tiburon Boulevard (California 131) exit. Go east on Tiburon Boulevard to Blackies Pasture Road, which is on the right (south) side of the highway along the waterfront. The Tiburon end point is about 3 miles farther south, also on the waterfront.

There is a large parking area at Blackies Pasture, but extremely limited parking in downtown Tiburon, which is often congested with tourists.

Transportation: Golden Gate Transit buses serve the Tiburon area. Contact the transit service by calling 511 (toll free in the Bay Area) or (415) 455–2000, outside the Bay Area. You can also visit the GGT Web site at www.golden gate.org.

Rentals: There are no rentals available along the trail.

Contact: Tiburon Town Hall, 1505 Tiburon Boulevard, Tiburon, CA 94920; (415) 435–7373.

|||||||||||||||||||||||||||||||||||||||||||||||||||||||||||||||||||||||||||||||||||||||||

The views from this rail trail, which winds through Tiburon Linear Park, couldn't be any richer. The trail runs along Richardson Bay, an arm of San Francisco Bay. Across the bay to the west, the sparkling white buildings of Sausalito glisten among the dark woods that cloak the hills. The tips of the towers of the Golden Gate Bridge rise above these hills, simple and elegant. Beyond Belvedere, its gentle slopes garnished with lavish homes, the jagged skyline of San Francisco glints above the bay waters.

Traveling back along the path from downtown Tiburon to Blackies Pasture, the reclining profile of the Sleeping Lady, Mount Tamalpais, dominates the view. The mountain's lower flanks shimmer with sunlight reflected off the windows of homes tucked into the woods of Mill Valley, and Richardson Bay laps calmly on the beach to the west.

And to the north? Well, the homes of Tiburon, neat and quite lovely, are perched over the trail and bay, allowing residents to live with the spectacular views that visitors only revel in for a short time.

The Tiburon Linear Park offers views of Richardson Bay and the surrounding hills.

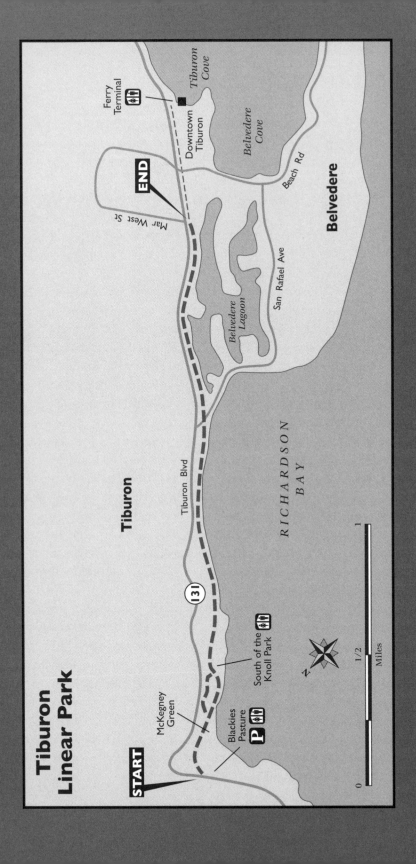

Tiburon
Linear Park

START

Tiburon

McKegney
Green

Blackies
Pasture

South of the
Knoll Park

131

RICHARDSON
BAY

Tiburon Blvd

Belvedere
Lagoon

San Rafael Ave

Belvedere

Mar West St

END

Downtown
Tiburon

Ferry
Terminal

Tiburon
Cove

Belvedere
Cove

Beach Rd

N

0   1/2   1
Miles

The path follows the route of the Northwestern Pacific Railroad, which provided passenger service through Marin County and points north from the early 1900s to the 1930s. At the south end of the trail, in downtown Tiburon, you will pass the depot, which was just one of many stops on the rail line that ran from San Francisco to Duncan Mills in the north.

The route is described beginning in Blackies Pasture. The broad path leads across Shapero Bridge at 0.1 mile to McKegney Green, where the trail forks, leading either bayside around the green or up and to the northeast of the broad lawn. A series of interpretive signs describing the ecology of the bay and its environs lines this section of the path.

McKegney Green presents the perfect site for a game of soccer or Frisbee, or for kite flying, and also offers a parcourse to those who are interested in a well-rounded workout. The lower trail leads to a trio of benches that look out over Belvedere and San Francisco Bay, then fades to dirt as it skirts a knoll that separates it briefly from the paved path to the northeast.

To remain on the pavement, take the high road, which passes behind the knoll that separates the trail from the bay. Tucked in the lee of the hill as South of the Knoll Park. It offers visitors a tot lot, a restroom, and a large grassy area upon which to relax. The lawn gradually narrows until the trail ends up tucked between Tiburon Boulevard and the bay. A strip of beach allows trail users to fish or rest and contemplate the views. Benches, garbage cans, and a couple of water fountains line the trail as it continues south, offering virtually unbroken views for the next mile or so.

At about the 1.5-mile mark, cross Lagoon Road at a stoplight. The path continues on the south side of the road, leaving the bay views behind as it dives into a bower of trees and blooming oleander that buffers the trail from the adjacent boulevard.

At 1.9 miles, pass a roadside parking lot and another small green studded with a couple of benches on the west. Just 0.2 mile beyond, the trail splits; stay right and proceed to the end of the rail trail proper, at Mar West Street.

You can turn around here, but if you've come this far, you ought to sample the pleasures of downtown Tiburon. A bike route has been delineated alongside the boulevard, and sidewalks offer pleasant roadside walking. At 2.4 miles, cross Beach Road, and at 2.6 miles, you will reach the train depot. At trail's end, at 2.7 miles, you arrive at the ferry terminal for the Blue and Gold Fleet and other transbay lines. Yet another small green overlooks Angel Island and San Francisco in the distance. Follow the same route back to the trailhead.

15 MILL VALLEY–SAUSALITO PATH

Traveling from the base of Mount Tamalpais in the north to the Sausalito shoreline in the south, the Mill Valley-Sausalito Path traverses the wetlands of Richardson Bay, where egrets, herons, and other seabirds forage at low tide. The path also passes the San Francisco Bay Model, a fascinating exhibit that demonstrates the dynamics of the bay.

Activities:

Location: From Mill Valley to Sausalito in Marin County

Length: 3.5 miles one way

Surface: Asphalt with a parallel path of crushed stone in some sections

Wheelchair access: The entire trail is wheelchair accessible.

Difficulty: Moderate, only because of the trail's length

Food: Savory meals are available at either end point of this trail. Both Mill Valley and Sausalito harbor eateries that range from fast-food outlets to gourmet burrito joints to upscale restaurants requiring reservations weeks in advance. It's a diner's delight.

Restrooms: Facilities are available in the various parks along the bike path, including Bayfront Park in Mill Valley and Earl F. Dunfy Park in Sausalito.

Seasons: The trail can be traveled year-round.

Access and parking: The best parking is at the north end of the rail trail in Mill Valley, where you will find a lot at Edna Maguire School, and more parking along the quiet residential streets that bound the school grounds. Limited parking is available at the Sausalito end point: There is a downtown parking lot, but because of the town's popularity with tourists, it is often full.

To reach the northern end point of the trail at Edna Maguire School from U.S. Highway 101 in Mill Valley, take the East Blithedale Avenue exit and follow East Blithedale for 0.7 mile to Lomita Drive. Turn right (north) on Lomita Drive and follow it for 0.6 mile to Edna Maguire School. The parking area is on the left (west), but you can also park on the streets nearby.

To reach the southern end point in Sausalito from US 101 at the north end of the Golden Gate Bridge, take the Sausalito exit and follow Bridgeway through the heart of town to the parking lot at Plaza Vina Del Mar. The lot is on the right (north) side of the road.

Transportation: Golden Gate Transit offers service between Sausalito and Mill Valley. Call 511 (toll free in the Bay Area) or (415) 455–2000 outside the Bay Area, or visit the GGT Web site at www.goldengate.org.

Rentals: In Sausalito, Mike's Bikes offers rentals; call (415) 332–3200 or visit www.mikesbikes.com.

Contact: Steve Petterle, Parks, Open Space & Cultural Services Department, Marin County Civic Center, San Rafael, CA 94903; (415) 499–6387.

|||||||||||||||||||||||||||||||||||||||||||||||||||||||||||||||||||||||||||||||||||||

From the base of Mount Tamalpais to the edge of San Francisco Bay, from the quaint neighborhoods of Mill Valley to bustling downtown Sausalito, this rail trail exemplifies perfectly the contrasts of a trail corridor that is both scenic and urban.

It begins in a tangle of blackberry and poison oak, skims through the manicured lawns of a neat suburban park, passes the shallow waters of Richardson Bay, where snowy egrets and other waterfowl do their best to ignore the hum of nearby traffic as they forage, then rams through civilization proper, briefly paralleling busy US 101 before plunging into the heart of historic Sausalito. It ends with postcard views of the bay and city of San Francisco, amid the sights and sounds that draw tourists from around the world to the cosmopolitan enclaves surrounding the Golden Gate.

The trail follows the former bed of the Northwestern Pacific Railroad, an interurban rail service that operated throughout the north bay counties of Marin and Sonoma. The electric line operated between 1903 and the early 1940s, and the trail was constructed in the late 1970s and early 1980s.

Keep in mind that cycling on the trail, while infinitely satisfying on the stretches in Mill Valley, is not easy when the trail merges with the crowded sidewalks of Sausalito. If you plan to ride or skate, consider stashing the bikes and the skates once you reach Gate 6 Road.

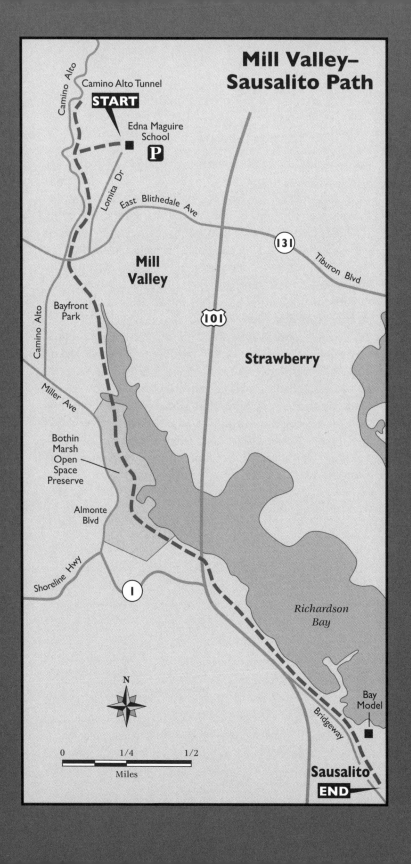

The Bay Model Visitor Center

Get an inside look at the waterworks of San Francisco Bay by visiting the San Francisco Bay Model, which is located adjacent to the Mill Valley–Sausalito rail trail. This working scale-model reconstruction of the bay and its delta allows both scientists and the public to observe the dynamics of tides and other influences on the bay. The model itself, built by the U.S. Army Corps of Engineers in 1956 and expanded in later years, is the centerpiece of the Bay Model Visitor Center, but there are other historical and environmental exhibits at the center as well.

The Bay Model Visitor Center is located at 2001 Bridgeway, but is reached via Harbor Road; follow the small brown-and-white Bay Model signs. The model is open from 9:00 A.M. to 4:00 P.M. Tuesday to Friday, and 10:00 A.M. to 5:00 P.M. on Saturday and Sunday during the summer; winter hours are 9:00 A.M. to 4:00 P.M. Tuesday to Saturday, except holidays. The model is closed Mondays. There is no fee. Call (415) 332–3871 for more information or visit www.spn.usace .army.mil/bmvc.

From the Edna Maguire School end point, a trail sign points you west of the school and onto the path, which is reached in 0.2 mile via a rough paved access road. Once on the paved path, you can either go left (south) toward the Sausalito end point, or head right (north) to the trail's true beginning.

If you choose to start from the beginning, go 0.1 mile north to Vasco Court; there is limited parking and trail access at this intersection. Cross Vasco and proceed north for another 0.15 mile on a dirt double-track that soon narrows to single-track in an area that remains moist and muddy through winter and into the spring. The Camino Alto Tunnel lies ahead, but is impossible to see from trail's end and impossible to reach without a hardy bushwhack. It's a half mile out and back from the Maguire school to this end point of the trail.

The primary trail heads south from the school. The pavement slopes gently downhill through a shady and flower-filled corridor bordered by homes to a major intersection at East Blithedale and Camino Alto at 0.7 mile. On the south side of East Blithedale, the trail becomes part of the San Francisco Bay Trail, and borders the marsh in Mill Valley's Bayfront Park. At 1 mile, pass more parking, for both trail and park, at the end of Sycamore, which can be reached by taking Camino Alto south from East Blithedale and turning left (east) at the Mill Valley Middle School.

Pass a dog run and a trail that leads left (east) and over the bridge to Bayfront Park's ball fields and tot lot. The next 1.5-mile section of trail meanders through the marshes of Bothin Marsh Open Space Preserve with glorious views of Mount Tamalpais, the wooded hills overlooking south Mill Valley and Sausalito, and the shimmering waters of Richardson Bay, which are frequented by snowy egrets, great blue herons, and other seabirds.

At 2.5 miles, the trail passes under the Richardson Bridge and emerges next to US 101. The route is wedged between the freeway and the bay for a short stint, eventually breaking away from the highway to border Bridgeway, Sausalito's main artery. Looking north toward the waterfront yields views of sailboats and fishing boats bobbing at docks and moorings, and across the bay to the extravagant homes of Tiburon and Belvedere.

At 3.3 miles, cross Gate 6 Road. At this point, walking is easier and more pleasant than cycling or skating. Shops and restaurants line Bridgeway, which follows the route of the railroad. At Napa Street (4.6 miles) the sidewalk splits, and riding or skating is a bit easier. Just beyond Napa and to the left (north and bayside) rise the grassy hummocks of Earl F. Dunfy Park, which invite both rest and picnics.

The rail trail proper ends after 3.5 miles, but if you've come this far, there's no point in missing the action in Sausalito. Reaching the heart of the town is simple—just continue along Bridgeway for another mile and a half. On summer weekends, you'll find the sidewalks crammed with people speaking a mélange of languages and gazing into the dazzling windows of bayfront shops. Just beyond the central shopping district, views open of San Francisco Bay and its forested islands, and of the glamorous city that glistens on the hills south of the Golden Gate. You can enjoy these views in greater peace by visiting off-season and during the week, but truly, half the fun is watching the people.

16 LANDS END TRAIL

Riding high on the cliffs overlooking the mouth of San Francisco Bay, the Lands End Trail offers unbeatable views of the Golden Gate Bridge, the most famous landmark of the city by the bay.

Activities:

Location: San Francisco, San Francisco County

Length: 2 miles one way

Surface: Dirt

Wheelchair access: Wheelchair users have access to sections of the trail at either end point, but the middle of the trail has been damaged by weather, narrows to single-track in spots, and includes a long staircase.

Difficulty: Moderate. The trail isn't long, but it includes steep stairs and uneven trail surfaces. Mountain biking is limited due to a steep staircase around cliff areas that requires riders to portage their bikes.

Food: There is no food available along the route, but San Francisco is famous for its fine dining.

Restrooms: There are restrooms at the U.S.S. *San Francisco* Memorial parking lot.

Seasons: The trail can be used year-round, but it is best to avoid Lands End during periods of heavy rainfall. Erosion has taken its toll on the grade, which suffered quite a bit of damage during the El Niño winter of 1997–1998. The trail has been repaired and improved, but erosion, always made worse when trails are used while muddy, constantly wears away at the spectacular cliffs of these headlands.

Access and parking: To reach the Point Lobos trailhead from the toll plaza on U.S. Highway 101 at the Golden Gate Bridge, take Lincoln Boulevard south and west to El Camino Del Mar. Follow El Camino Del Mar west, passing through the Lincoln Park Golf Course. At Legion of Honor Drive, turn left (south), passing the Palace of the Legion of Honor, to Clement Street. Go right (west) on Clement Street to its intersection with 48th Avenue and El Camino Del Mar. From here, you can go right (north) to the U.S.S. *San*

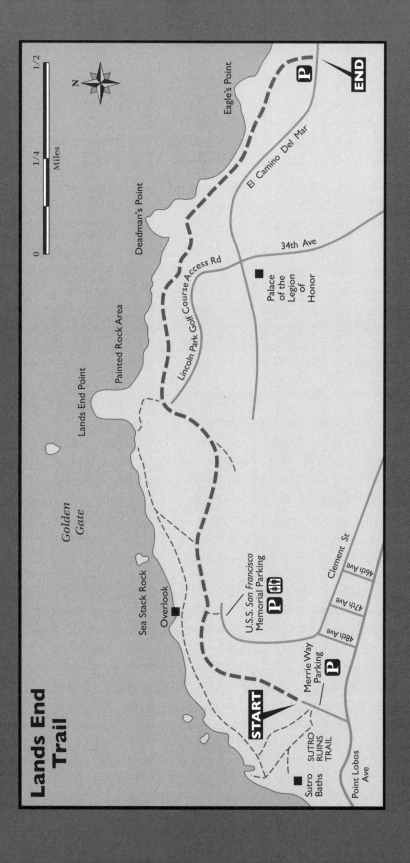

Francisco Memorial parking area or, to reach the trailhead proper, go left (south) on El Camino Del Mar for less than 0.1 mile to Point Lobos Avenue. Turn right (west) on Point Lobos Avenue and then turn right (north) almost immediately into the wheelchair-accessible Merrie Way parking lot.

There is limited streetside parking at the El Camino Del Mar end point; it's best to begin at the Point Lobos trailhead, where there is generous parking in the Merrie Way lot.

Transportation: MUNI, San Francisco's municipal transportation service, offers rail and bus access to the area, and can be reached by calling 311 in San Francisco or (415) 701–2311 outside San Francisco. The Web site is www.sfmta.com. Golden Gate Transit offers service to the Golden Gate National Recreation Area as well; call 511 (toll free in the Bay Area) or (415) 455–2000 outside the Bay Area, or visit the GGT Web site at www.golden gate.org.

Rentals: No rentals are available near the trail.

Contact: Golden Gate National Parks, Fort Mason, Building 201, San Francisco, CA 94123; (415) 561–4700; www.nps.gov/goga. You can also contact the Golden Gate Parks Conservancy at (415) 561–3000; www.parks conservancy.org. A link to trail information is www.parksconservancy.org/ visit/park.asp?pagekey=104.

|||||||||||||||||||||||||||||||||||||||||||||||||||||||||||||||||||||||||||||||||||||

It's not often that a man-made structure can compete with the elegance, grace, and beauty of the natural world. And it is no small feat when such a structure vies honorably with the majestic landscape at the mouth of San Francisco Bay. But the Golden Gate Bridge does just that. Because of its remarkable architecture, it transforms competition into compliment, so that the Golden Gate, lovely as it is, cannot be envisioned without its equally lovely bridge.

Both bridge and landscape are showcased along the Lands End Trail. The trail follows the former bed of a steam-powered railroad that was originally established by Adolph Sutro, one-time mayor of San Francisco. The railroad was operated by a number of companies from the 1880s to 1925, including the Cliff House and Ferries Railway, when landslides, which had plagued the area for years, finally forced the closure of the line. As former National Park Service ranger Dennis R. Glass notes in the history of the Lands End railroad lines that he has compiled, this closure was "the end of a rail era and the beginning of . . . public access" to the area.

After years of limited public access, the newly established Golden Gate National Recreation Area (GGNRA) cleaned up Lands End and opened the trail to the public in the mid-1970s. To quote Glass: "It is a site historically and presently for re-creation of the spirit."

The path, which circles crumbling cliffs with views of the narrow passage from the Pacific Ocean into San Francisco Bay, is part of the 9.1-mile Coastal Trail and is maintained by the GGNRA, an enormous park that spreads north to the spectacular Marin Headlands and abuts the Point Reyes National Seashore. Stewardship of the trail, from thinning the cypress forest to planting 40,000 native plants, falls under the auspices of the Golden Gate Parks Conservancy and Trails Forever (www.parksconservancy.com).

From the Merrie Way parking area, which in 2007 underwent improvements to make it more wheelchair-accessible and includes an overlook to the west over Sutro Baths, head north on the wide, obvious railroad grade

Cypress trees frame views of San Francisco's craggy coastline as seen from the Lands End Trail.

Two hikers take a brisk walk on the Lands End Trail.

to the right. The first third of a mile is wheelchair-friendly. Open canopies of cypress trees shade the trail and break the incessant wind that blows off the Pacific; the muffled roar of the ocean is a soothing companion for the entirety of the trail. Ignore narrow spur trails that branch off the main path. At the first major trail intersection, less than a quarter mile into the hike, go up and left (north) on the railroad grade.

The trail circles east to a staircase that leads up and south to the parking area at the U.S.S. *San Francisco* Memorial. An overlook offers lovely vistas from below the memorial. Views of both the craggy coastline guarding the mouth of the bay and of the Golden Gate Bridge open as the path bends eastward. The hillsides are thick with cypress, but an abundance of wildflowers and other native plants push up against the trail, glowing orange and pink beneath the green-bordering-on-black foliage of the evergreens. The trail is laid in a strip of wilderness that separates the city from the wind-whipped edge of the continent.

As you near the half-mile mark, the trail passes below the edifices of the Veterans Administration Memorial Hospital. Spur trails branch left and right; stay on the main, obvious track. A bit farther, a paved road drops to the rail trail; stay left (east and seaward) on the dirt route.

At about 0.75 mile, reach the Painted Rock Cliff, where DANGER signs warn you to stay on the maintained path. Enjoy the views from the Mile Rock overlook. Go up and right (southeast) on a long flight of railroad-tie steps; a bench at the halfway point on the staircase is a nice spot from which to enjoy the views. At the top of the stairs, rest before descending through eucalyptus and spindly Bishop pines to a trail intersection. Go left (northeast), back toward the ocean.

Once on the cliff again, views open of the Golden Gate. Bowers of cypress arc over the path, and the exclusive homes of Sea Cliff, with the beach below, can be seen. It's a bonanza of color on a clear day: the brick-red of the bridge, the pastels of the homes, the smoky green-blue of the ocean, the bleached sails of boats in the bay.

As you approach trail's end at about 2 miles, the path narrows again, and is bounded by thick underbrush. The rail trail leads to the edge of the Lincoln Park Golf Course near the Palace of the Legion of Honor. A wooden overlook at Eagle's Point offers yet another chance to savor the views before you retrace your steps to the Point Lobos trailhead.

17 BARBARY COAST TRAIL

Aside from the richness of San Francisco's food, shopping, cultural districts, and views, this rail trail offers something few others do: the chance to ride the rails for a leg of the route, in this case on one of the city's fabled cable cars.

Activities:

Location: San Francisco, San Francisco County

Length: 3-mile (give or take . . .) round-trip

Surface: The surface is mixed: concrete sidewalk, brick, asphalt, and boardwalk.

Wheelchair access: Though technically most of the trail is wheelchair accessible, negotiating the steep grades on Hyde and Powell Streets is tough for able-bodied walkers and cable car operators, let alone wheelchairs. The climb over the Stockton grade is also a potential challenge.

Difficulty: Moderate if you ride the cable car, hard if you don't.

Food: What can I say? Upscale, Continental, Chinese, Italian, fast food, seafood . . . if you can't find what you crave, it probably doesn't exist.

Restrooms: Public facilities are scattered along the route, including at the trailheads at Fisherman's Wharf and at Hallidie Plaza at the base of Powell on Market Street.

Seasons: The trail can be used year-round.

Access and parking: If walking, you can begin this loop route anywhere along the streets it follows. If you travel the trail as described, you'll begin with a cable car ride from Fisherman's Wharf, at the intersection of Hyde and Beach, where on-street and garage parking are available, all for a fee. Another option is to begin at Fifth and Mission. After parking at one of many parking garages or on the street (all for a generous fee), you can stroll 1 block north to the Market Street cable car stop, then ride to Fisherman's Wharf and take the rail clockwise.

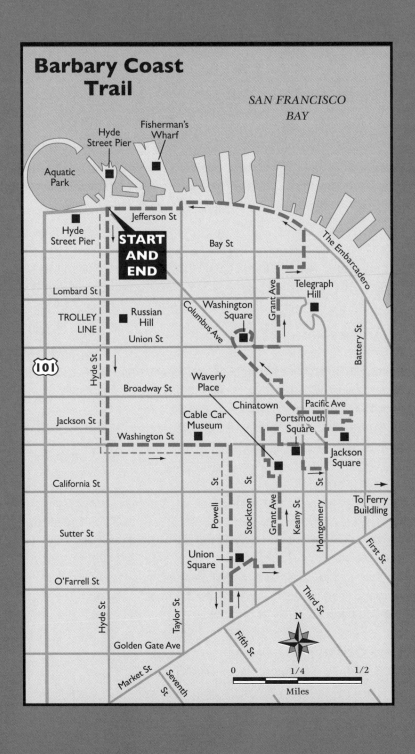

Barbary Coast Trail

SAN FRANCISCO
BAY

Aquatic Park

Hyde Street Pier

Fisherman's Wharf

Hyde Street Pier

START AND END

Jefferson St

Bay St

The Embarcadero

Lombard St

TROLLEY LINE

Russian Hill

Union St

Columbus Ave

Washington Square

Grant Ave

Telegraph Hill

Battery St

101

Hyde St

Broadway St

Waverly Place

Chinatown

Pacific Ave

Jackson St

Cable Car Museum

Portsmouth Square

Jackson Square

Washington St

California St

Powell St

Stockton St

Grant Ave

Kearny St

Montgomery

To Ferry Building

Sutter St

O'Farrell St

Union Square

First St

Hyde St

Taylor St

Golden Gate Ave

Fifth St

Third St

N

Market St

Seventh St

0   1/4   1/2

Miles

Transportation: MUNI, San Francisco's municipal transportation service, offers rail and bus access to Fisherman's Wharf, the financial district, and points between. It can be reached by calling 311 in San Francisco or (415) 701–2311 outside the city. The Web site is www.sfmta.com. Golden Gate Transit also serves the area; call 511 (toll free in the Bay Area) or (415) 455-2000 outside the Bay Area. The Web site is www.goldengate.org.

Rentals: While it's possible to rent bicycles and skates at various locations in San Francisco, this route is best traveled on foot. If cycling or skating is a must, contact the local telephone directory for options.

Contact: The trail is sponsored by the San Francisco Museum and Historical Society, which has placed bronze plaques in the sidewalks along the route and maintains Internet information on the trail. The historical society is at P.O. Box 420470, San Francisco, CA 94142-0470; the phone number is (415) 775–1111; the Web site is www.sfhistory.org. At the Web site, you'll find an interactive map describing the various historic sites you'll see along the trail.

Another good contact for the trail (and for Internet information on the route) is barbarycoasttrail.org. For information on tours or guides, you can e-mail info@barbarycoasttrail.org, or call (415) 454–2355.

The Barbary Coast Trail knits San Francisco's sights together in a perfect scenic overlay. From cable cars to Chinatown to Union Square, from the financial district to Coit Tower to Fisherman's Wharf, you'll see it all along this route.

The "trail" qualifies as a rail trail because a portion of it follows the Hyde and Powell Streets cable car lines. These tracks, and the open-air cars that ride upon them, are known the world over and provide the perfect start (or end) to an unforgettable tour of the city by the bay. The Hyde-Powell cable car route, which has been in existence since the late nineteenth century, is a National Historical Monument, and, according to the

The Barbary Coast Trail can either begin or end with a cable car ride.

historical society, was the brainchild of a gentleman who witnessed the ineffectiveness of a team of horses attempting to haul a load up one of the city's steep hills.

The route is described beginning with a cable car ride from the base of Hyde Street on Fisherman's Wharf. This $5 ride, which takes you to Market Street and Powell, will most likely involve a long wait in line, but is well worth both the money and the time. The route can be followed on foot, but given the choice . . .

The cable car takes you up and over Russian Hill, past lovely mansions with awesome views of the bay; the mansions have the easy views, while the cable car riders must twist around to see them. Dropping down Washington Street (the descent punctuated by the smell of the cable car's wooden brakes heating up), you'll pass the Cable Car Museum, housed in the old Ferries and Cliff House Railroad building. A final descent through crowded downtown via Powell Street lands you at Market Street, where you'll find a BART station, the San Francisco Visitor Center, and, a block south via Fifth Street, the Old U.S. Mint.

From this southernmost point of the trail, you'll head north. Locate the bronze marker at the corner of Powell and Market, and continue north along Powell, back toward the waterfront. Similar markers are set in the pavement at nearly every street intersection. Sponsored by area businesses and organizations, the markers include arrows that direct you along the route. A map will help, however: I did a couple of loops through Chinatown (not a bad place to get confused) but was easily able to find my way back on track using one of the free online maps provided by the San Francisco Museum and Historical Society (another map is offered at barbarycoasttrail.org). More complete guides available for purchase along the route and online include detailed information about the historic sites you'll see along the trail. The directions provided here will simply get you from one major attraction to the next.

The walk up Powell Street leads across Ellis and Geary to Union Square, San Francisco's shopping center. The markers lead through the heart of the square to the northeast corner at Post and Stockton. Cross Post and head south on Stockton to quaint Maiden Lane, which is closed to vehicle traffic and offers more upscale shopping options.

At the end of Maiden Lane, turn left on Grant and head north across Post, Sutter, and Bush into Chinatown, passing through the historic Dragon's Gate. The transformation is invigorating, as the streets clog with tourists and locals, bustling from shop to shop and restaurant to restaurant. The route leads uphill across Pine to the California Street intersection, where the brick facade of Old Saint Mary's Cathedral marks the northeast corner. Head left (west) on Sacramento to Waverly Place, a narrow alley dubbed the "Street of the Painted Balconies." Emerge onto Jackson and head east to Portsmouth Square, where you'll find restrooms and benches and clusters of local men hunkered over game boards, along with a monument that commemorates this as the site of the first public school in the city.

Head east from the square along Washington to cross Kearny and descend to Montgomery, at the base of the pyramid-shaped Transamerica Building, famous in the San Francisco skyline. Head right on Montgomery, across Clay, to Commercial Street, a narrow road that at one time, according to the historical society, was central to the city's commerce but now is lost in the steel and concrete of a much more modern financial district.

To continue toward Fisherman's Wharf, follow Montgomery north to Jackson; the markers lead you east to Jackson Square, then back north to Pacific and the site of the old Barbary Coast, home to the wild and prosperous businesses that made San Francisco infamous. Follow Pacific up to Kearny and then turn right along Columbus Avenue into North Beach, home of "beat San Francisco," where authors Jack Kerouac and Allen Ginsberg once hung out. The trail jogs onto Grant, then continues along Columbus, through a complicated intersection at Stockton and Green, and past numerous eateries with al fresco seating. (See why a map would be helpful?)

Cross Union to Washington Square, which features broad lawns, a tot lot, restrooms, and the spectacular Saints Peter and Paul Catholic Church on its northern front. Coit Tower, atop Telegraph Hill, is to the right (east). The main trail climbs to the top of the hill via Greenwich, then descends via Grant, Francisco, and Kearny to the Embarcadero; an alternative route, suitable for wheelchair users, follows Stockton and Northpoint to the waterfront.

At the Embarcadero, turn left (west) and follow the crowds and the MUNI tracks past the historic piers toward Fisherman's Wharf. The route (now also the Bay Trail) passes Pier 39, the Aquarium of the Bay, the headquarters for the Blue and Gold Fleet, which offers bay cruises as well as trips to notorious Alcatraz Island, and the busy restaurant and shopping district of the wharf itself. Finish the tour back at the cable car base at the bottom of Hyde Street; Ghirardelli Square and Aquatic Park are a block to the west.

18 BLACK DIAMOND MINES REGIONAL PRESERVE RAILROAD BED TRAIL

Mount Diablo dominates the skyline of the East Bay, and forms the bedrock upon which the rail trail in Black Diamond Mines Regional Preserve is built. The trail, short and sweet, leads to an abundance of historic sites within the preserve.

Activities:

Location: Black Diamond Mines Regional Preserve, Contra Costa County

Length: 1 mile one way

Surface: Dirt

Wheelchair access: The trail is not wheelchair accessible. Although the incline is relatively flat, the trail's surface is very rough.

Difficulty: Easy

Food: There is no food available along the trail or in the park, but ample food outlets, from fast food to restaurants to grocery stores, can be found a few miles east of the preserve in Pittsburg and Antioch.

Restrooms: Restrooms are available at the park office, which is near the lower end of the trail. Restrooms are also available near the trail's end.

Seasons: The trail is accessible year-round, but the path may be muddy after rains during the winter months.

Access and parking: To reach the park from California 4 in Antioch, take the Somersville Road exit. Go south on Somersville Road for 1.6 miles to where the road enters the Black Diamond Mines Regional Preserve. Go another mile up the canyon to the park entrance station. The lower trailhead for the Railroad Bed Trail is located here, at the south end of the large parking lot on the east side of Somersville Road. Head up the canyon for another mile to reach the upper parking area, where you will also find a good-size parking lot, a corral, and picnic sites. The parking is plentiful at both trailheads.

Transportation: There is no public transportation available within the park.

Rentals: There are no rental facilities in the park.

Contact: East Bay Regional Park District, 2950 Peralta Oaks Court, P.O. Box 5381, Oakland, CA 94605-5381; (888) EBPARKS or (510) 562–PARK. The Web site is www.ebparks.org/black-diamond. You can reach the park directly by calling (925) 757–2620.

IIIIIIIIIIIIIIIIIIIIIIIIIIIIIIIIIIIIIIIIIIIIIIIIIIIIIIIIIIIIIIIIIIIIIIIIIIIIIIIIIIIIIIIIII

The foothills of Mount Diablo fold into steep, shadowy canyons shaded by the occasional oak tree and carpeted in tall grasses and wildflowers. In winter, rain feeds these grasses, encouraging them to blush a vivid green; in summer, drought dries them golden and brittle.

This is the setting of the short rail trail that leads into Black Diamond Mines Regional Preserve. Although the trail itself is not breathtaking, it links with a trail system within the park that is rich in history and natural beauty. Consider it a gateway to a greater adventure or take it on its own merits. Regardless, you'll be delighted.

The railroad that once ran along this grade served the Black Diamond mines. Black diamonds were coal, and millions of tons were extracted from these hills over a forty-year period at the end of the nineteenth century. A thriving mining district blossomed around the mines, including five towns, the remains of which lie within the 5,000-acre preserve. The rail line, operated by the Black Diamond Coal & Railroad Company, ran for nearly 6 miles from Pittsburg to Somersville.

After the coal mines were abandoned, sand was mined in the area in the 1920s. And when those mines ceased operation, ranchers took over the hills, using the old mining equipment, including railroad ties, to help outfit their operations.

Because of its ease, this trail is perfect for children and fledgling mountain bikers. It begins beyond the gate at the south end of the parking lot near the park buildings and entrance station. The trail parallels Somersville Road as it heads up and south into the narrowing canyon. The stream that runs seasonally from the higher reaches of the park lies west of the road, overhung by pockets of oak trees. The rail trail itself is entirely open to the sun and the rain, bordered only in grasses, thistles, and wildflowers. Bring plenty of water and wear a hat if you plan to hike during the heat of a summer's day.

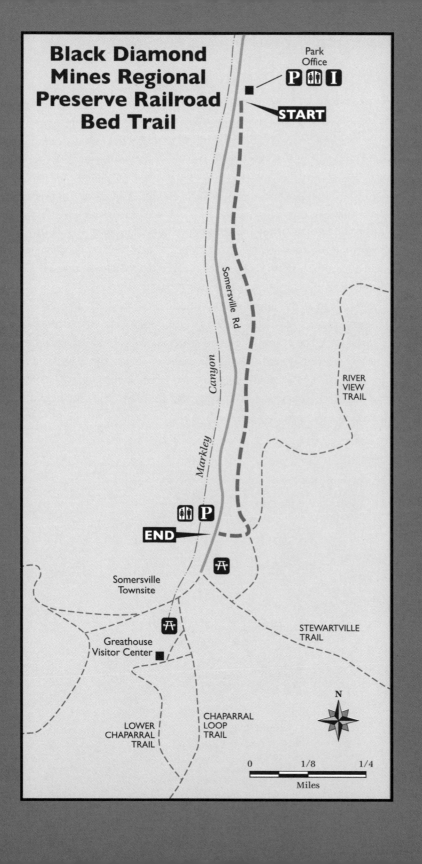

The canyon grows ever narrower and the adjacent paved road creeps closer to the trail as you climb toward the Somersville townsite. At about the 0.7-mile mark, the trail crosses a raised bed of gray ballast and sand. Once past this exposed section of the route, the trail drops below the elevation of Somersville Road, passing a stately shade tree. It fades from open roadbed to double-track, and climbs more steeply to the picnic area and corral at 1 mile.

This is the end of the rail trail, but there is much more to see. Another mile's worth of hiking will allow you to take a tour of the Somersville area, which includes the Greathouse Portal and the powder magazine, where explosives used in the mining process were stored.

The trailhead at the upper end point of the rail trail also offers abundant opportunities to take longer treks or mountain bike rides into other areas of the park. You can visit the end of the Black Diamond railroad line at Nortonville, stopping at the Rose Hill Cemetery along the way, or head east to the Stewartville townsite. The park brochure, which includes some general interpretive material, is a handy tool for planning other explorations, and is available at the entry station and online at www.ebparks.org/parks/maps.

19 OHLONE GREENWAY

Residents and visitors to three East Bay cities enjoy the amenities of this long rail trail, which offers access to community parks and experimental gardens. The trail also features intimate contact with the modern Bay Area Rapid Transit railway system.

Activities:

Location: Berkeley, Albany, and El Cerrito in Contra Costa County

Length: 6 miles one way

Surface: Asphalt

Wheelchair access: The trail is entirely wheelchair accessible.

Difficulty: Moderate. This is a relatively long trail, but it is easily broken into segments, which can reduce the difficulty.

Food: Although there are no restaurants or grocery stores along the path itself, a quick jog onto a neighboring street, especially in Albany and El Cerrito, will land you in shopping districts or malls presenting a parade of culinary outlets.

Restrooms: There are no public restrooms along the route.

Seasons: The trail can be used year-round.

Access and parking: To reach the Ohlone Park end point from Interstate 80 in Berkeley, take the University Avenue exit and head east on University Avenue toward the University of California at Berkeley campus. Turn left (north) on Milvia Street and go 2 blocks to Hearst Avenue. Ohlone Park is on your left (west). Park along the street.

To reach the Key Boulevard end point from I–80 in El Cerrito, take the San Pablo Avenue exit (California 123). Go south on San Pablo Avenue to Conlon Avenue and turn left (east). Follow Conlon Avenue east for 1 block to its intersection with Key Boulevard and turn right (south) onto Key Boulevard. The trail is located on the right (west) side of Key Boulevard. Again, park along the street.

Transportation: The San Francisco Bay Area Rapid Transit (BART) tracks fly directly overhead, offering the perfect opportunity for folks to travel the rail trail and then ride the train back to either end point. BART can be reached at P.O. Box 12688, Oakland, CA 94606-2688. The phone number for the Oakland/Berkeley area is (510) 465–2278; for the Richmond/El Cerrito area, call (510) 236–2278. The Web site is www.bart.gov. A/C Transit also provides service in the area. Call (510) 891–4700 or check the Web site at www.actransit.org.

Rentals: There are no rental shops on the path.

Contact: The trail passes through three cities. The contact for Berkeley is William Rogers, Director, Parks and Waterfront Department, Park Design Division, City of Berkeley, 2180 Milvia, Third Floor, Berkeley, CA 94704; (510) 981–6700. For the Albany section, contact Nicole Almaguer, Environment Resources Coordinator, Community Development Department, City of Albany, 1000 San Pablo Avenue, Albany, CA 94706; (510) 528–5754; www.albanyca.org. In El Cerrito, contact Bruce King, Manager of the City of El Cerrito's Maintenance and Engineering Department, 10940 San Pablo Avenue, El Cerrito, CA 94530; (510) 215–4382; www.el-cerrito.org.

|||||||||||||||||||||||||||||||||||||||||||||||||||||||||||||||||||||||||||||||||||||||||||||||||

A lthough it has a distinctly urban flavor and is foremost a safe route to schools and work, the Ohlone Greenway, also known as the Santa Fe Greenway, clearly doubles as a recreational trail. Its utilitarian worth is obvious: The trail allows workers and students to walk or ride from their homes to jobs or the University of California at Berkeley. But on any sunny day, you'll also find joggers, cyclists, families out for a stroll, and people walking their dogs on the route. From diapers to Lycra to three-piece suits, you'll see it all along the Ohlone Greenway.

Except for a short section in Berkeley, the trail runs directly beneath the elevated tracks of the San Francisco Bay Area Rapid Transit (BART). The trains are relatively quiet, but their passage is a noisome reminder that you travel on a rail trail. The route is nicely landscaped for its entire distance, passing through parks and near community gardens, and is long enough to give those seeking a workout just what they are looking for.

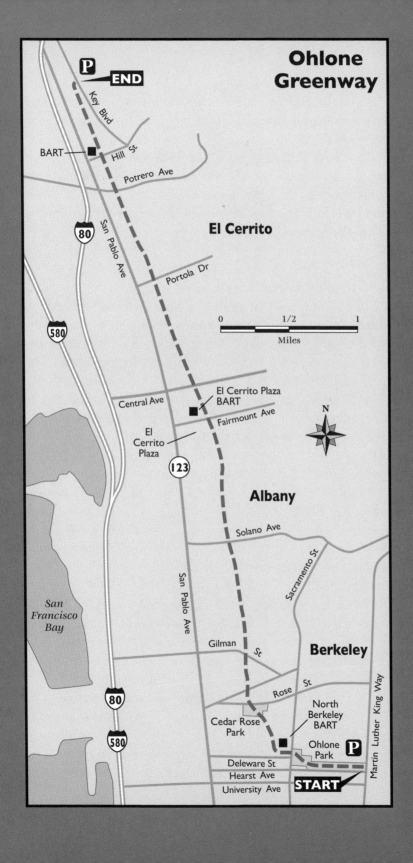

The trail is described here from south (Berkeley) to north (El Cerrito), but it is crossed by numerous city streets, and can be accessed from any of these points.

Ohlone Park, which, like the rail trail, is named for the native peoples that once populated the Bay Area, is an extremely pleasant starting point. A swath of greenery plunked in the middle of a quiet residential neighborhood, it offers a tot lot, basketball courts, and narrow fields that are nonetheless perfectly suited for a pickup game of soccer or Frisbee. The asphalt path heads west through the park, weaving back and forth to other meandering paths, until the park ends at the intersection of Delaware and Sacramento Streets, at the North Berkeley BART station.

Follow the bike lane that runs along Delaware Street for 2 blocks to its intersection with Acton Street and turn right (north), following the signs for the Ohlone Greenway. Go 2 blocks along Acton Street to its junction with Virginia Street. The signed Ohlone Greenway takes off from the northwest corner of the intersection at about the 0.3-mile mark.

The trail weaves across several quiet streets, passing basketball courts that ring with the sounds of men and women at play, to Cedar Rose Park at 0.5 mile. Another tot lot and a rolling lawn invite rest and fun.

At about the 0.8-mile mark, cross Peralta Avenue and pass two community gardens: The Karl Linn Garden is on the northeast side of the road, and the Peralta Community Garden is opposite, adjacent to the continuation of the trail.

The BART tracks rise up to meet the trail, then climb overhead. You pass underneath them at the intersection of Curtis and Gilman Streets at 1 mile. Cross the busy intersection with care and continue on the rail trail into the city of Albany.

At 1.2 miles, cross Codornices Creek. The street intersections that follow require concentration, especially the Solano Avenue crossing at about 1.7 miles.

The trail is nicely landscaped beneath the shade of the tracks and features a parcourse for those who want to add a few crunches or pull-ups to their walking or running routine. Pedestrians can avoid bicycle and skate traffic by stepping onto a winding dirt walkway that parallels the main paved route.

Enter the city of El Cerrito at the 2.4-mile mark and pass the El Cerrito Plaza BART station and the intersection with a link to the Bay Trail at Fair-

The Ohlone Greenway begins in Ohlone Park.

mount Avenue. Although the stretches of trail between street crossings become longer, and the streets seem less busy, these crossings demand you use caution.

Pass a retaining wall painted in splashes of green and blue, and another parcourse that runs along the rail trail. The trail's character changes as it passes from city to city, with the major difference between the El Cerrito and Albany sections being the landscaping; El Cerrito's is a bit more rustic than Albany's. Instead of manicured plants and shrubs, you'll encounter more opportunistic flora. In spring the trail is sprinkled with the brilliant orange blooms of poppies and the vivid yellows and greens of clover, as well as the riotous colors of calla lilies and other plants that have escaped the confines of gardens. Trail signs become more frequent in El Cerrito as well, pointing the way to the local library and other public facilities that can be reached from the trail.

As you near the 4-mile mark, you will enter a section of trail designated a Dinosaur Forest. No dinosaurs are present; the name refers to some prehistoric-looking plants that grow in the area. The section of trail between Schmidt Lane and Potrero Avenue is the site of another unique plant environment. In the Urban Forest Demonstration Area, a wide variety of exotic trees and shrubs has been planted; they are marked with small interpretive signs.

Reach Hill Street at the 4.6-mile mark and pass the El Cerrito Del Norte BART station. Beyond the station the trail skirts the parking lot for a neighboring apartment building, then climbs to Baxter Creek, which is nicely accented with small, well-tended flower beds. The creek is the subject of a preservation effort by a grassroots organization called Friends of Baxter Creek. Part of that effort involves promoting an extension of the Ohlone Greenway along the creek to the San Francisco Bay Trail, by linking it with the Richmond Greenway.

Until such an extension is reality, the trail ends beyond Key Boulevard, continuing for about 0.25 mile along Baxter Creek, which has been nicely restored and features a seating area. At about the 6-mile mark, either return as you came or backtrack to the BART station and catch a ride back to Berkeley.

20 IRON HORSE REGIONAL TRAIL

A short description for a trail of this length will, of necessity, resemble the proverbial laundry list. Oak-shaded greenbelts through quiet neighborhoods, modern business districts, and quaint shopping areas, long stretches that work the muscles of the most dedicated athletes, sunshine, rolling hills—the Iron Horse Trail adds up to a wonderful recreational experience.

Activities:

Location: Alameda and Contra Costa Counties

Length: 25.5 miles from Concord to the Dublin/Pleasanton BART Station

Surface: Asphalt and concrete with a parallel dirt walkway in some areas

Wheelchair access: The trail is accessible to wheelchairs for its entirety.

Difficulty: Hard if taken as a whole, but when broken into smaller chunks, the rail trail is easy to moderate.

Food: There are innumerable places to pick up a bite to eat along the northern reaches of the trail. You will find grocery stores, fast-food joints, snazzy restaurants, and coffeehouses at the trail's midpoint in the Danville area. South of Danville, the trail passes through more residential areas; it is not until you reach the mall at Alcosta Boulevard that you again encounter convenient eats.

Restrooms: There are a few public restrooms scattered along the trail, at the BART station and Walden Park in Walnut Creek, at Hap McGee Park in Danville, and at the San Ramon Community Center and Park in San Ramon.

Seasons: This paved route is accessible year-round.

Access and parking: The trail parallels Interstate 680 through the towns and cities of Concord, Pleasant Hill, Walnut Creek, Alamo, Danville, San Ramon, and Dublin. It can be accessed at numerous points along its route. There is limited parking at the Monument Boulevard trailhead, which is located east of I–680 on Monument Boulevard at Mohr Lane. You can also pick up the trail at the Walnut Creek BART station on Treat Boulevard; this too is east of I–680, with parking located to the north of the station on Coggins Drive.

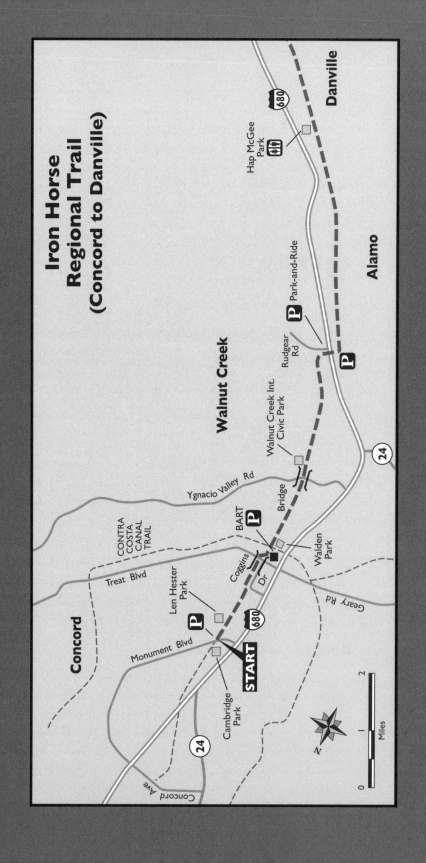

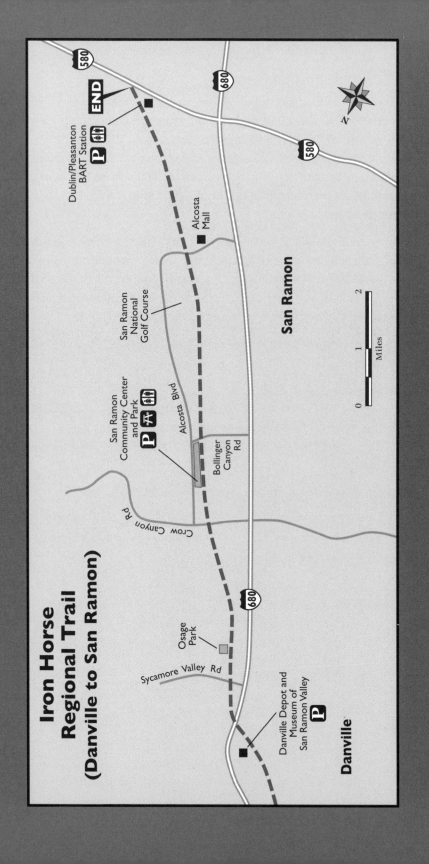

Iron Horse Regional Trail (Danville to San Ramon)

580

680

580

END

P 🚻

Dublin/Pleasanton BART Station

Alcosta Mall

San Ramon National Golf Course

San Ramon

2

1

Miles

0

San Ramon Community Center and Park

P A 🚻

Alcosta Blvd

Bollinger Canyon Rd

Crow Canyon Rd

680

Osage Park

Sycamore Valley Rd

Danville Depot and Museum of San Ramon Valley

P

Danville

N

The Park-and-Ride parking lot on the east side of the interstate at Rudgear Road in Danville also offers good parking and trail access. Cross to the west side of the freeway and go about 25 yards north along the frontage road to the trailhead. There is limited parking right at the trailhead at this location. You can also pick up the trail in downtown Danville, near the Danville Depot on West Prospect Avenue, which is on the west side of the interstate at Diablo Road.

Near the southern end of the trail, you can park at the San Ramon Community Center and Park, which is located east of I–680. Take Bollinger Canyon Road east toward Alcosta Boulevard; the park is on the north side of the road. San Ramon, you can hop on the trail near the Alcosta Mall, which is located east of the interstate on Alcosta Boulevard.

The southernmost access is at the Dublin/Pleasanton BART station, just off Interstate 580.

Transportation: A/C Transit provides bus service in the area. Call (510) 891–4700 for bus schedules, write to 1600 Franklin Street, Oakland, CA 94612, or check the Web site at www.actransit.org. Bay Area Rapid Transit (BART) also serves the trail; call (925) 676–2278 or (510) 441-2278, or visit www.bart.gov.

Rentals: There are no rentals available along the trail.

Contact: East Bay Regional Park District, 2950 Peralta Oaks Court, P.O. Box 5381, Oakland, CA 94605-5381; (888) EBPARKS or (510) 562–PARK; www.ebparks.org/parks/trails/iron_horse.

|||||||||||||||||||||||||||||||||||||||||||||||||||||||||||||||||||||||||||||||||||

From Silicon Valley–esque business districts to trailside lemonade stands, you'll see it all along the friendly and popular Iron Horse Regional Trail.

At its northern end, the Iron Horse Trail is very urban, almost metropolitan, passing through business districts with high-rise buildings and busy four-lane roads. At its center, in Alamo and Danville (arguably the prettiest section of the trail), the rail trail passes through wealthy suburbia on a swath of oak-shaded pavement bordered by lush grasses, wildflowers, and well-kept homes. Downtown Danville is quaint, outfitted with upscale supermarkets and coffee shops.

South of Danville, both the neighborhoods and the trail are more exposed. Gone are the shady oaks, replaced by a wide treeless greenbelt upon which the grasses are vividly green in winter and spring, and dry to a crackling yellow in summer and fall. Wooden fences delineate the boundary between the trail and the neighborhoods on either side of it.

Beyond Crow Canyon Road, the trail passes through industrial complexes boxed neatly in glass and masonry, with large parking lots abutting the trail. Near its southern terminus, the trail passes through the San Ramon National Golf Course, where trail users are protected from wayward golf balls by a bower of meshlike fencing. The setting is gritty and urban at trail's end in Dublin.

The rail trail follows the right-of-way of the Southern Pacific Railroad, which established a branch line in the San Ramon Valley in 1890 to serve the farming and ranching communities that had sprung up in the then sparsely populated area. The railroad served the valley and its burgeoning towns for about seventy years, until improved roadways through the region rendered the rail line unnecessary. The tracks were abandoned in 1975, and by the early 1980s, cities in the valley had begun to acquire the right-of-way and set it aside for a trail. By the end of the 1980s, sections of the trail had been constructed, paved, and dedicated, and the Iron Horse Trail was well on its way.

The East Bay Regional Park District (EBRPD) continues to focus on further development of the rail trail corridor, with plans to extend the trail south and east to Livermore and the Shadow Cliffs Regional Recreation Area. When completed, the route will be 34 miles long.

As mentioned above, the existing trail can be done in its entirety or in segments. I found the section from Rudgear Road to Danville to be the prettiest—and probably the most enjoyable for hikers and runners—with the segment in San Ramon the most conducive to exercise-oriented cycling, running, and in-line skating. Every part of the trail offers wonderful recreational opportunities to neighborhood residents.

The trail is described beginning in the north at Monument Boulevard in Concord and running southward to the Dublin/Pleasanton BART station.

A short trail segment heads north from Monument Boulevard for about 0.5 mile, through tiny Cambridge Park and alongside the channel

A cyclist climbs a bridge on the Iron Horse Trail.

that holds Walnut Creek, to an underpass at I–680. A fence bars passage under the freeway; traveling this segment is an out-and-back affair.

The streetlight at Mohr Lane offers safe passage across Monument Boulevard, where you pick up the southbound trail. The trail passes through well-kept subdivisions, crossing intersections with tree-lined neighborhood streets via crosswalks, railroad bridges, and underpasses, to Coggins Drive. A bridge spans busy Treat Boulevard at 2.7 miles, arcing over the eight-lane roadway and landing at the BART station on the south side of the thoroughfare.

The next intersection is with the Contra Costa Canal Trail (3 miles). Continue straight (south) through the greenbelt (or goldbelt once the grasses dry in summer). At 3.1 miles, you can turn right (west) to Walden Park, which features a tot lot, picnic tables, water, and restrooms.

Beyond this trail junction, the rail trail proceeds south to the Ygnacio Valley Road bridge in Walnut Creek at about 4.2 miles; this is followed by a more traditional trestle bridge.

A couple of street crossings come in quick succession at about the 5-mile mark; the first at Mount Diablo Boulevard, the second leading to the west side of Newell Avenue. Beyond Newell, the trail is squeezed between apartment buildings on the west and an ivy-draped wall that serves as a barrier to South Broadway on the east.

At about 6.5 miles, arrive at the intersection of Rudgear Road and I–680. The Park-and-Ride parking lot is on the northeast corner of the intersection. Pass under the interstate and cross the frontage road (Danville Boulevard); the trail continues about 25 yards north of the stoplight on the frontage road.

The setting of the rail trail now gives the impression of being almost rural, passing through an oak woodland spread with knee-high grasses and wildflowers, and bordered by large homes with tasteful fences and ornamental shrubbery. Cross a number of small neighborhood roads before the trail's intersection with Stone Valley Road at 9 miles, where the scenery becomes more urban. Cross a bridge at Hemme Avenue. At about 10 miles, follow Camille Avenue left (east) to Hap McGee Park, where you will find water and restrooms.

Cross another small bridge before Hartford Road, then travel south for a mile to West Prospect Avenue, where the Danville Depot and the Museum of San Ramon Valley border the path. The museum is open Tuesday through Friday from 1:00 to 4:00 P.M. and Saturday from 10:00 A.M. to 1:00 P.M. The Web site is www.museumsrv.org.

Now in downtown Danville, the trail circles the west side of a shopping center and traces Railroad Avenue. Cross Prospect Avenue and San Ramon Valley Boulevard before passing under the interstate at about the 12.5-mile mark.

By the time the rail trail crosses Sycamore Valley Road at 13.2 miles, it has taken on a decidedly suburban aspect, passing through a broad greenbelt that resonates with noise from the nearby freeway. From this point to Alcosta Boulevard, the rail trail can be hot and dry—especially in summer—with no water available save that found at the San Ramon Community Center and Park, which is at about the 17.5-mile mark.

Between Sycamore Valley Road and the park, cross several streets, including Fostoria Road, where a large "golf ball" and power station adorn the east side of the path. Cross Crow Canyon Road as well, which is bordered by industrial buildings. You can reach the community park from the trail via either Norris Canyon Road or Bollinger Canyon Road. At 18 miles, pass a park with a tot lot at Monte Video Road.

The power poles that have been shadowing the trail since Crow Canyon Road end at Pine Valley Road. At about 19.5 miles, you will reach the San Ramon National Golf Course, passing beneath the arch of fencing that protects trail users from stray golf balls.

At about the 23-mile mark, cross Alcosta Boulevard; the trail skirts a shopping mall, crosses a bridge, and drops into a greenbelt bordered by a canal on the west side. Look for egrets, herons, ducks, and other waterfowl in the waterway as you pass.

At about 24 miles, the Iron Horse crosses Amador Valley Boulevard, then follows the canal for another 0.2 mile to a bridge. On the far side of the span, the rail trail intersects the Alamo Canal Trail. Go left, then quickly right, on the Iron Horse; a signpost marks the way, and an old trestle reminds you of the origins of the path.

Cross Dougherty Drive at 24.5 miles, and the route enters a decidedly more industrial setting. Another bridge and the Dublin Boulevard crossing signal the approaching end of the route as of late summer 2007; the last segment deposits you at the Dublin/Pleasanton BART station in the shadow of I–580 at 25.5 miles. Unless you've arranged a pickup or want to ride the train back to Walnut Creek, return as you came.

21 LAFAYETTE–MORAGA TRAIL

Rolling, grassy hills trimmed with spreading oaks form the backdrop for this long, scenic rail trail. The route links tidy residential communities with St. Mary's College, the community park at Moraga Commons, and the more rustic trails of the neighboring watershed.

Activities:

Location: From Lafayette to Moraga in Contra Costa County

Length: 7.6 miles one way

Surface: Asphalt and concrete

Wheelchair access: The trail is accessible to wheelchairs for its entire length, with the exception of the dirt Valle Vista Staging Area parking lot.

Difficulty: Moderate, due to the trail's length

Food: The northern part of the trail, through Lafayette's residential districts and past St. Mary's College, offers few gastronomic opportunities. Once you enter Moraga, however, you will find grocery stores and restaurants near the path.

Restrooms: There are no restrooms at the Olympic Boulevard Staging Area, but restrooms are available at the Moraga Commons and at the Valle Vista Staging Area.

Seasons: The trail can be used year-round.

Access and parking: To reach the northern end point in Lafayette, take the Pleasant Hill Road exit from California 24. Go right (south) on Pleasant Hill Road for 0.9 mile to Olympic Boulevard. Go right (west) on Olympic Boulevard for about 0.1 mile to the parking area, which is on the right (north) side of the road. There is ample parking here and at another lot located about 0.2 mile farther west on Olympic Boulevard.

To reach the Valle Vista Staging Area from CA 24, take the Pleasant Hill exit, go south onto Pleasant Hill Road, then turn right (west) on Mount Diablo Boulevard. Follow Mount Diablo Boulevard to Moraga Road and turn left (south). Go south on Moraga Road to St. Mary's Road, and turn left (east). Follow St. Mary's Road which traces the route of the rail trail, south to Canyon Road. Canyon Road continues south to the Valle Vista Staging Area parking lot.

Transportation: The County Connection provides local bus service; call (925) 676–7500 or visit www.ccta.org.

Rentals: No rentals are available along the trail.

Contact: East Bay Regional Park District, 2950 Peralta Oaks Court, P.O. Box 5381, Oakland, CA 94605-5381; (888) EBPARKS or (510) 562–PARK; www .ebparks.org/parks/trails/lafayette_moraga.

|||||||||||||||||||||||||||||||||||||||||||||||||||||||||||||||||||||||||||||||||||||||||

The beauty of the Lafayette–Moraga Trail sneaks up on you. It has many facets: the neat and quiet neighborhoods of Lafayette, the pastoral setting of St. Mary's College, the playful Moraga Commons, the relative wildness of the Valle Vista Staging Area. Each of these facets, taken alone, has a certain sparkle, but when combined, the trail glitters with possibilities.

The rail trail lies on the former bed of the Sacramento Northern Railroad; a scattering of railroad crossing signs hints at its past. But where passengers once let electric trolleys transport them from one destination to the next, these days hikers, cyclists, and in-line skaters propel themselves through the sun-splashed hills.

The trail is described from north to south, but direction makes no difference, as the trail is an up-and-down affair, with the high point at the "pass" near St. Mary's College.

From the Olympic Boulevard trailhead, go west on the paved path, which meanders among the old trees of an orchard for 0.2 mile to the second parking lot at the intersection of Reliez Station Road and Olympic Boulevard. Cross Reliez Station Road to continue on the trail, which lies within a narrow greenbelt that passes between residences.

At about 0.5 mile, the trail crosses Hawthorne Drive; pass a railroad sign, then cross Foye Drive at about the 1-mile mark. Beyond, the path weaves through the Moraga Pumping Plant complex, crosses a bridge, then proceeds through more neighborhoods. A brief section of the trail

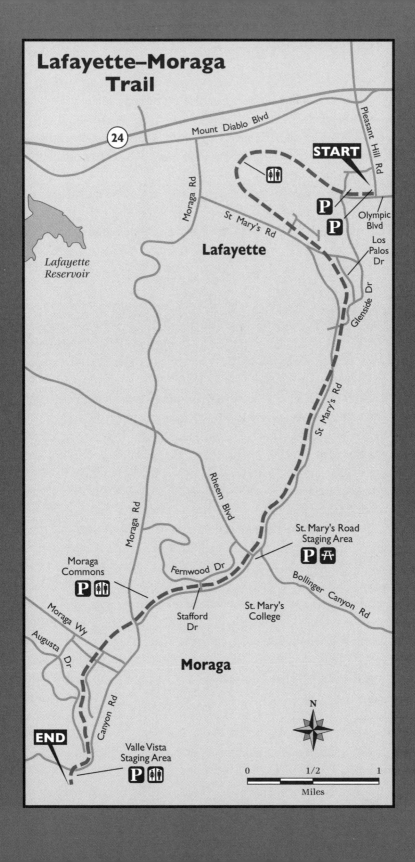

is on Brookdale Court, a residential street, but resumption of the rail trail proper is just ahead.

By the 2-mile mark, intersections with neighborhood streets are spaced a bit farther apart. Pass the Las Trampas Pool complex at about 2.5 miles and continue south.

At about 3 miles, cross busy St. Mary's Road. Parking is available midway along the trail at South Lucille Lane.

Once across St. Mary's Road, the trail passes into more scenic terrain in the folds of the oak-covered hills. At about 3.5 miles, a waterfall drips from the rocks on the right (west) side of the trail during the spring and winter months.

The route climbs to cross Rheem Boulevard at about 4 miles. To the left (east) is the St. Mary's College campus, its buildings sparkling white among the greens and golds of the surrounding hills. There is parking for trail users here as well, and the rail trail itself, which begins its descent at this point, is accompanied by a parcourse.

The trail wanders down to Moraga Commons at 5.5 miles, where users will find restrooms, water, ample parking, lawns for picnicking, and a playground for the wee ones. The trail skirts the park, then crosses Moraga Road.

On the other side of Moraga Road, the trail surface changes from asphalt to concrete. The trail also becomes markedly less scenic—in fact, it's merely a glorified sidewalk—as it passes Moraga Ranch and a shopping center, where you can purchase groceries if necessary.

Continue southwest along School Street to Country Club Drive. Cross Country Club Drive; trail signs indicate the bike route forks, but to continue to Valle Vista on the rail trail, you must go right (west) along Country Club Drive to the separate path, which heads left (southwest) before the bridge. The route snakes between homes and a creek to an S-curve behind apartment buildings, then climbs beside Canyon Road to hilltop views at about the 7-mile mark. From this high point, the trail drops down and south to the Valle Vista Staging Area. There are restrooms here, as well as lots of parking. The staging area also serves as the trailhead for the Rocky Ridge Trail and other trails in the watershed managed by the East Bay Municipal Utility District (EBMUD). You can obtain a permit to hike in the watershed by contacting EBMUD at (510) 287–0469.

Unless you have arranged for a shuttle, this is the turnaround point. Return as you came.

22 CREEK TRAIL

Tucked in a steep canyon in the hills east of San Jose, this rail trail passes through beautiful country that once attracted visitors not simply with its natural setting, but also with mineral waters that bubbled to the surface near a creek shaded by alders and oaks.

Activities:

Location: Alum Rock Park in San Jose, Santa Clara County

Length: 1.8 miles of the 2.4-mile Creek Trail is on the abandoned railroad corridor.

Surface: The section from Penitencia Canyon to Quail Hollow Picnic Area is dirt single-track. The surface is paved from Quail Hollow to the dirt road 100 yards west of the railroad bridge, then a broad dirt track to the western border of the developed section of the park near the visitor center. The route is paved past the visitor center and Youth Science Institute, then narrows to a dirt track for the last mile, ending at the confluence of Penitencia and Aguague Creeks.

Wheelchair access: The paved portion of the trail is wheelchair accessible.

Difficulty: Moderate, due to the changing trail surface and the trail's length

Food: There is no food available in Alum Rock Park, so bring a picnic lunch. Water is available in the park. Nearby South Bay cities, including San Jose, offer a bonanza of grocery stores and restaurants.

Restrooms: Facilities are available at the Eagle Rock and Quail Hollow picnic areas in the western part of the park, at the visitor center, and at the Live Oak Picnic Area in the eastern reaches of the park.

Seasons: The paved section of the trail is passable year-round. The dirt section, however, may be difficult or impassable when rains turn the surface to mud.

Access and parking: To reach the park, take the Alum Rock Avenue/California 130 exit from either U.S. Highway 101 or Interstate 680 in San Jose. Go east on Alum Rock Avenue to the park entrance, which is 4.6 miles from US 101 and 3.5 miles from I–680. A small fee is charged to enter the park.

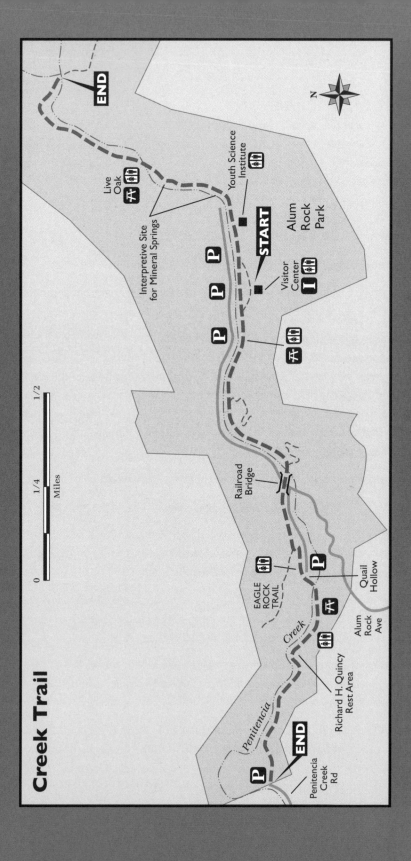

Creek Trail

END

Live
Oak

Interpretive Site
for Mineral Springs

Youth Science
Institute

Alum
Rock
Park

START

Visitor
Center

I

P

P

P

P

Railroad
Bridge

EAGLE
ROCK
TRAIL

Quail
Hollow

Alum
Rock
Ave

Richard H. Quincy
Rest Area

Creek

Penitencia

P

END

Penitencia
Creek
Rd

P

N

0   1/4   1/2

Miles

To reach the west end of the rail trail, turn left (west) at the intersection immediately north of the entrance station onto Penitencia Creek Road and drive approximately 0.2 mile to the Quail Hollow Picnic Area. A Creek Trail signpost directs you over the bridge and through the picnic area; the trail continues west along the creek to the Penitencia Creek Road end point. There is plenty of parking at this location.

To reach the east end of the rail trail, follow the main park road east for 0.6 mile from the entrance station to the large parking lot near the visitor center. The Creek Trail runs along Penitencia Creek on the north side of the visitor center. From this point, you can head either east toward the creek confluence or west toward Quail Hollow.

Transportation: Contact the Santa Clara Valley Transportation Authority by calling (408) 321–2300, or writing 3331 North First Street, San Jose, CA 95134-1906. The Web site is www.vta.org.

Rentals: No rentals are available in the park.

Contact: Rob Reynolds, Alum Rock Park, 16240 Alum Rock Avenue, San Jose, CA 95132; (408) 259–5477. The park Web site is www.sjparks.org; click on the Directory of Parks link.

|||||||||||||||||||||||||||||||||||||||||||||||||||||||||||||||||||||||||||||||||||

Alum Rock Park, tucked in a steep canyon in the hills east of sprawling San Jose, has been a retreat for the city-weary for more than a century. Its mineral springs—some infused with soda, others smelling of sulfur—as well as a tea garden, restaurant, and dance pavilion, were among its lures in the early part of the twentieth century. These days you cannot soak in the mineral waters, but you can enjoy the scenery and history of the park from the rail trail that rolls through it.

The park was a popular resort from 1890 to the early 1930s. For two bits you could ride the steam trains of the San Jose and Alum Rock Railroad into the park. Apparently, riding up to the resort wasn't too bad, but the open cars behind the "steam dummies," or engines, frequently jumped the tracks on the ride back down into town.

At the turn of the twentieth century, railroad owner Hugh Center converted his Alum Rock steam line to an electric narrow-gauge line, and the

Mineral spring grottoes can be found along the Creek Trail.

railway continued to prosper until the Great Depression, when the line gradually fell into disuse. The hard times culminated for the San Jose and Alum Rock Railroad in 1934, when it was dismantled and the rails and other equipment salvaged.

Remnants of the line that couldn't be salvaged can be seen along the Creek Trail, which follows Penitencia Creek through much of the park. The flat track takes visitors past concrete abutments that once supported the tracks, and across an old trestle near Alum Rock. A forest of great variety, including buckeye, maple, walnut, and alder, lines the shores of the creek, with the steep walls of the Penitencia Creek canyon rising to grassy heights to the north and south.

The best place to begin the rail trail is at the visitor center. The Creek Trail is the paved path wedged between the creek and the lawns fronting the center. Go west on the trail, past the log cabin. The trail's surface changes from pavement to dirt on the west side of the cabin.

The track continues west along the creek, passing intersections with the Woodland Trail at 0.2 mile and 0.5 mile. At both, stay right (west) on the old railroad bed. At about 0.8 mile, you reach the concrete trestle, which arcs around Alum Rock to an intersection with the Eagle Rock Trail. At this point, leave the railroad bed for about 0.2 mile. Go left (south), then right (west) in a quick switchback down to Penitencia Creek Road, and follow this west to the Quail Hollow Picnic Area at 1 mile.

At Quail Hollow, cross the creek on a ramshackle bridge, then head west to pick up the trail at the western edge of the picnic area. The route narrows to single-track as it winds down the south side of Penitencia Creek, passing a couple of concrete abutments and a section of trail supported by a lovely stone retaining wall.

At about 1.8 miles, the trail leaves creekside and enters an open, rustic picnic area. A steep dirt-and-railroad-tie staircase leads down to the parking area on Penitencia Creek Road. Return along the same route to the visitor center.

Exploring Alum Rock Park

Although the section of the Creek Trail that heads east from the visitor center to the confluence of Penitencia and Aguague Creeks is not entirely on the railroad grade, it makes a fascinating addition to the route.

From the visitor center, follow the trail east past the greens, the Ramada, and the Youth Science Institute to the mineral springs, grottoes, and picnic area. Pools, fonts, and alcoves shelter the different mineral springs, and an interpretive display describes some park history. About a half mile from the visitor center, the trail crosses to the north side of the creek, the pavement ends, and the route narrows to single-track. Follow the gently climbing route for another half mile, amid the crackling shade of the oaks, buckeyes, and maples, to the shady overlook at the confluence of Penitencia and Aguague Creeks.

23 LOMA PRIETA GRADE

The trees within the Forest of Nisene Marks are so thick and the environment seems so pristine that it's hard to fathom the rail trail upon which you tread was once part of an extensive logging operation in the Aptos Creek Canyon.

Activities:

Location: The Forest of Nisene Marks State Park in Aptos, Santa Cruz County

Length: 9 miles round-trip

Surface: Dirt

Wheelchair access: The trail is not wheelchair accessible.

Difficulty: Hard. The rail trail is relatively steep, and completing the entire loop will take most of a day.

Food: There is no food or water available along the trail. Pack in what you will need. There are a couple of restaurants in Aptos, and lots of eateries in nearby Santa Cruz.

Restrooms: The nearest restrooms are located at the Porter Family Picnic Area, which is 0.2 mile south of the trailhead.

Seasons: The trail is best tackled when dry, between the months of May and October.

Access and parking: To reach the Forest of Nisene Marks State Park from California 1 (the Pacific Coast Highway) in Aptos, take the State Park Drive exit. Go north on State Park Drive for 0.1 mile to Soquel Drive and turn right (east). Go 0.5 mile on Soquel Drive to Aptos Creek Road, which is just before the Aptos Station and turn left (north). Follow Aptos Creek Road for about 0.7 mile to the Forest of Nisene Marks entrance station, where a fee is levied. The pavement ends at this point. Follow the park road another 1.2 miles to George's Picnic Area, which is the trailhead during the winter season. There is plenty of parking at the picnic area and along the park road. In the summer, you can proceed another 1.1 miles to the Porter Family Picnic Area, where you will find ample parking as well.

Transportation: There is no public transportation available within the park.

Rentals: There are no rentals near the trail. Mountain biking is not allowed on the Loma Prieta Grade Trail.

Contact: The Forest of Nisene Marks State Park can be reached by writing to the California Department of Parks and Recreation, 600 Ocean Street, Santa Cruz, CA 95060; (831) 763–7064. The Web site is www.santacruzstateparks .org/parks/nisene. You also can support the park by contacting the Advocates for the Forest of Nisene Marks State Park at P.O. Box 461, Aptos, CA 95001-0461; the Web site is www.advocatesfnm.org.

|||||||||||||||||||||||||||||||||||||||||||||||||||||||||||||||||||||||||||||||||||||

In the Forest of Nisene Marks, nature proves that it can renew itself. The original redwoods and Douglas firs that grew here, thriving on moisture from the nearby Pacific Ocean, were extensively logged in the early 1900s, but you'd never know it now. The evergreens, along with oaks, madrones, and bays, have grown back with a vengeance, creating a jungle that envelops park trails in a translucent green light. This benevolent light even shines on the trail that runs along the grade of the railroad that was used to haul the ancestor trees down and out of the canyon.

That's not to say the landscape doesn't bear the scars of the operations run by the Loma Prieta Lumber Company. Along the former Loma Prieta Railroad grade, which was used to transport logs to the mill site and beyond, you will see a few old railroad ties half-buried in the loamy soils and stacked trailside. Other signs of human activity in the Aptos Creek Canyon, like the site of the Porter House and the remnants of the Loma Prieta Mill Site, huddle in clearings amid the encroaching trees.

The railroad operated in the steep canyon beginning in 1910 and was abandoned in the early 1920s. A Dutch woman named Nisene Marks later purchased the lumber company's property, and under her ownership the forest began to revive. It was her children who donated the area to the California state parks system, in honor of their mother.

The history of the park, both natural and human-made, is documented in interpretive signs scattered along the trails and in books and

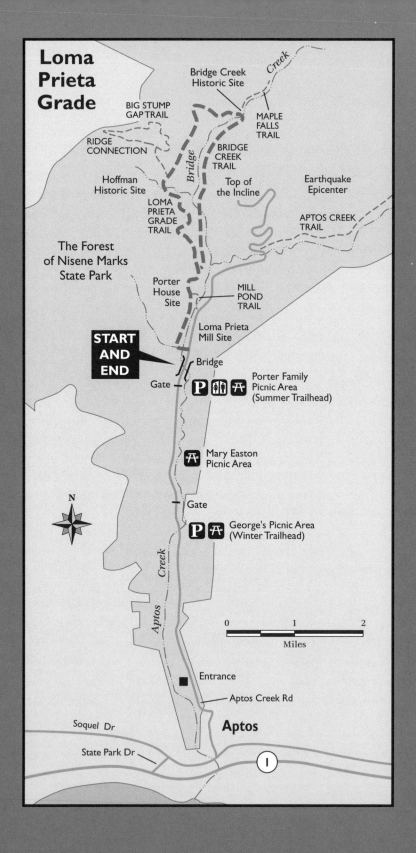

Loma Prieta Grade

Bridge Creek Historic Site

Creek

BIG STUMP GAP TRAIL

MAPLE FALLS TRAIL

RIDGE CONNECTION

Bridge

BRIDGE CREEK TRAIL

Hoffman Historic Site

Top of the Incline

Earthquake Epicenter

LOMA PRIETA GRADE TRAIL

APTOS CREEK TRAIL

The Forest of Nisene Marks State Park

Porter House Site

MILL POND TRAIL

Loma Prieta Mill Site

START AND END

Bridge

Gate

P

Porter Family Picnic Area (Summer Trailhead)

Mary Easton Picnic Area

Gate

P

George's Picnic Area (Winter Trailhead)

Aptos Creek

N

Entrance

Aptos Creek Rd

Soquel Dr

Aptos

State Park Dr

0   1   2
Miles

1

materials available from the park and from the Advocates for the Forest of Nisene Marks.

As if all the logging and railroading and natural beauty weren't enough, the park is also the site of the epicenter of a major earthquake that rocked the San Francisco Bay Area in 1989. One of the other trails in the park takes you past this interesting point of more modern history.

The Loma Prieta Grade Trail is a lollipop loop, starting and ending about 0.4 mile beyond the gate that blocks the roadway to motor vehicles at the Porter Family Picnic Area. No bikes are allowed on the trail, and a bike rack is provided for those who pedal to the trailhead.

The grade takes off past the gate on the left (northwest) side of the main park road, with Aptos Creek running loud and clear to the right (east). The forest chatters in the almost ever-present ocean breeze, which stirs the treetops, rattles limbs, and sends cones and branches tumbling to the ground. The path is soft and duff-covered, muffling the footfalls of those who pass on it, and the shade is so thick that it's almost dark beneath the canopy, even at noon on a bright, sunny day.

Within a quarter mile, the trail narrows to a footpath etched in the mountainside, dropping through a drainage and crossing a small bridge. Climb back onto the railroad grade; a pile of moss-covered railroad ties is stashed on the right (east) side of the trail.

Continue gently upward on the grade. You'll pass a clearing that hosts the Porter House site, with its interpretive sign and bench, at about the 1.5-mile mark. A side

The Loma Prieta Grade Trail burrows through a dense forest.

trail leads east to the Aptos Creek Fire Road, which serves as the main route through the park. The rail trail then loops through another drainage, using yet another small bridge, to the trail fork at the intersection with the Bridge Creek Trail at 1.8 miles.

You can do the loop in either direction. If you travel to the left (northwest), you will climb first to the Hoffman Historic Site at 3.7 miles. Named for the man who was camp superintendent, and nicknamed Camp Comfort, this logging camp operated between 1918 and 1921. The railroad grade was used to haul huge redwoods out of Big Tree Gulch.

Beyond the camp, the trail continues to the intersection with Big Stump Gap Trail, which leads to the ridge in the western reaches of the park. Remain on the rail trail, which continues northward and reaches its apex as it leaves the railroad grade and makes a sharp right-hand (eastward) turn.

Drop to the Bridge Creek Historic Site at the 6-mile mark. Not much remains of this logging camp, which was washed downstream by El Niño–strengthened storms that battered California in 1982. A side trail leads left (north) off the loop at this point and follows Bridge Creek to Maple Falls.

The next leg of the loop, which follows the Bridge Creek Trail down along the creek that bears the same name, won't rejoin the railroad grade until it nears the end of the loop and the Porter House site again. From the Bridge Creek Camp, turn right (south) and follow the eastern bank of Bridge Creek, which you will cross about 1.5 miles below the historic site. Pick up the railroad grade again and continue down to the junction with the Loma Prieta Grade. From here retrace your steps back to the trailhead and the Porter Family Picnic Area.

More Rail Trails

SONOMA REGIONAL PARK PATH

D This lovely little park features a single paved path, part of which lies on the abandoned bed of the Sonoma Valley Railroad Company line that once traveled the length of the area's fabled Wine Country, from downtown Sonoma to Glen Ellen and beyond. The route links the two major thoroughfares through the valley, and passes through lovely oak woodland alongside shady Sonoma Creek.

Activities:

Location: Glen Ellen, Sonoma County

Length: 1.4 miles one way

Surface: Asphalt

Wheelchair access: The trail is wheelchair accessible.

Difficulty: Easy

Food: There are no food outlets along the route, but nearby Glen Ellen is famous for the saturation of fine restaurants and grocery stores in its tiny downtown.

Restrooms: Portable toilets are located at the northern trailhead on Sonoma Highway, adjacent to the Elizabeth Anne Perrone Dog Park.

Seasons: The trail can be used year-round.

Access and parking: The trail stretches between Sonoma Highway (California 12) and Arnold Drive in Glen Ellen, which is about 7 miles north of the town of Sonoma. The Sonoma Highway entrance is located midway between the Madrone Road intersection and the Arnold Drive intersection, just north of the California Department of Forestry fire station. It is on the left (west) side of the road as you head north on Sonoma Highway, and is well signed. There is a large parking lot at this trailhead. A parking fee is levied.

The Arnold Drive park entrance is about 2 miles south of downtown Glen Ellen, just north of the bridge over Sonoma Creek at the entrance to the Sonoma Developmental Center. There is limited on-street parking at this trailhead, and no fee is charged.

Transportation: Sonoma County Transit provides bus service in the Sonoma Valley. Call (707) 576–7433 for more information. The Web site is www .sctransit.com.

Rentals: There are no rentals near the trail.

Contact: County of Sonoma Regional Parks Department, 2300 County Center Drive, Suite 120A, Santa Rosa, CA 95403; (707) 565–2041. The park Web site is www.sonoma-county.org/parks/pk_snoma.htm.

E LARKSPUR–CORTE MADERA PATH

From the banks of estuarine Corte Madera Creek to the tangled undergrowth that has wrapped itself around the long-unused Alto Tunnel, the Larkspur–Corte Madera rail trail runs through a lovely slice of Marin County that illustrates why the area has become a desirable place to live. It is primarily a neighborhood path, used by locals walking their dogs and teaching their kids to ride bikes. The trail also links to other recreational paths in the area.

Activities:

Location: Larkspur, Marin County

Length: 1.7 miles one way

Surface: Asphalt and dirt

Wheelchair access: Most of the trail is paved and wheelchair accessible. The extreme southern end of the trail is dirt and narrows to overgrown single-track as you approach the Camino Alto Tunnel.

Difficulty: Easy

Food: The trail passes through downtown Larkspur, where you will find grocery stores and both upscale and café-style dining establishments. Downtown Larkspur is also home to Larkspur Station, a stop on the now-defunct Northwestern Pacific Railroad.

Restrooms: No public restrooms are available along the route.

Seasons: The trail is passable year-round, but the dirt section of the route may be muddy during and following winter rains.

Access and parking: Parking is limited at both trailheads. To reach the southern trailhead from U.S. Highway 101 in Corte Madera, take the Tamalpais Drive exit and head west on Tamalpais Drive, which becomes Redwood Avenue, to Corte Madera Avenue. Turn left (south) on Corte Madera Avenue, which merges into Montecito Drive. Continue south on Montecito Drive, following it for about 0.3 mile to a dirt parking area that is wedged between the roadway and the dirt trail.

To reach the northern trailhead from US 101 in Larkspur, take the Sir Francis Drake Boulevard exit. Go left (west) on Sir Francis Drake Boulevard to Bon Air Drive. Turn left (south) on Bon Air Drive and go over the bridge; a paved trail takes off to the north from the right (west) side of the road. The rail trail begins on the left (east) side of Bon Air Drive on the far side of the bridge, heading south.

Larkspur Station on the Larkspur rail trail is a classic small-town railroad depot.

Transportation: Golden Gate Transit operates buses in this area. Contact the transit service at 511 or (415) 455–2000, or visit the GGT Web site at www.goldengate.org.

Rentals: There are no rentals along the route.

Contact: Debra Johnson or Tony Gokoffski, Public Works, Town of Corte Madera, 300 Tamalpais Drive, Corte Madera, CA 94925; (415) 927–5064.

F RICHMOND GREENWAY

This urban rail trail provides a short recreational opportunity for local residents, a ribbon of open space in an otherwise heavily developed cityscape. The route sits on the old Santa Fe railroad grade, which runs parallel to Ohio and Chanslor Avenues through a relatively depressed industrial/residential area of Richmond. Plans call for the rail trail to extend west to the San Francisco Bay Trail, and east to the Ohlone Greenway in El Cerrito.

Activities:

Location: Richmond, Contra Costa County

Length: 1 mile one way (1.5 miles with linked roadside bike path)

Surface: Asphalt

Wheelchair access: The trail is wheelchair accessible.

Difficulty: Easy

Food: There are no food outlets along the route.

Restrooms: No facilities are provided on the trail.

Seasons: The trail can be used year-round.

Access and parking: To reach the greenway from Interstate 580 in Richmond, take the Canal Boulevard exit. Head north on Canal Boulevard for 0.3 mile to the West Ohio Avenue/Garrard Boulevard (Richmond Parkway) intersection. Turn right (east) on West Ohio; there is a Richmond Greenway sign here. Go 0.5 mile to Second Street and turn left (north). A small parking area is at the trailhead on the right (east) side of Second Street just north of the intersection with West Ohio Avenue.

There is on-street parking available along the route where it intersects other residential avenues. No parking is available at the busy 23rd Street end point.

Transportation: The San Francisco Bay Area Rapid Transit (BART) serves the Richmond area. BART can be reached at P.O. Box 12688, Oakland, CA 94606-2688. The

The Richmond Greenway looking east toward the Berkeley Hills.

phone number for the Richmond/El Cerrito service area is (510) 236–2278. The Web site is www.bart.gov. A/C Transit also provides service to the area. For route information call (510) 891–4700 or visit www.actransit.org.

Rentals: No rentals are available along the trail.

Contact: The City of Richmond Parks Department, 1401 Marina Way South, Richmond, CA 94804; (510) 231–3004; www.ci.richmond.ca.us. The city's trail Web site is www.ci.richmond.ca.us/greenway. The Friends of the Richmond Greenway are dedicated to promoting improvements along the greenway. The phone number is (510) 236–5812.

G BOL PARK BIKE PATH

The Bol Park Bike Path is a brief charmer that threads through a peaceful neighborhood in the hills of Palo Alto, south of San Francisco. At its heart is Bol Park, a strip of playground and lawn laid alongside Matadero Creek. The short path is primarily used by local residents.

Activities:

Location: Palo Alto, Santa Clara County

Length: 1.5 miles one way

Surface: Asphalt

Wheelchair access: The entire trail is wheelchair accessible.

Difficulty: Easy

Food: No food is available along the trail, but you can find restaurants and grocery stores in nearby areas of Palo Alto.

Restrooms: There are no restrooms available along the route.

Seasons: The trail can be used year-round.

Access and parking: There is very limited parking along the road at the Hanover Street end point. Parking lots in the area are for private businesses. To reach this end point from Interstate 280 near Palo Alto, take the Page Mill Road exit and go north on Page Mill Road for about 1.5 miles to Porter Drive. Turn right (southeast) on Porter Drive, which bends to the northeast and becomes Hanover Street. Drive a total of about 0.9 mile to the trailhead, which is wedged between the parking lots of two businesses on the right (southeast) side of Hanover Street.

There is parking at Bol Park itself, which can be reached by continuing down Page Mill Road to El Camino Real. Turn right (southeast) on El Camino Real and follow it to Matadero Avenue. Turn right (southwest) on Matadero Avenue and proceed to Laguna Avenue. Go left (southeast) on Laguna Avenue for a short distance to the park.

Transportation: Contact the Santa Clara Valley Transportation Authority by calling (408) 321–2300, or writing 3331 North First Street, San Jose, CA 95134-1906. The Web site is www.vta.org.

Rentals: No rentals are available along the trail.

Contact: Gayle Likens, Senior Planner, City of Palo Alto, P.O. Box 10250, Palo Alto, CA 94303; (650) 329–2136. You can visit the Bol Park Web site at www.city.palo-alto.ca.us; use the search function.

H SHEPHERD CANYON TRAIL

The Shepherd Canyon Trail follows Shepherd Canyon Road up into a residential area in the hills above Oakland. Built on a grade established by the Sacramento Northern Railroad, it provides area residents with a scenic path through the oak woodlands from which the surrounding city drew its name.

Activities:

Location: Oakland, Alameda County

Length: 1.25 miles of the 3-mile trail is on a former railroad grade.

Surface: Asphalt

Wheelchair access: The trail is wheelchair accessible.

Difficulty: Easy

Food: No food is available along the route, but Oakland hosts a variety of restaurants and markets.

Restrooms: There are no restrooms along the route.

Seasons: The trail can be used year-round.

Access and parking: To reach the Shepherd Canyon Park access point, which lies near the midpoint of the trail, from California 13 in Oakland take the Park Boulevard exit. Head east (uphill) on Park Boulevard to Mountain Boulevard and go left (north), paralleling the freeway. At the first stoplight, go right (east) on Snake Road. Follow Snake Road to where it splits and go right (southeast) on Shepherd Canyon Road. Follow Shepherd Canyon Road to the light at the fire station; Shepherd Canyon Park, with parking, is northeast of the fire station on the right (south) side of Shepherd Canyon Road. Walk or ride about a quarter mile farther up Shepherd Canyon Road to Paso Robles Road and Bishop Court. Cross to the left (north) side of Shepherd Canyon Road.

Transportation: A/C Transit provides buos service in the area. Call (510) 891–4700 for bus schedules, write to 1600 Franklin Street, Oakland, CA 94612, or check the Web site at www.actransit.org. Bay Area Rapid Transit also serves the area; call (510) 465–2278 or visit www.bart.gov.

Rentals: There are no rentals along the trail.

Contact: Martin Matarrese, Parkland Resources Supervisor, City of Oakland, 3590 Sanborn Drive, Oakland, CA 94602; (510) 482–7857. You can also visit www.shepherdcanyon.org; to view an image of the railroad interpretive sign, append /images/ShepherdCanyonRailroadHistorycompressed.jpg.

LOS GATOS CREEK TRAIL

This short, unpaved, nicely graded rail trail follows Los Gatos Creek from the historic Forbes Mill Museum in downtown Los Gatos to the spillway at Lexington Reservoir at the base of the Santa Cruz Mountains. Both trail and creek continue east from town, but only the trail segment in Los Gatos follows a former railroad right-of-way.

Activities:

Location: Los Gatos, Santa Clara County

Length: 1.6 miles one way

Surface: Dirt

Wheelchair access: The trail is not wheelchair accessible.

Difficulty: Moderate. There are two steep sections: one that takes you down onto the railroad grade and another that leads up to the pedestrian bridge across the spillway.

Food: The trail begins in charming downtown Los Gatos, where you will find a selection of restaurants. There is no water available along the trail, so be sure to bring what you'll need. Water fountains are at the Main Street trailhead and on the trail below Main Street.

Restrooms: There are no restrooms along the route.

Seasons: The trail is accessible year-round, but it may be muddy during and after winter and spring rainstorms.

The Lexington Dam is visible from the Los Gatos Creek Trail.

Access and parking: To reach the trailhead from California 17, take the Los Gatos/Saratoga/California 9 exit. Go south on CA 9 to where it ends on Los Gatos Boulevard. Turn right (southwest) on Los Gatos Boulevard, which becomes East Main Street. The trailhead is 0.8 mile south of CA 9 at the intersection of East Main and Maple Lane. Parking is available along the street and on the bridge.

Transportation: Contact the Santa Clara Valley Transportation Authority by calling (408) 321–2300, or writing 3331 North First Street, San Jose, CA 95134-1906. The Web site is www.vta.org.

Rentals: There are no rentals along the trail.

Contact: Tim Boyer, Park Maintenance Supervisor, Town of Los Gatos, Parks and Public Works Department, P.O. Box 949, Los Gatos, CA 95031; (408) 399–5770. Santa Clara County Park and Recreation Department, (408) 355–2200. The Web site is www.sccgov.org; follow links to the park department and an excellent trail Web site with maps.

Los Gatos Creek

To visit the History Museum of Los Gatos in historic Forbes Mill, a nice start to any hike or ride on Trail, turn right (east) on the dirt track, which leads under the bridge and through a garden of trees and grasses to the old stone building. Originally four stories tall, the mill was built in 1853 and 1854 and was served by a spur of the South Pacific Coast Railroad. The two-story structure that houses the museum today was built in 1880. The museum is open from noon to 4:00 P.M. Wednesday through Sunday, and can be reached by calling (408) 395–7375; the Web site is www.museumsoflosgatos .org/historymuseum.html.

Best Rail Trails
SIERRA NEVADA

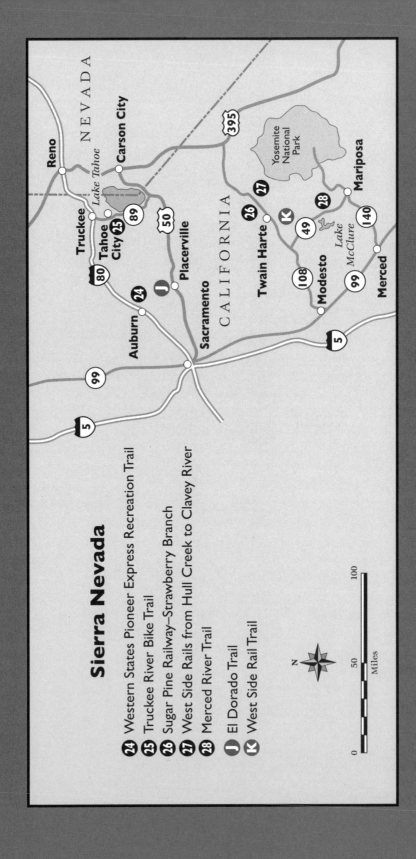

Sierra Nevada

24 Western States Pioneer Express Recreation Trail
25 Truckee River Bike Trail
26 Sugar Pine Railway–Strawberry Branch
27 West Side Rails from Hull Creek to Clavey River
28 Merced River Trail
J El Dorado Trail
K West Side Rail Trail

24 WESTERN STATES PIONEER EXPRESS RECREATION TRAIL

The abundant riches of California's Gold Country this rail trail. Not the riches that are ripped from the ground, mind you, but a wealth of wilderness, which in this case encompasses spectacular vistas of the American River and its canyon.

Activities:

Location: El Dorado and Placer Counties near Auburn

Length: 2 miles of this one-way trail are on the railroad grade. The entire Western States Pioneer Express Recreation Trail is 100 miles long.

Surface: Gravel and dirt

Wheelchair access: None. The trail is rough and quite narrow in places.

Difficulty: Moderate

Food: No food is available along the trail, nor is there potable water, so pack in what you will need.

Restrooms: There are no restrooms along the rail trail.

Seasons: The trail is passable year-round, although you may encounter snow in the winter and early spring.

Access and parking: To reach the trailhead at the American River bridge on California 49, from Interstate 80, take the CA 49/Placerville and Grass Valley exit in Auburn. Go south on CA 49, following the signs through the quaint downtown area. Just out of town, CA 49 dives into the American River Canyon. Drive 2.3 miles down the canyon to near riverside and veer right (south) over the bridge. It's a total of 3.3 miles from Auburn to the bridge parking area.

The section of trail on the former railroad grade ends 2 miles downriver; at this point the trail climbs steeply to a gravel road that leads west toward Auburn and east into the other areas of the Auburn State Recreation Area. The unmaintained railroad grade continues west from this point. The best access to this end point is from the American River bridge trailhead.

Parking for the section of trail on the railroad grade is available on the south side of the bridge on CA 49 just beyond its intersection with Foresthill Road. If there is no parking available here, you can park in the small lot 0.2 mile east of the intersection along Foresthill Road. Be cautious crossing the bridge as there is no pedestrian walkway or shoulder.

Transportation: None available.

Rentals: Bikes and boats may be rented in Auburn. This section of trail, however, is off-limits to mountain biking.

Contact: California Department of Parks and Recreation, P.O. Box 3266, Auburn, CA 95604; (530) 885–4527. Information on the Auburn State Recreation Area's trails can be found at www.canyonkeepers.org; complete recreation information is available at www.parc-auburn.org.

|||||||||||||||||||||||||||||||||||||||||||||||||||||||||||||||||||||||||||||||||||||

The American River is one of California's major waterways, nourishing the fertile soil of the Central Valley and carrying the precious metal wealth that spawned the great formative event of the state in the mid-nineteenth century: the Gold Rush.

This rail trail follows a portion of the Mountain Quarry Railroad, which carried limestone from quarries on the Middle Fork of the American River to Auburn and the Southern Pacific line that continued to Sacramento. The railroad's future—as well as the future of the entire Auburn State Recreation Area—was thrown into limbo when plans to build the Auburn Dam were announced in the 1960s. But the dam was never built, and the canyons that were to be part of a reservoir were developed as a recreational area instead. The railroad grade is now part of an extensive trail system within the Auburn State Recreation Area, a large section of Gold Country

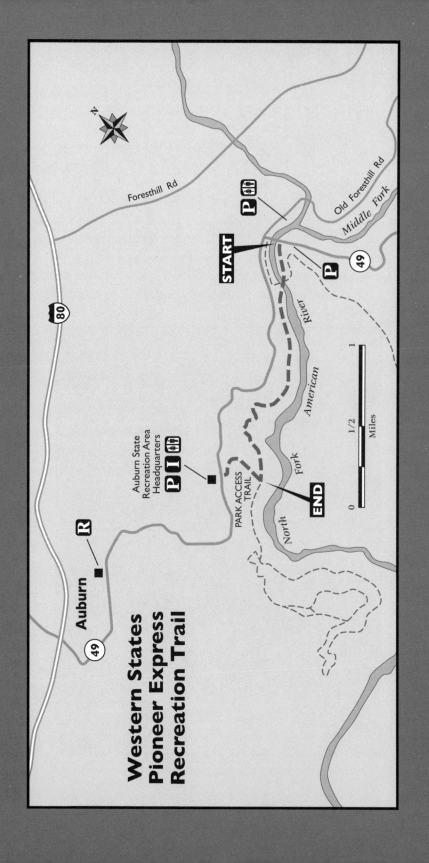

mined these days for the pleasure of hikers, mountain bikers, anglers, paddlers, and other outdoor enthusiasts.

The rail trail portion of the Western States route begins on the south side of the bridge spanning the American River. There is no sign, but the trail is obvious, heading west down the river. You'll pass a trail intersection at 0.1 mile: The left (south) trail leads 3.1 miles to the hamlet of Cool. Stay right (west) and cross the bridge that spans the river. Heed the warning signs posted on the bridge for safety reasons. It's 4.2 miles to Auburn from here.

The trail is broad and easy, with open and dynamic views of the river and canyon. A gravel road breaks off to the left (south and to the riverside) at 0.6 mile. Continue straight (west) on the very obvious railroad grade,

Hikers walk their dog on the Western States Pioneer Express Recreation Trail.

hiking along the south-facing hillside above the river. In summer this hillside is hot and dry, covered with a sparse scrub that grows in sharp contrast to the dense evergreen forest thriving on the moister north-facing slope of the river canyon.

At a Western States Pioneer Trail sign, a path merges onto the rail trail from the right (north). Stay left on the grade; beyond here the path narrows.

Round a bend marked by the first of several concrete buttresses that were the foundations of short trestles that spanned ravines along the river. The trail narrows to single-track and loops through the gully. Pass the second foundation on the other side; the date 1921 is inscribed in the concrete. The path widens briefly, and then plunges through another drainage where the foundation is dated 1915.

At about 1.2 miles, you'll dip through a third foundation-bordered drainage. This one hosts a lovely waterfall that flows in spring and early summer; it is thick with undergrowth that includes poison oak, so watch your step.

Climb away from the waterfall, passing yet another trestle foundation, to a trail marker. The trail continues west, about 100 feet above the river, which flows green and deep in its bed. As you walk beneath a towering black-streaked rock formation, views of the river are unimpeded by brush or trees.

Pass a mile marker that reads 2.5 miles. At this point, the rail trail ends on the concrete foundation to the left (west). The Western States Recreation Trail arcs sharply right (north), leaving the railroad grade behind.

If you choose to continue on the Western States Pioneer Trail, follow switchbacks that lead steeply up the sun-baked hillside before the trail dips through a brush-choked creek bed. Continue up past two more switchbacks and a trail sign to a dirt fire road that is 0.5 mile above the end of the railroad grade. Go left (west) on the road to reach Auburn; heading right (east) will lead to CA 49 between the Auburn State Recreation Area headquarters and the town itself. Either return as you came, or enjoy other trails and activities in the recreation area.

25 TRUCKEE RIVER BIKE TRAIL

Boisterous. If a single word could describe the Truckee River Trail in summer, that would be it. The trail hums with activity during the height of the summer season, as colorful rafts packed with paddlers spill down the Truckee River, and hikers, cyclists, and skaters trace a parallel course downstream on the rail trail that also originates on the shores of Lake Tahoe.

Activities:

Location: Tahoe City, Placer County

Length: 5.3 miles one way

Surface: Asphalt

Wheelchair access: The entire trail is wheelchair accessible, but snow precludes wheelchair use during the winter months.

Difficulty: Moderate, due only to the trail's length

Food: There are two grocery stores and a number of restaurants in Tahoe City, at the eastern end point of the trail. River Ranch, near the trail's western end point, also offers the opportunity for riverside dining.

Restrooms: Restrooms are available at the Tahoe City end point, at various locations along the trail, and at River Ranch.

Seasons: The trail can be used year-round.

Access and parking: To reach the trailhead from the intersection of California 89 and 28 in Tahoe City, follow CA 89 south for 0.2 mile to the trailhead, which is on the right (west) side of the road. To reach River Ranch from the Tahoe City intersection, follow CA 89 west, toward the town of Truckee, for 3.6 miles to Alpine Meadows Road. The trail crosses Alpine Meadows Road at River Ranch. Limited parking is available along the roadway. The western end point is 1.3 miles beyond River Ranch, at the intersection of CA 89 and Squaw Valley Road.

There is a huge parking lot at the Tahoe City end point, but this lot may be packed during the summer season, when both trail users and river rafters flock to the Truckee River.

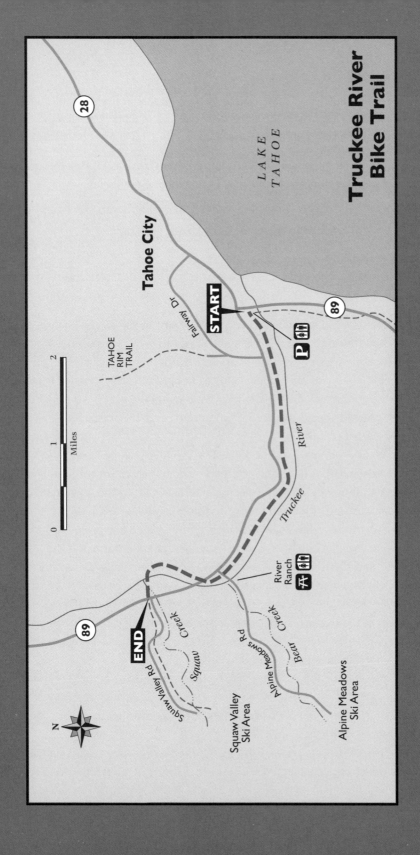

Truckee River
Bike Trail

Transportation: TART, the Tahoe Area Regional Transit organization, provides bus service in the area. TART may be reached by calling (530) 550–1212. The Web site is www.tahoesbest.com/Transportation/tart.htm.

Rentals: Several shops in the Tahoe City area rent bicycles. Consult the local telephone directory for shop names and telephone numbers.

Contact: Bob Bolton, Director of Parks and Recreation, Tahoe City PUD, P.O. Box 33, Tahoe City, CA 96145; (530) 583–3796 ext. 22.

|||||||||||||||||||||||||||||||||||||||||||||||||||||||||||||||||||||||||||||||||

The Truckee River has carved an easy passage from Lake Tahoe to the historic town downriver that shares the river's name. The Truckee, though swift moving, is remarkably gentle between lake and town, sweeping in broad meanders along the floor of a heavily wooded valley. This placid but invigorating demeanor has made the river the destination of an army of river rafters in the summertime, and the site of a rail trail of unparalleled popularity.

On any summer weekend, the Truckee River rail trail and the river itself are packed with brightly clothed recreationalists. The rafts are vivid orange, sunburst yellow, and electric blue, accented by the bright garb of those bouncing along, whooping and singing, inside them. On the trail, folks are dressed with equal brilliance, and they travel by many modes— walking, cycling, or in-line skating—with equal enthusiasm. It is the ultimate family trail, with strollers, training wheels, and dogs on leashes as much in evidence as the Lycra and intensity of more serious athletes.

If you feel the urge to forsake the trail temporarily for the translucent waters of the Truckee, by all means, jump in. The water is clear and reflects the mottled browns of the sand and river cobbles that pave its bed, fading to a cool blue in deeper swimming holes.

It was the relative flatness of the river valley that no doubt made it inviting to the railroad operated by the Lake Tahoe Railway and Transportation Company, which once used the bed upon which day hikers, dog walkers, and bicyclists now play.

The trail begins on the west side of the Truckee River access parking area, which is located off CA 89 just south of the main intersection in Tahoe

City. Cross the bridge, then go left (west), following both the highway and the river downstream.

A couple of driveways and side roads intersect the trail in its first mile, then the path drops riverside. The Truckee initially is hidden in a dense cover of riparian vegetation, but soon comes into view as the rail trail passes a scattering of private homes.

Beyond, the trail is uninterrupted for a long stretch. For the most part the route is open to the sun and river views, broken only by brief shady stretches overhung by evergreens and crowded with willows and lush riverside undergrowth. Portable restrooms are placed at intervals along the route, and short side trails lead to beaches where you can rest or swim.

Rafters can be seen from the Truckee River Trail.

It's not until about the 3.5-mile mark that the scenic routine is broken. At that point, climb a short hill and pass through a parking/staging area for Truckee River rafting companies. By now, having watched the antics and overwhelming joy of those floating downriver, you are probably more than intrigued by the prospect of trying a rafting excursion yourself, so you might want to jot down the names of the companies using the area.

This is just the beginning of a busy and often crowded stretch of trail, so proceed with courtesy and caution. River Ranch and Bells Landing lie just downstream; from the trail you can observe the bustle of bodies and rafts, a bonanza of color and activity, at the landing. Patrons of River Ranch watch from the deck of this riverside resort, which lies at the intersection of CA 89 and Alpine Meadows Road.

To continue on the rail trail, cross Alpine Meadows Road. The trail changes demeanor immediately, as though the gate that marks the beginning of this portion of the path is more than a barrier to cars. Although still paved, the trail is wilder and seems more secluded: There are no rafts on the river, and the highway noise fades a bit as the trail drops below its grade. It's a lovely stretch, complete with restrooms and paved ramps that offer access to the Truckee. Pass the 4-mile marker as you approach the highway bridge that spans the Truckee.

Cross the river and continue downstream on the opposite side, enjoying the shade provided by the forest on the west-facing slope. About a mile downstream, the route again crosses the Truckee and deposits travelers at the entryway to Squaw Valley USA, at the intersection of CA 89 and Squaw Valley Road. Gather your strength for the return journey by channeling athletic prowess from the Olympic flame and rings at the ski area entrance . . . unless you have arranged a car ride back to the trailhead at the lake, of course.

Plans call for the trail to be extended to the east side of Tahoe City by 2011; only a portion of that extension, to the Tahoe Marina, will be on the former railroad grade.

26 SUGAR PINE RAILWAY–STRAWBERRY BRANCH

This segment of rail trail, which follows the historic Sugar Pine Railway, is captured within the forested gorge of the South Fork of the Stanislaus River. It is lined with interpretive signs keyed to a brochure that describes the logging operations that were carried out here in the early and mid-1900s.

Activities:

Location: Strawberry, Tuolumne County

Length: 3 miles one way

Surface: Gravel and dirt

Wheelchair access: The trail is not wheelchair accessible.

Difficulty: Moderate

Food: Although there are no food outlets along the trail, you can find eateries and grocery stores in nearby Twain Harte. Bring food and water, and you can picnic along the route.

Restrooms: There are no restroom facilities at either trailhead or along the trail. The nearest facilities are in the Fraser Flat Campground, which is located about a half mile farther down the forest service road.

Seasons: The trail is accessible year-round. Hiking and mountain biking are best in the spring, summer, and fall; you may cross-country ski on the trail during the winter months when snow permits.

Access and parking: Access to the trail varies depending on the time of year. In summer, you can reach the Fraser Flat trailhead by heading east from Twain Harte on scenic California 108 to Stanislaus Forest Road 4N01, which is well signed. Turn left (north) on FR 4N01 and follow the winding road for about 2.5 miles to the bridge over the South Fork of the Stanislaus River. The trailhead is on the right (east) side of the road before you cross the river.

The eastern trailhead serves as the only access to the trail in the winter months. To reach this end point, continue on CA 108 to Old Strawberry

Road, which is about 2 miles east of the turnoff to Fraser Flat. Turn left (north) on Old Strawberry Road and go about 2 miles to the trailhead, which is on the left (west) side of the road and is marked by a couple of posts that can be difficult to see from the roadway.

Transportation: There is no public transportation to the trailheads.

Rentals: There are no rentals in the area.

Contact: Chuck James, Recreation Technician, Stanislaus National Forest, Mi Wok Ranger District, P.O. Box 100, Mi-Wuk Village, CA 95346-0100; (209) 586–3234.

The Stanislaus River gains momentum in the canyon traced by this section of the Sugar Pine Railway, tumbling with the vigor of an adolescent through a narrow passage cut from smoky granite. Evergreen trees— timber to those who built the railroad to harvest lumber—grow thickly on either side of the river, enveloping the route in shade and insulating it from signs of civilization clustered in villages along CA 108.

This is but a short section of the Sugar Pine rail trail, which currently spans approximately 16.5 miles from Twain Harte to Strawberry and, if all proceeds as planned, will eventually extend for about 30 miles. Indeed, an extensive web of rail lines and spurs winds through this neck of the woods. The Sugar Pine Railway alone included about 70 miles of mainline and approximately 400 miles of spurs, branches, and sidings. The rails were laid down in the rugged foothills just after the turn of the twentieth century, and were used to transport harvested old-growth trees to sawmills for processing. The railroad ceased operation in 1965. The abandoned grades—including the grade spanned by this segment of the rail trail— are very mild, belying the steepness of the terrain that surrounds them.

The rail trail is lined with interpretive posts, which are keyed to an informational packet that is available from the Mi-Wok Ranger District in Mi-Wuk Village.

The trail makes for fine hiking; the mountain biking, especially for the beginner, is sublime. The trail is described here climbing northeast from the bridge that spans the Stanislaus near the Fraser Flat Campground to

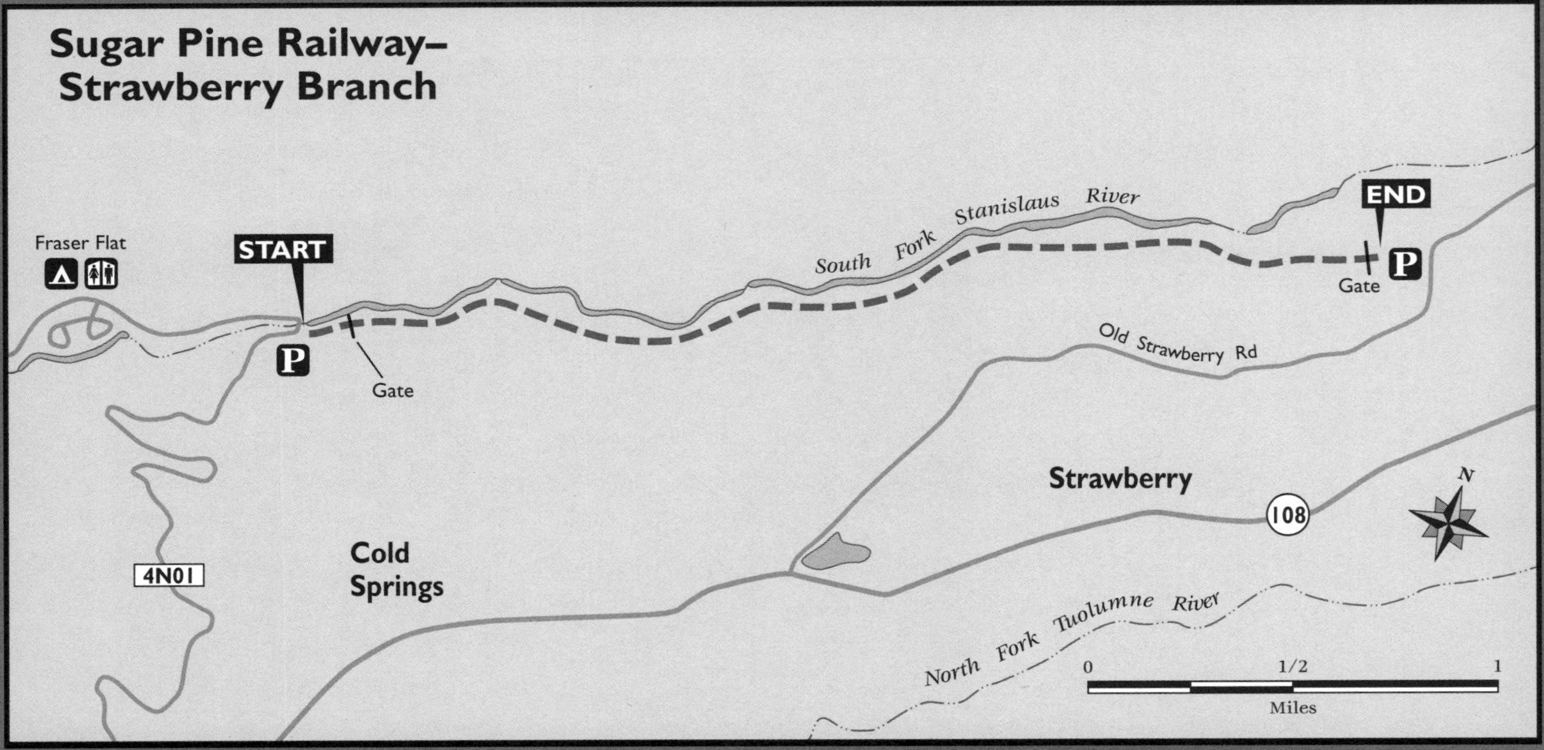

Sugar Pine Railway–
Strawberry Branch

Fraser Flat

END

P
Gate

Stanislaus River

South Fork

Old Strawberry Rd

N

108

Strawberry

North Fork Tuolumne River

1

1/2
Miles

0

Gate

START

P

Cold
Springs

4N01

Old Strawberry Road, but can be traveled in either direction easily. This is the optimal starting point for an out-and-back journey, however, because it is all downhill on the return trip.

Begin on the south side of the bridge over the Stanislaus River. An informational billboard is posted at the trailhead, and the route is barricaded to prohibit use by motorized vehicles.

Posts 1, 2, and 3 are passed within a third of a mile of the trailhead, calling your attention first to the old logging camp at Fraser (now the Fraser Flat Campground); then to Camp Lowell, a logging camp used for a single season in the early twentieth century; and finally to the rigors of building a railroad in the foothills. The path is a gentle roller coaster, dip-

A family enjoys the Sugar Pine Railway trail.

ping through shallow gullies as it climbs through thick stands of conifers. You can catch glimpses of the South Fork of the Stanislaus in the canyon to the left (north) through brief openings between the trunks of the trees.

At about the 1.1-mile mark, the gorge deepens, and the remains of a flume appear on the opposite side of the canyon. Called the Philadelphia Ditch, the flume was used by gold miners a century ago. Less than a quarter of a mile beyond, pass post 4 and a diversion dam, which is still used for power generation.

At about the 1.5-mile mark, pass a green gate, then continue up through the lovely woodland to post 6, where the forest opens a bit and filtered sunlight illuminates the glistening river. The grade splits here; remain on the main (and obvious) path that continues northeast to the Old Strawberry Road trailhead. The trail veers away from the riverside at about the 2.5-mile mark and crosses through yet another of the gullies that lend the trail its rolling profile.

Continue in an easterly direction to post 8. This marks the remnants of research projects conducted within the U.S. Forest Service's Stanislaus–Tuolumne Experimental Forest, which served as a laboratory for foresters and other scientists from 1927 to 1969. The research station is located across the South Fork of the Stanislaus and now houses forest service employees.

Post 8 stands at the edge of a small meadow, which the trail crosses before returning to the woods. At the trail intersection at 2.8 miles, go right (northeast) and up on the narrow footpath. The railroad grade can be seen heading off to the left (north).

The path leads up steeply to Old Strawberry Road, where two orange-and-brown trail posts mark the trailhead. Although these are obvious from the path, they aren't easily seen from the roadway, as they are tucked below grade. Unless you have arranged a shuttle, this is the turnaround point; return as you came.

27 WEST SIDE RAILS FROM HULL CREEK TO CLAVEY RIVER

The foothills of the Sierra Nevada are expansive and remarkably untouched by modern life. The West Side rail trail travels into the depth of this isolation, winding through dense stands of timber on a track that once rang with the squeal of wheels on metal and now rings with the songs of the wind and the birds.

Activities:

Location: Southeast of Long Barn in Tuolumne County

Length: 8 miles one way

Surface: Dirt

Wheelchair access: The trail is not wheelchair accessible.

Difficulty: Hard

Food: There is no food or water available along the trail, so bring all you'll need. There are restaurants and grocery stores in Twain Harte and other villages along California 108.

Restrooms: There are no restrooms along the trail. Practice leave-no-trace principles by burying waste at least 8 inches underground and packing out toilet paper.

Seasons: The trail is accessible year-round. Hiking and mountain biking are best in the spring, summer, and fall; you may cross-country ski on the trail during the winter months if snow permits.

Access and parking: An absolutely gorgeous road leads to the remote trailheads for this route. To reach the Hull Creek end point from CA 108 in Long Barn, turn east off the highway at the Merrell Springs turnoff, where there are signs for Hull Creek and Clavey River. Turn right (south) onto Long Barn Road and go 0.1 mile to Forest Road 3N01 (also known as Stanislaus County Road 31 and North Fork Road). Follow FR 3N01/CR 31, cross the North Fork of the Tuolumne River at 2 miles, then continue for about 6.3 miles to Forest Road 3N07, which sports a sign for the West Side Rail Tour.

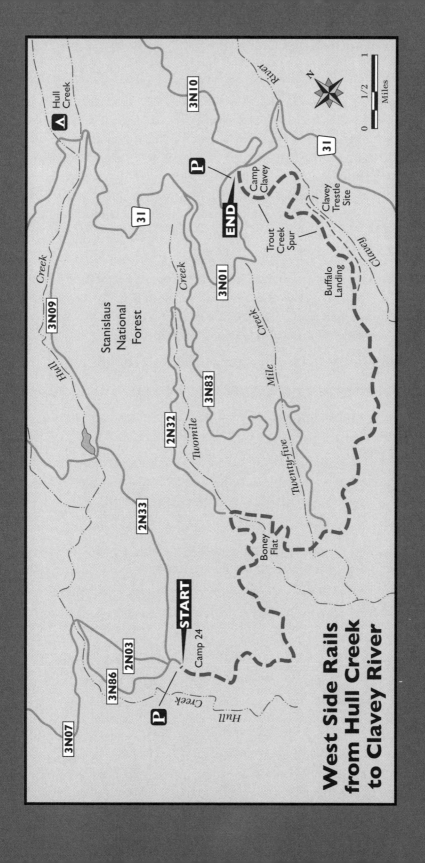

West Side Rails
from Hull Creek
to Clavey River

Stanislaus National Forest

Hull Creek

3N10

31

3I

3N09

2N32

3N83

2N33

2N03

3N86

3N07

3N01

Twomile Creek

Mile Creek

Twenty-five

Boney Flat

Buffalo Landing

Trout Creek Spur

Camp Clavey

Clavey Trestle Site

Clavey River

Hull Creek

Camp 24

START

END

P

P

▲

River

0   1/2   1
Miles

N

Turn right (south) on FR 3N07. This well-graded dirt road leads for about 3 miles (9.3 miles from CA 108) to an intersection; stay on FR 3N07, which leads to a second road fork 0.1 mile farther, at the William R. Rolland Memorial Plantation. Go left (east) on Forest Road 3N86; a sign indicates that parking for the West Side Rail Tour is 2 miles ahead. The trail begins just above the crossing of Hull Creek, where you will find limited parking. You can continue for another mile to a parking pullout at post 2, the site of Camp 24, which was home to a thriving logging operation until 1960. Several Forest Service roads converge here.

To reach the Clavey River trailhead, continue past the turnoff at FR 3N07, traveling a total of 15.5 miles on North Fork Road (FR 3N01/CR 31) to its intersection with FR 3N86 at Camp Clavey. This is the terminus of the rail trail. There is parking in pullouts along the dirt road.

Transportation: There is no public transportation to this rail trail.

Rentals: There are no rentals available along the trail.

Contact: Chuck James, Recreation Technician, Stanislaus National Forest, Mi-Wok Ranger District, P.O. Box 100, Mi-Wuk Village, CA 9346-0100; (209) 586–3234.

The dense woods of the Stanislaus National Forest envelope this section of the former West Side Lumber Company railway. Now a rough-and-tumble rail trail, the evergreen setting harkens back to the height of the area's lumberjack days.

The Stanislaus National Forest revived this segment of the West Side line, which was abandoned in the 1960s, as a recreational trail and has compiled a wonderful brochure detailing the route via a good (and necessary) map and interpretation keyed to signposts along the trail. Quite a bit of the route can be traveled in a passenger car, still more in a four-wheel-drive vehicle, but the heart of the rail trail is best managed on foot. The trail has become popular with off-highway vehicles, especially on weekends, so be prepared to share the route.

The rail trail follows a leg of one of the four railroads that provided access to the abundant timber in the region. Like its neighbors, including the Sugar Pine Railway, the West Side Railroad Company laid down a remarkable amount of track, including a mainline that reached nearly 70 miles from the town of Tuolumne south toward the Hetch Hetchy Valley in Yosemite National Park.

The West Side rails were a narrow-gauge line, which made it easier to carve into steep mountainsides but resulted in less stability for the trains on the tracks. The width of the grade these days, however, is perfect for hikers, cyclists, or equestrians who wish to travel side by side, discussing the railroad history that unfolds along with spectacular views of the high country. The rail trail doubles as FR 3N86.

Interpretation begins just above FR 3N86's intersection with Hull Creek, where signpost 1 marks one of the railroad's sidings. But the best parking

A mountain biker speeds along the West Side Rails near the Clavey River.

is at signpost 2, at about the 1-mile mark, which was the site of Camp 24, once a bustling hub and now little more than a wide spot in the road.

The route continues across open, scrub-covered hillsides, passing post 3 at the site of an old oil tank. Leave open ground for the duration of the journey once you enter the forest, with views opening only occasionally southward as you traverse the mountainside.

Pass posts 4 and 5 at about 2.5 miles, which direct your attention to various types of railroad paraphernalia and to the meadow at Boney Flat. Just beyond, two large stakes stand on either side of the trail, forming a rustic portal. If you are still in a passenger car, this marks the end of the line for you; if you're in a four-wheel- drive vehicle, you've got another mile and a half or so to travel before you will have to bail out.

The route cuts a broad switchback around Boney Flat. Negotiate an easy detour around a missing bridge at the Twomile Creek crossing, which is at about 3 miles. The trail also intersects Forest Road 2N32, which is signed. At this point, the track is no longer passable to motor vehicles. Arc south on the gently inclining rail trail, which dips into another drainage that is washed out and clogged with fallen logs.

At post 6, you reach the halfway point of the rail trail. The post marks the site of Camp 25 and Twenty-Five Mile Creek. The rail trail curves back to the east beyond the creek and winds through the woods to its intersection with Forest Road 3N83 (also signed). This service road branches off first to the right (south), and then to the left (north) at signpost 7 (about 5.5 miles). A cedar tree bearing the scars of chains used by steam donkeys, large machines that pulled logs from where they were cut to where they could be loaded onto railroad cars, is the focal point of this interpretive post.

The trail gently meanders northeast beyond FR 3N83, winding through a pleasant forest that opens to fleeting views down into the Clavey River drainage. Cross the occasional creek, usually dry by late summer, and pass a few interpretive signposts: Post 8 points up the difficulty these seasonal streams posed to railroad builders, post 9 marks the location of yet another logging camp, and post 10 brings your attention to the telephone line that served the loggers and railroad workers, sections of which now lie on the ground along the route.

At about the 6.5-mile mark, reach post 11, which marks the start of the Trout Creek Spur. The spur will lead you to trail's end at Camp Clavey—

again, an old logging camp. But it's worth your while to branch off to the right (northeast), dropping from Buffalo Landing, once the site of feverish logging activity, toward the Clavey River, where you can view the remains of the Clavey River trestle. The wooden trestle, which stood more than 75 feet above the river, has burned, but its foundations are still visible.

To finish the hike, climb up to Camp Clavey via the Trout Creek Spur, which ascends more steeply than the rest of the grade before topping out among the evergreens that encroach upon the clearings at Camp Clavey. The end of the rail trail (and of FR 3N86) is at its intersection with FR 3N01 at about the 8-mile mark.

Unless you have arranged a shuttle, the quickest return is along the same route. But a web of Forest Service roads winds through the woods, offering wonderful opportunities for exploration for those with a good map, a compass, and the wits to use them both.

28 MERCED RIVER TRAIL

As rough and tumble as the river it follows, as enchanting as the canyon that cradles it, the Merced River Trail is one of the most challenging and beautiful of California's rail trails.

Activities:

Location: West of Yosemite National Park in Mariposa County

Length: 16 miles round-trip; there is no bridge at the Bagby end point.

Surface: Original ballast and dirt

Wheelchair access: None

Difficulty: Hard

Food: There are no restaurants or stores along the route, but food is available in the nearby town of Mariposa, at the lodges located east of Briceburg along California 140, and in Yosemite National Park.

Restrooms: Restrooms are available at Briceburg, in the campgrounds that lie at the end of the gravel access road, and at the campground in Bagby.

Seasons: The trail can be traveled year-round. Hiking is best in the summer and autumn months. You can cross-country ski on the trail during the winter when there is sufficient snow cover. The trail is least hospitable when wet and should be avoided if flooded.

Access and parking: Parking is available at both end points, but it is not easy to do this trail as a one-way shuttle venture because there is no bridge spanning the Merced River at Bagby. Most travelers begin at the Briceburg end point and travel downstream to the confluence with the North Fork of the Merced River, then return as they came.

To reach the Briceburg end point, head east on CA 140 from Mariposa for almost 12 miles to the Briceburg Visitor Center. Ample parking is available at the picnic area that is wedged between the Briceburg building and the Merced River.

To reach the Bagby end point from Mariposa, follow California 49 north for

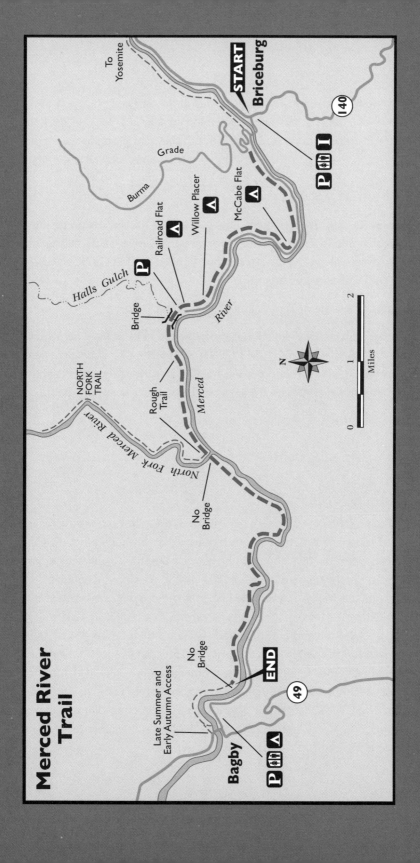

Merced River Trail

START Briceburg

To Yosemite

Burma Grade

Railroad Flat

Willow Placer

McCabe Flat

140

P

Halls Gulch

Bridge

P

Merced River

N

Miles

0   1   2

NORTH FORK TRAIL

Rough Trail

North Fork Merced River

No Bridge

No Bridge

Late Summer and Early Autumn Access

Bagby

END

49

P

about 16 miles to Bagby, which is located at the east end of Lake McClure. Turn right (east) into the Bagby recreation area; a small fee is levied here. Follow the campground road for 0.7 mile to the campground area. Trail access from this end point, only feasible in late summer and fall when water levels in the lake are low, is via the old, unmaintained railroad grade at the north end of the Bagby bridge.

Transportation: While there is no direct public transportation to either trail end point, Yosemite Area Regional Transportation System (YARTS) provides service along the CA 140 corridor. Contact YARTS at (877) 989–2787 (98–YARTS) or at www.yarts.com.

Rentals: There are no rentals available along the trail.

Contact: Jim Eicher, Recreation Planner, Bureau of Land Management, 63 Natoma Street, Folsom, CA 95630-2671; (916) 985–4474. During the summer months, you can also get information by contacting the Briceburg Visitor Center at (209) 379–9414. The trail Web site is www.blm.gov/ca/st/en/fo/folsom/mercedrivertrail.2.html.

⁝⁝⁝

This one is far from tame.
Most of the rail trails you'll read about in this guide are relatively easy paved routes that earn their difficulty by virtue of their length. Not the Merced River Trail. This comes as close to a wilderness experience as you will find on any rail trail in California, with the possible exception of the Bizz Johnson Trail. And even the Bizz Johnson doesn't present the same kinds of challenges that the Merced River Trail does.

Lest I scare you off, rest assured that this trail is eminently passable and wanders through some of the most spectacular country in the mountains of California. It follows the scenic Merced River Canyon of Yosemite National Park, passing through a steep-walled gorge before spilling into a wider river valley shaded with spreading oaks and cloaked in wildflowers in spring. The river is immensely popular with white-water rafters, so look for these adventurers in the summer season.

But I'd be remiss not to mention its challenges. The trail is a superlative hike, especially during wildflower season in March and April, but is an extremely technical (and marginally enjoyable) mountain bike ride. You must ford the North Fork of the Merced River at the trail's midpoint, which can be a challenge when rainfall raises the water level in the river. *And be forewarned:* There is no bridge at the Bagby end point, rendering the journey a round-trip affair totaling 16 miles. Most hikers venture only as far as the North Fork confluence, then return as they came.

The Bountiful Merced River Valley

The area surrounding the Merced River Trail positively blossoms with opportunities to enjoy the outdoors. Hiking, mountain biking, and horseback riding on the rail trail are just a few of the possibilities. More than 70 miles of the river have been designated "wild and scenic," and all along its upper sections you will find high-caliber white-water rafting and fishing. The rustic campgrounds west of Briceberg, which are managed by the Bureau of Land Management (BLM), cradle delightful sites that front the river. And Yosemite National Park, undoubtedly one of the most spectacular places on earth and the birthplace of the Merced, lies less than 20 miles upstream.

There is also abundant history to be explored in the canyon, including the unimproved portion of the old Yosemite Valley Railroad, which continues along the north side of the Merced from Briceburg to El Portal outside Yosemite National Park. The Briceburg Visitor Center itself is a historic site, having served as a store, a post office, and a regular stop for the railroad (among other incarnations), before it was sold to the BLM in the late 1980s. The quaint stone structure was restored to its pristine condition, and has since served as a public information center and gateway to the wonders of the Merced River valley.

To learn more about this area, contact the Mariposa Visitor Center at (209) 966–7081 or (866) 425–3366; the Web site is www.homeofyosemite.com.

Finally, in late season when water levels in Lake McClure are low, trek-kers might be able to follow the old railroad grade out of the canyon to the bridge on CA 49 at Bagby, but when the water is up, the last 2 miles of the route are flooded. Contact the trail manager or check at the Briceburg Visitor Center to learn more about the status of the trail at the time of your visit.

The rail trail follows the right-of-way of the Yosemite Valley Railroad. Trains ran through the Merced River valley to El Portal, just downriver of Yosemite National Park, from 1906 to 1945, serving the logging, mining, and tourist industries in the scenic canyon. The railroad began to fall into disuse once CA 140 was completed in 1926. Both Briceburg at the east end of the trail and Bagby at the west end, where the Merced flows into Lake McClure, were once way stations along the railroad.

The Merced River Trail winds through a steep-walled gorge.

In the summer season, you can either begin at the Briceburg Visitor Center, where you will find ample parking, or you can drive 4.5 miles down the good gravel road to the trailhead at Railroad Flat Campground, where you will find more limited parking. If you are planning on bicycling the route, the road from Briceberg to Railroad Flat is an enjoyable warm-up. It too follows the old railroad grade and offers wonderful views of the neighboring river.

The trail proper begins at the west end of the Railroad Flat Campground, beyond the white gate. The trail reaches a bench at about the quarter-mile point, at the bridge that spans Halls Creek. A private home is perched on the north slope of the river canyon beyond the creek crossing, and another little bridge spans a seasonal stream just below the house. The trail narrows to single-track amid a jumble of rocky debris deposited by floods. Stay straight (west) on the riverside track at the switchback that leads up toward the residence. At about the 0.6-mile mark, you will reach a Merced River Trail sign.

The footpath winds through the narrowing gorge, with steep cliffs overhanging the route on the north. Unless you are an exceptionally skilled mountain biker, you'll be walking your bike through this section. The walk is absolutely wonderful, because the slower pace—and the diminished fear of crashing and burning—will permit you to truly enjoy the lovely canyon.

The bike portage/single-track hike, accented by the occasional dogwood tree, continues for about 1 mile, then the canyon opens a bit and you can look across to the rusted flume that traces the canyon's southern wall.

The rail trail, now bordered by thin grasses, continues its gentle descent through the broadening canyon, to the confluence of the North Fork of the Merced River at about the 3-mile mark. There is no bridge here; you must ford the brisk river, which can be knee-deep even in late season, and may be impassable when heavy rains raise the water level. The trail leads to the most obvious ford. The concrete remains of the trestle that spanned the confluence are at the mouth of the North Fork; upstream (north) of the trestle and ford are the remains of a rustic stone structure. This makes a fine picnic and turnaround point for those seeking a pleasant day hike.

Once across the North Fork, you can use one of two routes to climb back onto the railroad grade. The right (northern) route leads directly to the path; the left (southern) leads about 50 yards to an inviting clearing in which you will find the sun-splashed pilings for the defunct trestle, then goes up and west to the rail trail.

The route west of the North Fork of the Merced is broad, pebbly, and bordered by grasses that grow blonder as the summer progresses. A narrow creek, which may be dry in late season, spills down from the north to cross the trail at about the 5-mile mark.

Farther downstream, the path pulls northwest, away from the Merced, and is shaded by a sparse canopy of thin pines. Brush and shade encroach on the route before it spills back into the more open river basin, where the Merced threads through channels that it has carved in its cobbled bed. The canyon now wears the mantle of the lower foothills, including shady oak and buckeye trees and thickening grasses peppered with wildflowers. These tufts of grass squeeze the trail, confining it to a narrow swath on the broader grade.

The rail trail ends at the remains of the bridge that used to span the stream that spills from Solomon Canyon into the Merced. To the west, the river thickens into an arm of Lake McClure. This is the trail's turnaround point.

More Rail trails

J EL DORADO TRAIL

El Dorado County has worked diligently on the evolving El Dorado Trail, which runs through oak woodlands and evergreen forests between the charming Gold Country towns of Placerville and Camino. It's both a neighborhood trail and a scenic excursion, long enough in its present iteration to offer a good workout, and promising more length and beauty in the future.

Activities:

Location: Placerville to Camino, El Dorado County

Length: Approximately 6 miles one way

Surface: Asphalt, ballast, and dirt

Wheelchair access: The paved portions of the trail are wheelchair accessible.

Difficulty: Easy. The trail has a 3 percent grade.

Food: Restaurants and grocery stores are available in Placerville.

Restrooms: There are restrooms at the Placerville trailhead and at the Jacquier Road staging area.

Seasons: The trail can be used year-round. Despite its location in the foothills of the Sierra Nevada, the elevation is too low to maintain adequate snow cover for cross-country skiing in winter.

Access and parking: To reach the Jacquier Road staging areas from westbound U.S. Highway 50 in Placerville, take the Broadway exit. Go left on Broadway and follow this to Smith Flat Road. Turn left (east) on Smith Flat Road and follow it to Jacquier Road. The Jacquier Road staging areas offer access to both the eastbound portion of the trail, which ascends to Camino, and the westbound section, into downtown Placerville.

To reach the Mosquito Road end point in Placerville, take the Broadway exit from westbound US 50 and go right (west) on Broadway to Mosquito Road. Go right (north) on Mosquito Road, under the bridge. Continue left (north) on Mosquito Road for about 25 feet; the trailhead is on your right, opposite the bus station.

Transportation: El Dorado Transit provides bus service to the area. Call (530) 642–5383 or visit www.eldoradotransit.com.

Rentals: There are no rentals available along the trail.

Contact: Parks and Recreation Department, City of Placerville, 549 Main Street, Placerville, CA 95667; (530) 642–5232. The El Dorado County Transportation Web site, at www.edctc.org/_eldoradotrail.htm, contains a link to a great trail map.

K WEST SIDE RAIL TRAIL

This trail follows another of the many railroad grades plowed through the foothills of the Sierra Nevada by the West Side Lumber Company. The grade, carved in the mountainside by Chinese and Native American laborers, traces the steep canyon of the North Fork of the Tuolumne River, passing leftover rails and ties, to the River Ranch Campground. The last leg of the trail is not well maintained and may be overgrown.

Activities:

Location: Tuolumne City, Tuolumne County

Length: 5.5 miles one way

Surface: Dirt and original ballast

Wheelchair access: This rough path is not wheelchair accessible.

Difficulty: Hard, due to the trail's length and rough surface

Food: There is no food available along this rail trail, but restaurants and grocery stores are available in Twain Harte and other towns along California 108. No water is available along the trail either, so be sure to pack plenty.

Restrooms: There are no restrooms available along the trail. Practice leave-no-trace principles by burying waste at least 8 inches underground and packing out toilet paper. Restrooms are available at River Ranch Campground at the Cottonwood Road end point.

Seasons: The trail is accessible year-round. Hiking and mountain biking are best in the spring, summer, and fall; you may cross-country ski on the trail during the winter months if snow permits.

Access and parking: To reach the trailhead from the Mi-Wok Ranger Station in Mi-Wuk Village, follow CA 108 west for 2.9 miles to Tuolumne Road. Go left (east) on Tuolumne Road and follow it for 6.7 miles to Cottonwood Road (a.k.a. Stanislaus Forest Road 1N04/Forest Route 14). Go left on Cottonwood Road for 0.2 mile to the trailhead parking area, which is located at the intersection of Miramonte Road and Buchanan Road.

Transportation: Tuolumne County Transit serves Tuolumne City; phone (209) 532–0404 or visit www.tuolumnecountytransit.com.

Rentals: Bicycles may be rented at Pinecrest Lake Resort, located off CA 108 in Pinecrest, south of Strawberry. Call (209) 965–3411; the Web site is www.pinecrestlakeresort.com.

Contact: Chuck James, Recreation Technician, Stanislaus National Forest, Mi-Wok Ranger District, P.O. Box 100, Mi-Wuk Village, CA 95346-0100; (209) 586–3234.

Best Rail Trails
CENTRAL CALIFORNIA

Central California

29 Monterey Peninsula Recreational Trail
30 Ventura River Trail
31 Ojai Valley Trail
L Fresno Sugar Pine Trail and Clovis Old Town Trail
M Santa Maria Valley Multipurpose Trail
N Fillmore Trail

126 Fillmore
N Fillmore
Ojai
30 31 Ventura
Santa Barbara
99
41 L Clovis
Fresno
5
San Luis Obispo
M 101
1
Salinas
Monterey 29
101
1

PACIFIC OCEAN

N

0   50   100
Miles

29 MONTEREY PENINSULA RECREATIONAL TRAIL

This rail trail immerses you in the culture of a seaside town. If you are lucky, otters will be frolicking in the kelp off the coast of Pacific Grove when you pass. There is no doubt that sparkling sailboats will be moored in Monterey Bay near Fisherman's Wharf, and seabirds will take wing over the estuary in Seaside. It's a lovely outing.

Activities:

Location: Pacific Grove, Monterey, and Seaside in Monterey County

Length: 4.8 miles one way; the rail trail is part of the Monterey Bay Coastal Trail, which extends from Pacific Grove to Castroville.

Surface: Asphalt and concrete, with a dirt walking path alongside the paved trail in Pacific Grove

Wheelchair access: The entire trail is wheelchair accessible.

Difficulty: Easy

Food: You will find an abundance of restaurants along the trail in Monterey's Cannery Row and Fisherman's Wharf areas.

Restrooms: There are no restrooms along the trail, but facilities can be found in parks, beaches, and private business establishments along the route.

Seasons: The trail can be used year-round. Although temperatures are usually moderate, Monterey Bay is subject to the marine influence, and the fog can be dense and cold when it is in. Be prepared for swift changes in temperature.

Access and parking: To reach the parking lot at Lovers Point in Pacific Grove, follow U.S. Highway 1 to the California 68 exit. CA 68 leads into Pacific Grove. After about 2.2 scenic miles, the highway veers left (south) onto the famed 17-Mile Drive; stay right (straight) on Forest Avenue. Follow Forest Avenue about 2 miles to Lighthouse Avenue. Turn left (south) on Lighthouse Avenue, go 2 blocks to 17th Street, and turn right (west). Follow 17th Street for about 0.3 mile to the Lover's Point parking lot, which is on the right (north) side of the road about 100 yards before the big, pink Lovers Point Inn.

To reach the Pacific Grove/Lover's Point trailhead from downtown Monterey, head toward the ocean to Del Monte Avenue. From the intersection of Del Monte Avenue and Washington Street, which is south of Cannery Row and the Monterey Bay Aquarium, head north on Del Monte Avenue, through the tunnel, to the first road fork. Ignore the signs for Cannery Row and the aquarium, staying north on Lighthouse Avenue. Once you enter Pacific Grove, stay left (north) on Central Avenue to 17th Street. Turn right (east) on 17th and go down toward the bay for about 0.2 mile to the trailhead on the right (north) side of the road.

To reach the Seaside trailhead from US 1, take the Seaside/Del Rey Oaks exit. Go east on California 218 (Camino Del Rey), drive about 50 yards, and turn right (south) onto Roberts Avenue and into the parking lot, which faces a small estuary. The bike path that begins here leads to the rail trail, which is located on the far (east) side of the estuary.

There are parking areas at both end points.

Transportation: Monterey–Salinas Transit serves the area. MST can be contacted by writing 1 Ryan Ranch Road, Monterey, CA 93940, or by calling (831) 899–2555 or 424–7695. The Web site is www.mst.org.

Rentals: Bay Bikes (831–655–BIKE) has a shop on the rail trail at Cannery Row in Monterey. The Web site is www.baybikes.com.

Contact: For the portion of the trail in Monterey, contact Kay Russo, Director of the Monterey Recreation and Community Service Department, 546 Dutra Street, Monterey, CA 93940; (831) 646–3866. For overall trail information, contact the Monterey Peninsula Regional Park Disrict at (831) 372–3196. The address is 60 Garden Court, Suite 325, Monterey, CA 93940. The trail Web site is www.mprpd.org/parks/coastaltrail.htm.

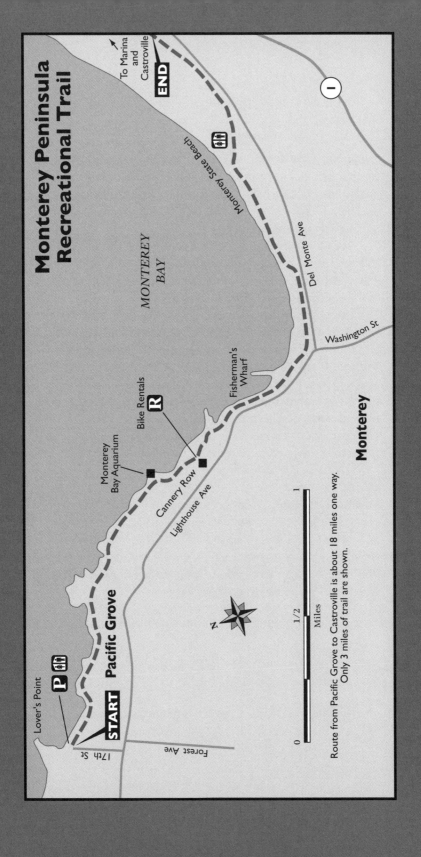

Monterey Peninsula Recreational Trail

MONTEREY BAY

To Marina and Castroville

END

Monterey State Beach

Del Monte Ave

Washington St

Fisherman's Wharf

Monterey

R Bike Rentals

Monterey Bay Aquarium

Cannery Row

Lighthouse Ave

Pacific Grove

Lover's Point

P

START

17th St

Forest Ave

N

Miles

0   1/2   1

Route from Pacific Grove to Castroville is about 18 miles one way. Only 3 miles of trail are shown.

Peek into the Deep

Luminous jellyfish that look like egg drops. Leopard sharks and sunfish that fly from inky darkness to blue light in a tank that holds a million gallons of seawater. Otters that play, eat, and rest in kelp that grows two stories high. Anchovies that spin a silvery, swirling web.

The Monterey Bay Aquarium is home to some incredible creatures, offering glimpses into a mysterious undersea world and displaying animals and plants that thrive in a realm we can admire from behind glass.

This amazing aquarium, which shelters and provides a forum for study of the wildlife protected within the Monterey Bay National Marine Sanctuary, is located 1 block south of the Monterey Peninsula Recreational Trail in Monterey's Cannery Row. From the trail you can enjoy the flat, glittering expanse of Monterey Bay and the wildlife that abides on or near its surface. Within the aquarium, you can observe the environment below the bay's surface, from the magic of tide pools to the mysterious depths of the Monterey Canyon.

The aquarium is open from 10:00 A.M. to 6:00 P.M. daily except Christmas Day, and from 9:30 A.M. to 6:00 P.M. from Memorial Day through Labor Day and during major holiday periods. Ticket prices are $24.95 for adults, $22.95 for seniors, and $15.95 for children ages 3 to 12 and for the disabled. Children 3 and younger are free. Contact the aquarium at (831) 648–4800 for more information, or visit the aquarium's Web site at www.mbayaq.org.

There are some who might gaze with longing upon the gingerbread dollhouses that overlook the craggy shoreline of Pacific Grove. There's no denying it: The folks who live in these historic homes reside in an area of unsurpassed scenic and cultural beauty. But the sea otters have it pretty darn good, too. From the sun-splashed kelp beds on which they lounge, the views are just as spectacular, and because they work from home, they get to enjoy it day in and day out. That's living!

The Monterey Peninsula Recreational Trail affords hikers, cyclists, and skaters many opportunities to check out the sea otters—and the sea lions, and the seabirds—as well as the chance to sample many other amenities offered by the popular resort town. The path wanders through historic Cannery Row, past the eateries and museums of Fisherman's Wharf, along the beaches at San Carlos Park and Monterey Bay Park, and through a colonnade of eucalyptus to a seabird-speckled estuary in Seaside.

The rail trail follows the former bed of a Southern Pacific line that began in Spanish Bay and ran north to San Francisco. During the heyday of the area's fisheries, in the 1930s and 1940s, the line served the canneries, taking goods to the markets in the north and bringing supplies back south to Monterey. It also served as a passenger line, with a turntable located at Lovers Point in Pacific Grove.

You can begin anywhere along the route, but the trail is described here starting at Lover's Point and ending at Seaside. The spectacular rocky shoreline borders the path on the west; on the east, the charming Victorians of Pacific Grove overlook the bay. Head north up the rail trail; bicyclists and in-line skaters are restricted to the paved portion, while hikers and walkers stroll along the dirt pathway that parallels the pavement. At 0.3 mile, pass a mural

This cyclist enjoys a marina view along the Monterey Peninsula Recreational Trail.

on the (right) east that describes the history of the area; to the west, the lumpy crags poking out of the bay host cormorants, seagulls, and pelicans, and clumps of kelp serve as beds for the frolicsome otters. A small park, with manicured grass and benches shaded by cypress, lies at the half-mile point.

At 0.8 mile, historic homes give way to historic warehouses, and the trail passes the Hopkins Marine Station of Stanford University on the west. Cross Eardley Avenue at 1 mile and enter Cannery Row proper. The trail is now concrete, and walkers, cyclists, and skaters share the same path. A series of street crossings follows. Pass the Monterey Bay Aquarium, the cannery buildings, the carousel in the Edgewater Packing Company building, and the Southern Pacific railway cars that house the Cannery Row Welcome Center.

The route continues north to San Carlos Beach and Fisherman's Shoreline Park at 1.5 miles. A sloping lawn shaded by cypress drops to a blue bay dotted with sparkling fishing and sailing vessels. Pass a small beach. At 2 miles, the trail deposits you on Fisherman's Wharf in the square that fronts the Custom House Museum.

Beyond the wharf, the trail splits briefly, with hikers staying waterside, users on wheels shunted east around a parking lot. The bike path crosses Washington Street and parallels Del Monte Avenue to Monterey Bay Park at 2.5 miles.

The rail trail, now asphalt again, veers left (west) into the park, rejoins the walking path, then heads north between the small dunes sheltering the beach on the west side and a large lawn on the east. Beyond the park, the path is used primarily by local residents. It passes between warehouses and businesses into a strip of eucalyptus that serves as a barrier between it and the adjacent roadway. At 3.5 miles, a boardwalk offers access to the tall dunes to the west of the path; there is no dune access for the next half mile or so, as the beachside property belongs to a U.S. naval installation with restricted access. The railroad tracks, unseen to this point except in Cannery Row, reappear to the east of the trail, cross beneath it, and pop in and out of view as the route continues north.

The trail rolls beneath a couple of overpasses, then enters the city of Seaside at 4.1 miles, near the intersection of Del Monte Avenue and Roberts Avenue. The emergent railroad tracks pass through a small bower of cypress; the paved trail runs alongside them for another 0.2 mile to Camino Del Rey. The rail corridor continues ahead, running between shopping centers and the busy thoroughfare, continuing to Marina and on toward Castroville. Unless you have arranged a shuttle, you must return as you came.

30 VENTURA RIVER TRAIL

While hardly the most scenic trail in this guidebook, the Ventura River Trail is definitely one of the most fascinating. More than any other, this route points up the intriguing and provocative juxtaposition of what the railroads often bring to a community—namely, industry—and what they leave behind when they are abandoned.

Activities:

Location: City of Ventura, Ventura County

Length: 6.3 miles one way

Surface: Asphalt

Wheelchair access: The trail is wheelchair accessible. There aren't many easy ways to access the trail other than at the end points, however, so all users, whether in wheelchairs or not, should be prepared to go the distance.

Difficulty: Moderate, due only to the trail's length

Food: There is no food or water available along the trail, so pack what you will need. Picnic tables are available at Foster Park. You can find restaurants and stores in Ventura, if you want to stock up at that end point.

Restrooms: There are no restrooms at the Ventura end point, nor are there any along the trail. Restrooms are available at the Foster Park end point.

Seasons: The trail is accessible year-round.

Access and parking: To reach the Ventura end point from the southbound lanes of U.S. Highway 101 in Ventura, take the Main Street exit. Turn right (east) on Main Street and follow it less than a quarter mile to the trailhead parking lot, which is on the right (south/ocean) side of the road opposite Peking Street and before the California 33 overpass. From northbound US 101, take the CA 33/Ojai exit. Head north to Main Street. Turn left (west) on Main Street and follow it to the parking lot.

To reach Foster Park, continue northeast on CA 33 for about 5.5 miles to the Casitas Vista/Foster Park exit. The park is adjacent to the freeway on its northwest side. There is plenty of parking available.

Transportation: The Ventura County Transportation Commission runs the VISTA bus system, which can be reached by dialing (800) 438–1112 or (805) 642–1591. The Web site is www.goventura.org.

Rentals: Bikes can be rented from Ventura Bike Depot, Inc., which is near the trailhead at 239 West Main Street in Ventura. The phone number is (805) 652–1114; the Web site is www.venturabikedepot.com.

Contact: Department of Public Works, City of Ventura, 501 Poli Street, P.O. Box 99, Ventura, CA 93002-0099; (805) 654–7702. You can also visit the city Web site at www.cityofventura.net; go to the maps link, then the Ventura River Trail map link.

||||||||||||||||||||||||||||||||||||||||||||||||||||||||||||||||||||||||||||||||

S tretching from ocean to mountain, like the river that lends it its name and the railroad that preceded it, the Ventura River Trail presents a conundrum. This unusual route showcases both the natural world and the industrial in an interesting and contradictory visual tableau. There is the willow-lined Ventura River, and there are the rusted scraps of machinery. There is the noisy freeway, and there are the rugged mountains that frame the valley. There are lemon trees, works of art, and tractors. It's a provocative and very worthwhile journey for a thoughtful traveler.

The rail trail cuts through Ventura's industrial underpinnings. Oil wells sucking black gold from the earth nod a slow hello to passersby; the tanks that store the crude rise adjacent to the trail in stark, fenced yards; tractors and trucks, which will burn the oil once it is refined, are parked in orderly rows awaiting dispatch. The Ventura River, a sluggish flow in a broad bed bordered by a fragile veil of riparian plants, writhes in and out of view on the northwest side of the rail trail, not dominating the scene until the route bends toward its finish in the Ojai Valley. And all along the route, artists have placed evocative works—a sculpture of an egret, a scattering of "oranges," animals set in bas relief on the trash cans—that draw from nature. Most striking of these are the "Midden Markers," etched with sayings that are as thought-provoking as the setting.

The trail follows the lower portion of the former Ventura and Ojai Rail Road, which was purchased in 1890 by the Southern Pacific Rail-

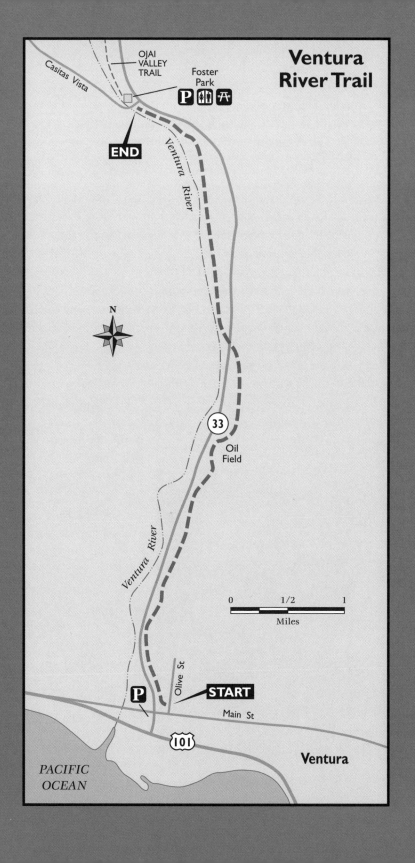

road Company. Fighting a losing battle with flood damage to the rails, Southern Pacific slowly abandoned the line, a process that started in the 1960s and wasn't completed until the late 1980s. The right-of-way was acquired as open space, and the trail was opened to the public in October 1999.

Begin by following the on-street bike lane east down Main Street, passing under CA 33 to Olive Street. Turn left (north) on Olive Street; there is a Ventura River Trail sign here. Turn left (north) off of Olive Street at Dubbers Street (marked with another Ventura River Trail sign). The obvious trail begins at the sharp curve in Dubbers Street.

The paved path, marked by mile and kilometer markers and accented with the "Midden Markers," is wedged between the freeway and the ball fields and community center at West Park, then spills into the industrial complexes. At 1.4 miles, the trail crosses Stanley Avenue. The neighboring freeway is screened by eucalyptus for a stretch, then the trail pulls away from the busy roadway as it winds through a series of gates that

offer access to various industrial operations. Watch for trucks, and walk bicycles around the gates if they are closed.

The first oil rigs appear on the left (northwest) at about the 2.5-mile mark. Cross a series of small access roads as you pass through the oil fields, then cross under the freeway again at 3.4 miles.

The trail is now adjacent to the willow-screened Ventura River, which runs seasonally, and may be completely

A dilapidated bridge spans the Ventura River Trail.

A Tale of Two Trails

The Ventura River Trail and its older sibling, the Ojai Valley Trail, lie on the former right-of-way of the Ventura and Ojai Rail Road Company. This railroad, which traveled between Ventura and Ojai carrying both passengers and freight, including the succulent citrus of the region's ubiquitous orchards, was established in 1898, and was purchased by Southern Pacific soon after its completion.

But floods, scourge of roadways and railroads throughout California into modern times, beset the rail line. The Ventura and Ojai line washed out many times before Southern Pacific decided to discontinue passenger service in the early 1930s. By the time record rains drenched the area in the late 1960s, the tracks had been damaged so many times that Southern Pacific decided it wasn't worth the fight and abandoned all but a limited section of track that served the oil industry in Ventura. Eventually floods damaged that last link as well, and the line was completely abandoned by the late 1980s.

The Ojai Valley Trail, which runs from Foster Park to Ojai, was built over a period of nearly ten years, and completed in 1989. The Ventura River Trail, also ten years in the making, opened in October 1999. Linking the trails makes for a fantastic bike ride, totaling 15.8 miles and encompassing all of the fascinating scenery from the mountains surrounding the Ojai Valley to the flatlands near the Pacific Ocean.

dry in summer and early fall. On the east side of the trail rise the storage tanks, painted a pastel green and accented with rust and drips of oil.

The route takes on a more rural aspect as you continue inland toward the Ojai Valley, with orchards decorating the slopes of the nearby mountains, and a few lemon trees growing adjacent to the trail. Cross a bridge at 4.6 miles, where you will be treated to the best views of the Ventura River.

By the 5.4-mile mark, the trail again runs adjacent to the freeway but has curved away from Ventura into the scenic Ojai Valley. The mountains, with a scrappy covering of grayish green scrub, rise steeply away from the river bottom. Pass a trail entrance at 5.7 miles and stay straight on the obvious route.

The trail ends in Foster Park, with its picnic tables, tot lot, lawns, and other amenities, at 6.3 miles. This is the turnaround point, unless you plan to continue on the Ojai Valley Trail, which begins here.

31 OJAI VALLEY TRAIL

Though it sits on the edge of the ever-changing and expanding Los Angeles metropolitan area, the Ojai Valley has retained its rural charm. Part of that charm is the rail trail that follows the Ventura River into the valley, passing broad open spaces and wonderful views of the surrounding mountains as it climbs.

Activities:

Location: From Foster Park to Ojai in Ventura County

Length: 9.5 miles one way

Surface: Asphalt, except for a short section from Fox Street in Ojai to the Soule Park Golf Course, which is dirt and limited to equestrian and pedestrian use

Wheelchair access: Except for the brief unpaved section in Ojai, the trail is wheelchair accessible.

Difficulty: Hard. The trail is long, and climbs steadily from Foster Park to Ojai.

Food: You will find fast food and a market near the midpoint of the trail, when it briefly parallels California 33 in Oak View. There are plenty of restaurants and stores in downtown Ojai, at the trail's northeastern end point.

Restrooms: There are public restrooms at Foster Park. No other public facilities are available along the trail.

Seasons: The trail can be used year-round, but the portion of the path that crosses the Ventura River may be flooded during and after winter and spring rains.

Access and parking: To reach the Foster Park end point from CA 33 northeast of Ventura, take the Casitas Vista/Foster Park exit. The park is adjacent to the freeway on its northwest side. There is plenty of parking available here.

To reach the Fox Street end point, continue on CA 33 into the town of Ojai. At the intersection of CA 33 and California 150 in Ojai, go right (east) on CA 150, and proceed through the charming downtown area. Fox Street intersects the highway on the east side of town; turn right (south) and drive a couple of blocks to the trail. Limited parking is available along the residential streets.

Transportation: The Ventura County Transportation Commission runs the VISTA bus system, which can be reached by dialing (800) 438–1112 or (805) 642–1591. The Web site is www.goventura.org.

Rentals: There are no rentals available along the route.

Contact: Theresa Lubin, Ventura County Parks Reservations and Information Office, 800 South Victoria Avenue, Ventura, CA 93009; (805) 654–3951. Visit www.countyofventura.org and follow the link to the Parks Department.

The spectacular Ojai Valley, cradle of the Ventura River, is surrounded—you might even say insulated—by the sharp, dry peaks of Los Padres National Forest. Carpeted with grasses that are verdant in winter and spring and golden in summer, the valley has fended off suburban sprawl, retaining the rural, agricultural atmosphere that once dominated the coastal valleys of south-central California.

The Ojai Valley Trail, awarded the Cal-Trans Award for Excellence in Transportation Facilities in 1989, is the perfect path from which to enjoy the valley. At its southern end, Foster Park offers abundant amenities, including riverside picnicking and a playground for the wee ones. The trail dips away from busy CA 33 into the wildlands bordering the river for an infinitely appealing mile or so, then climbs into quiet neighborhoods as it approaches Ojai. Within the quaint town itself, the trail, a shady pathway frequented by local residents walking dogs and pushing strollers, offers a wonderful alternative to the bustling main street.

The rail trail lies on the bed of the former Ventura and Ojai Rail Road, which followed the Ventura River from Ojai to the oceanside town of Ventura. The railroad carried passengers and freight between the two towns from the turn of the twentieth century to the 1930s. When Southern Pacific, which acquired the railroad shortly after it was completed, decided to abandon the line, the county of Ventura purchased it and installed the trail, which was completed in 1989.

The trail begins in Foster Park, which is also the end point of the Ventura River Trail; combining these two routes makes for an extremely

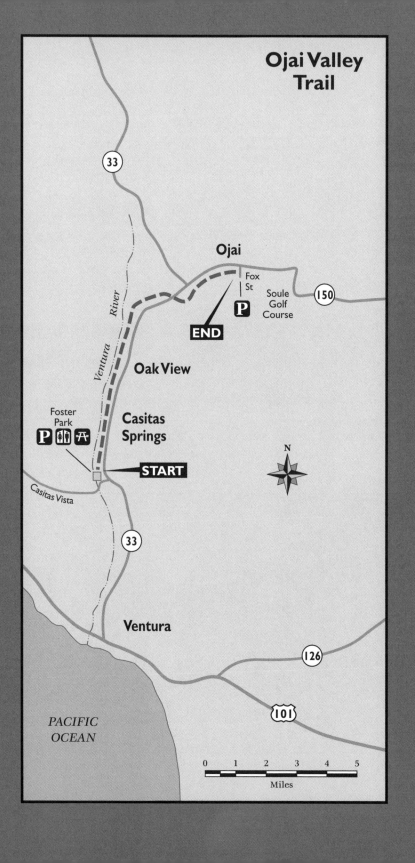

pleasant, lengthy bike ride. The first half mile of the trail borders the park, passing the picnic areas, tot lot, and ball fields. Beyond, the trail passes through a bower of eucalyptus, then cruises by the open backyards of homes wedged between the trail and CA 33, which the route roughly follows. A dirt walkway, ideal for horses and trail runners, parallels the paved path, but is separated by a rustic fence.

At the 1-mile mark, the trail curves east along the two-lane highway through Casitas Springs for a half mile, crossing several side streets. On the north side of the town, the trail hooks back west toward the river, bordered on one side by the broad, rocky channel and on the other by dense brush and oaks. Climb a short hill onto the railroad grade proper and wind through the oak woodland to a low, concrete-covered culvert that bridges the river at 1.8 miles. This section is subject to flooding during and after rainstorms.

The splendid seclusion ends at the 3-mile mark, where the trail slowly makes the transition from relative wildness to the quiet neighborhoods of Oak View. Cross Santa Ana Boulevard, then Monte Via, where you will find a small parking area.

The rail trail passes behind Oak View Community Park, with its lawns, playground, and ball field, then climbs onto an exposed stretch of grade that

Here pavement and railroad grade meet along the Ojai Valley Trail.

offers commanding views of the river valley. Beyond the elevated section, the trail drops into a shady gully and continues through area neighborhoods.

At 5.3 miles, the trail again bends eastward to parallel the highway. At the Woodland Avenue intersection in Oak View, you have easy access to fast food and a market. The trail crosses a number of side streets before it reaches a large meadow that opens on the left (northeast) side of the trail near the 6.5-mile mark. This lovely open space, with its scattering of oak trees, stretches to the wooded mountains in the distance.

At the 8-mile mark, the trail crosses the major intersection of CA 33 and 150 in Ojai; there is a large shopping center at this juncture. Use traffic signals to cross CA 150 safely, then pick up the obvious trail on the south side of the highway.

The rail trail plunges back into a peaceful neighborhood setting, cruising through the greenbelt that separates these Ojai backyards. At 9 miles, pass through Libbey Park, which offers parking, an amphitheater, restrooms, picnicking, and access to a trail leading north to the downtown area.

The paved trail ends in a cul-de-sac at Fox Street, although horseback riders can continue on the dirt track to Soule Park and Golf Course. Unless you have arranged a shuttle or plan to return to the trailhead via public transportation, return as you came. It's all downhill from here!

More Rail Trails

L FRESNO SUGAR PINE TRAIL AND CLOVIS OLD TOWN TRAIL

The development of the Fresno and Clovis route exemplifies how community support can foster the birth and growth of an urban rail trail. The path passes through Old Town Clovis, and connects with trails along the San Joaquin River in northern Fresno. The trail is urban and suburban in nature, linking routes to work, school, retail shops, and community parks for local residents. More than 4,000 trees planted by volunteers in the spring of 2000 mark a world record and make the route scenic and shady.

Activities:

Location: Fresno and Clovis in Fresno County

Length: 13 miles one way

Surface: Asphalt

Wheelchair access: The paved route is wheelchair accessible.

Difficulty: The two sections, taken independently, are easy, but the entire route is moderate due to its length.

Food: Restaurants, grocery stores, and fast-food outlets are available throughout the Fresno and Clovis areas.

Restrooms: There are restrooms at the Tarpey Village Rest Stop, Treasure Ingmire Park, and John R. Wright Park on the Clovis trail segment. Restrooms are also available in Woodward Park in Fresno. .

Seasons: The trail can be traveled year-round.

Access and parking: To reach the southern end point of the Clovis Old Town Trail from California 99 northbound, take California 41 north to California 180. From southbound CA 99, exit onto CA 180 eastbound. Follow CA 180 west to California 168 to Clovis/Huntington Lake (also known as the Sierra Freeway). Take the Ashlan Avenue exit off CA 168. At the stoplight, turn right (east) on Ashlan Avenue and go about 3 miles to its intersection with Clovis Avenue. Go right (south) on Clovis Avenue and proceed to Dakota Avenue; the trailhead is on your left at the Clovis Recreation Center.

Transportation: The Clovis Transit Stageline can be reached at (559) 324–2770. You can also visit the City of Clovis Web site at www.ci.clovis.ca.us.

Rentals: There are no rentals along the route.

Contacts: The Fresno City Parks and Recreation Department is at 2326 Fresno Street, Room 101, Fresno CA 93721; (559) 621–CITY (2489). The Web site is www.fresno.gov; follow the links to the Parks, Recreation, and Community Services Department.

For the Clovis Old Town Trail, contact John Lovejoy, Clovis Engineering Department; (559) 324–2600. The Web site is www.ci.clovis.ca.us; follow links to the Parks Department and a great trail map.

For more trail information, you can contact Mark Keppler, formerly with the Coalition for Community Trails, which has merged with the nonprofit Tree Fresno. The Web site is www.treefresno.org. Keppler's e-mail address is mkeppler@csufresno.edu.

SANTA MARIA VALLEY MULTIPURPOSE TRAIL

The Santa Maria rail trail is short, but it offers neighborhood access to a lovely and diverse urban park, well-manicured ball fields, a lush private golf course, and the active tracks of the Union Pacific railroad. The trail, built in 2004, lies on the right-of-way of the Santa Maria Valley Railroad, with active rail lines running alongside.

Activities:

Location: Santa Maria, Santa Barbara County

Length: 1.1 miles one way

Surface: Asphalt

Wheelchair access: The trail is wheelchair accessible.

Difficulty: Easy

Food: There is no food or water along the trail, but water is available in Waller Park.

Restrooms: No restrooms are on the trail, but you will find them in adjacent Waller Park.

Seasons: The trail can be used year-round.

Access and parking: To reach the Waller Park trailhead from U.S. Highway 101 in Santa Maria, take the Betteravia Road exit. Go right (west) on Betteravia Road toward Lompoc for 1 mile and turn left (south) on Broadway/California 135, again headed for Lompoc. Follow Broadway for 1 mile to Waller Park; turn right at Waller Lane at the brown county park sign.

The best parking for the trail is near the ball fields and dog park in the southwest quadrant of the park. To reach this area, head south on the park road for about 0.5 mile to Goodwin. Turn right on Goodwin and go about 0.5 mile to the signs for Woof Park (the dog park). The narrow Woof Park access road circles around to the Hagerman Sports Complex and a decomposed granite path that drops past the ball fields to the rail trail. The trail formally begins a bit south of the fields, near the intersection of Airpark Drive and Hagerman Lane; the Santa Maria YMCA is across the street to the south.

There is no parking on the north end of the trail at McCoy Lane.

Transportation: Santa Maria Area Transit (SMAT) provides public transportation to the area. For more information call (805) 928–5624, or visit the Web site at www.ci.santa-maria.ca.us/3075.html.

Rentals: There are no rentals available along the trail.

Contact: Alexander Posada, director of the City of Santa Maria's Parks and Recreation Department, can be reached at (805) 925–0951. The city Web site is www.ci.santa-maria.ca.us.

Larry Lavagnino, Santa Maria representative to the Santa Barbara County Area Government Board, can be reached by calling (805) 925–0951 ext. 191.

FILLMORE TRAIL

This short rail trail begins at the Fillmore end of the historic Fillmore & Western Railway. The dynamic collection of railroad cars clustered around the Fillmore Station—including one that houses a museum—is the highlight of the route, which parallels existing rail lines to Shiells Park. The trail offers access to the historic Fillmore & Western Railway, which runs vintage railcars on its line; call (800) 773–8724 or visit www.fwry.com for more information.

Activities:

Location: Fillmore, Ventura County

Length: 2 miles one way

Surface: Asphalt

Wheelchair access: The rail trail is wheelchair accessible.

Difficulty: Easy

The Fillmore rail trail runs along the tracks of the Fillmore & Western Railway.

Food: There are no restaurants on the trail, but you can find restaurants and markets nearby in downtown Fillmore.

Restrooms: There are restrooms at the Fillmore City Hall trailhead and at Shiells Park.

Seasons: The trail can be used year-round.

Access and parking: To reach the Fillmore Central Station Park from California 126 (Ventura Street) in Fillmore, head north for 1 block on Central Avenue to City Hall. Parking is available in the designated lots off of Main Street and along the street itself.

Transportation: The Ventura County Transportation Commission runs the VISTA bus system, which can be reached by dialing (800) 438–1112 or (805) 642–1591. The Web site is www.goventura.org.

Rentals: There are no rentals available on the trail.

Contact: Bert Rapp, City Engineer, City of Fillmore, 524 Sespe Avenue, Fillmore, CA 93015; (805) 524–3701.

Best Rail Trails
SOUTHERN CALIFORNIA

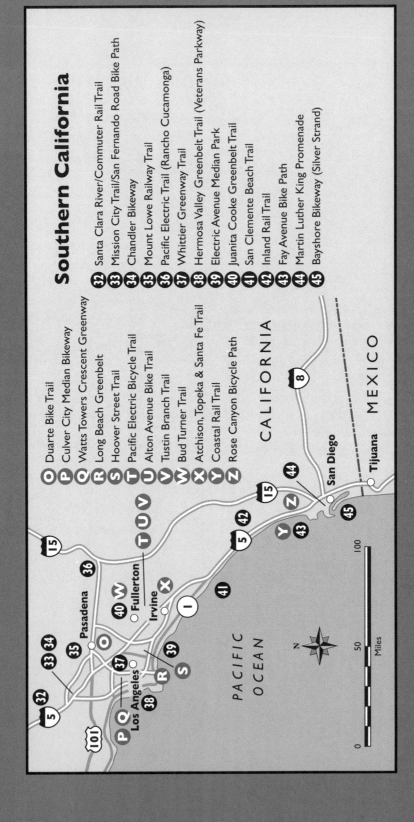

Southern California

- ⓄDuarte Bike Trail
- ⓅCulver City Median Bikeway
- ⓆWatts Towers Crescent Greenway
- ⓇLong Beach Greenbelt
- ⓈHoover Street Trail
- ⓉPacific Electric Bicycle Trail
- ⓊAlton Avenue Bike Trail
- ⓋTustin Branch Trail
- ⓌBud Turner Trail
- ⓍAtchison, Topeka & Santa Fe Trail
- ⓎCoastal Rail Trail
- ⓏRose Canyon Bicycle Path

- ㉜Santa Clara River/Commuter Rail Trail
- ㉝Mission City Trail/San Fernando Road Bike Path
- ㉞Chandler Bikeway
- ㉟Mount Lowe Railway Trail
- ㊱Pacific Electric Trail (Rancho Cucamonga)
- ㊲Whittier Greenway Trail
- ㊳Hermosa Valley Greenbelt Trail (Veterans Parkway)
- ㊴Electric Avenue Median Park
- ㊵Juanita Cooke Greenbelt Trail
- ㊶San Clemente Beach Trail
- ㊷Inland Rail Trail
- ㊸Fay Avenue Bike Path
- ㊹Martin Luther King Promenade
- ㊺Bayshore Bikeway (Silver Strand)

32 SANTA CLARA RIVER/COMMUTER RAIL TRAIL

The Santa Clara River and its tributaries form the skeleton of a network of well-developed trails through Santa Clarita, with the San Gabriel Mountains forming a stark, sharp-edged backdrop.

Activities:

Location: Santa Clarita, Los Angeles County

Length: 4.5 miles one way

Surface: Asphalt with an unpaved parallel pathway

Wheelchair access: The trail is wheelchair friendly.

Difficulty: Moderate, due only to length

Food: There are no restaurants or stores on the trail, but the Promenade trailhead is located in a shopping center with a supermarket and fast-food outlets. Water is available at the South Fork trailhead.

Restrooms: There are no restrooms along the route, but facilities are available in the trailhead shopping center.

Seasons: Year-round, though you should avoid the trail in winter if the river is high.

Access and parking: To reach the trailhead from Interstate 5 in Santa Clarita, take the Magic Mountain Parkway exit. Travel about 1 mile east to McBean Parkway and turn left, then turn left into the large shopping center. The trailhead is at the northwest corner of the parking lot; there is plenty of parking available.

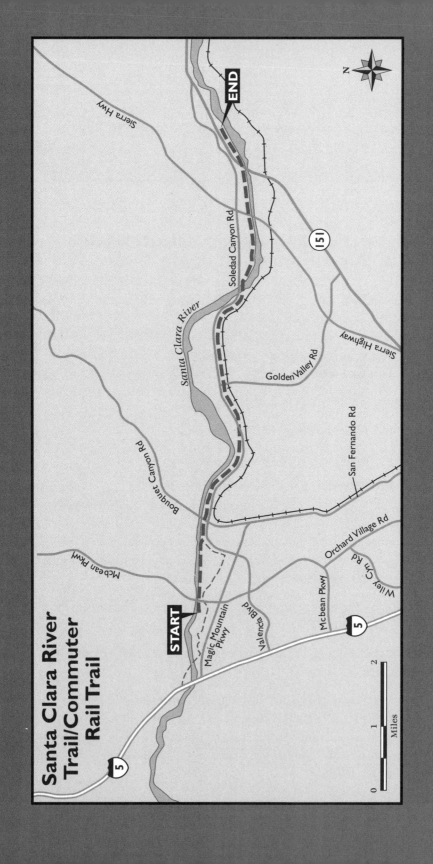

Transportation: City of Santa Clarita Transit, which provides bus service to the area, can be reached at (661) 295–6300. Schedules are available by calling (661) 294–1BUS (1287); you can also visit the Web site at www .santa-clarita.com/cityhall/admin/transit. Information about transit services in Los Angeles County may be obtained by dialing (800) COMMUTE. The Los Angeles Metropolitan Transportation Authority Web site is www. mta.net.

Rentals: There are no rental outlets on the route.

Contact: The City of Santa Clarita's Parks Department, located at 23920 Valencia Boulevard, Suite 120, can be reached by calling (661) 286-4000. The trail system Web site is www.santa-clarita.com/cityhall/parks/trails. A wonderful trail map can be downloaded from the site; just follow the links.

I n late summer, the Santa Clara River dries to a crackly crunch. But its liquid heart is evident in the riparian habitat that thrives even in the heat

Shade bathes a cyclist on the Santa Clara River Trail/Commuter Rail Trail.

of southern California's trademark season. Willows and alders line the riverside, with sycamore and eucalyptus providing additional shade along sections of the paved trails that trace the waterways.

The route described here follows a portion of the commuter rail trail, then arcs away from that trail to meander alongside the western bank of the south fork of the Santa Clara River, with the Metrolink rail line on the east shore.

Begin at the Promenade trailhead, located in the northwest corner of the shopping center parking lot at the intersection of the Magic Mountain and McBean Parkways. A circular stone bench marks the entrance to the path, which branches off to both east and west; a trash can and a receptacle for doggie-doo bags also are located here. It's obvious that you're on the river path whether the river has water in it or not, given the wall of willows that delineates the north side of the trail.

Heading west (left) drops you a mile downstream to the end of the trail near the junction of I–5 and the Magic Mountain Parkway. Instead, turn east (right) and head upstream along the double-wide paved path. The route drops almost immediately below the McBean Parkway via an underpass, then climbs back to a level grade. A chain-link fence separates trail users from power lines, which pass overhead at about 0.2 mile, and a wooden fence guards the riverside. The San Gabriel Mountains rise ahead, mottled brown, gray, and gold against a backdrop of blue sky. Pass a trail access path at about 0.4 mile, which offers access to the commercial/business district up and right of the trail. The trail dips under a roadway and continues east along the riverbank, exposed and following the power lines.

At about 1 mile, you'll reach the Valencia Boulevard underpass and trail intersection for the South Fork Trail and the commuter rail trail. This intersection was not well signed when I visited in the summer of 2007; I mistakenly ended up on the South Fork Trail, which heads south from this intersection and follows the south fork of the Santa Clara River. No worries: If you make the same mistake, you'll follow a nice, flat route that mimics a rail trail, with an unpaved trail for equestrians alongside the paved route, both shaded by sycamore and eucalyptus. Neighborhood access paths periodically intersect the route; it also dips under a major roadway overpass at about the 2-mile mark, and there's a single major trail intersection, which leads into the adjoining residential areas, at about 3 miles. The trail ends at about 3.5 miles at Orchard Village Road. There are no amenities at this trailhead (parking would be on side streets), and there are no restrooms or water fountains on this stretch of trail. Return as you came.

To stay on the commuter rail trail, go left at the Valencia Boulevard trail junction, across the south fork of the Santa Clara River, and stay right at the next two trail intersections. The trail definitely lives up to its designation as a commuter route, as it is frequented by workers on bicycles (we saw a bicycling chef in a uniform the color of whipped egg whites on our visit). This section parallels Valencia Boulevard to San Fernando Road at about 1.3 miles.

After passing San Fernando Road, cruise along the south bank of the Santa Clara River, with the river on the left (north) and Soledad Canyon Road and the Metrolink rails on the right (south). Pass trail access to a Metrolink station at about the 2.3-mile mark; the station lies to the right (south) of the trail.

Beyond the Metrolink station, the trail diverges from the riverside, sticking close to the roadway and the rail line. Near the 3-mile mark, the route crosses Soledad Canyon Road and continues eastward, with the roadway on the north (left) and the train tracks on the south (right). At about 3.5 miles, the commuter rail trail intersects Golden Valley Road; stay left on the commuter rail trail, which proceeds east in the rail corridor toward the mountain backdrop.

The trail and rail line bend southward at about 4.5 miles, with the river coming back into play again. At about 5 miles, the commuter rail trail and Soledad Canyon Road cross the river to the Camp Plenty Road trailhead, where you will find parking and a drinking fountain. This is the end of the rail trail, though the Santa Clara River Trail continues east along the north bank of the waterway for another couple of miles to the Lost Canyon trailhead.

33 MISSION CITY TRAIL/SAN FERNANDO ROAD BIKE PATH

Running adjacent to the active Metrolink lines through downtown San Fernando, the Mission City Trail offers recreationalists and locals access to area businesses and communities, a close-up view of the railroad, a lesson in successful urban landscaping, and a small memorial park.

Activities:

Location: San Fernando, Los Angeles County

Length: 3 miles one way

Surface: Concrete and asphalt

Wheelchair access: The trail is wheelchair accessible.

Difficulty: Easy

Food: Restaurants and markets, while not fronting the trail, are located along adjacent San Fernando Road. There is no water along the route.

Restrooms: There are no restrooms along the rail trail.

Seasons: The trail can be used year-round.

Access and parking: To reach the northern trailhead at Roxford Road from Interstate 5 in San Fernando, take the Roxford Road exit. Go east on Roxford Road for 0.5 mile to the intersection of Roxford and San Fernando Roads. There is on-street parking at this location.

To reach the southern end point, where you will also find on-street parking, follow San Fernando Road south from Roxford Road to Wolfskill Street. Turn left on Wolfskill, then right on First Street; a trail sign marks the trailhead.

Transportation: Mission City Transit, which offers transportation to local residents, can be reached at (818) 366–4119. The Web site is www.ci.san-fernando.ca.us; click on "For Residents" and follow the links. Information about transit services in Los Angeles County may be obtained by dialing (800) COMMUTE. The Los Angeles Metropolitan Transportation Authority

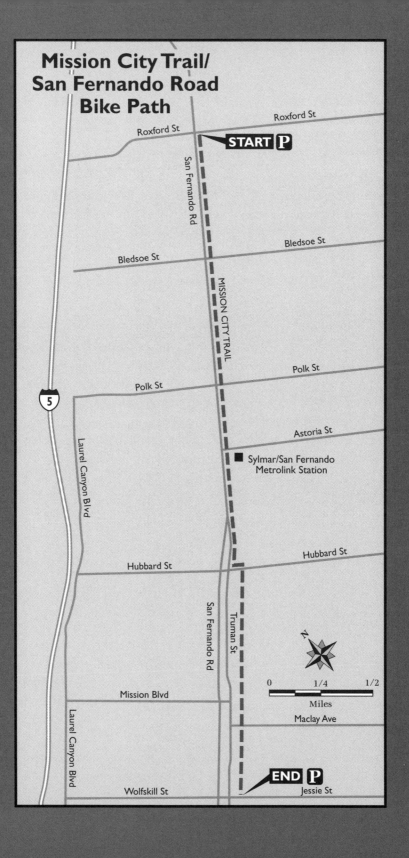

Mission City Trail/
San Fernando Road
Bike Path

Roxford St

Roxford St

START P

San Fernando Rd

Bledsoe St

Bledsoe St

MISSION CITY TRAIL

Polk St

Polk St

Astoria St

■ Sylmar/San Fernando
Metrolink Station

Laurel Canyon Blvd

Hubbard St

Hubbard St

San Fernando Rd

Truman St

5

N

0   1/4   1/2
Miles

Mission Blvd

Maclay Ave

Laurel Canyon Blvd

END P

Wolfskill St

Jessie St

Web site is www.mta.net. For information specific to the Metrolink system, visit www.metrolinktrains.com or call (800) 371–LINK (5465).

Rentals: There are no rentals along the path.

Contact: Michelle Mowery, Senior Project Manager for the City of Los Angeles Bicycle Program; (213) 972–4962; www.bicyclela.org. For information on the portion of the trail in the city of San Fernando, call (818) 898–1222.

|||||||||||||||||||||||||||||||||||||||||||||||||||||||||||||||||||||||||||||||||||||||||

This rail-with-trail runs adjacent to the active railroad line that passes through downtown San Fernando, offering a safe route for local residents to rail transportation, local businesses, and adjacent neighborhoods. While not a scenic destination, the route fills a necessary utilitarian role, as all good rail trails should, and is nicely outfitted with vibrant landscaping and a sweet little park with a fountain, rose garden, and public art.

The north end point of the trail is at the intersection of Roxford Street and San Fernando Road; there is no formal trailhead here. The solar-lighted, two-lane paved path heads south, wedged between the rail line and the roadway and sparsely shaded by towering palms. A high fence separates the trail from the rails. The setting is mostly commercial, with hotels and other businesses lining San Fernando Road.

At 0.4 mile, the trail intersects Bledsoe Street; at 1 mile, cross Polk Street, and the scattered palms give way to scattered eucalyptus. Pass the Astoria Street pedestrian access route at 1.3 miles, and continue southeast on the pencil-straight route.

The trail drops below the railroad tracks at about 1.6 miles, at the Sylmar/San Fernando Rail Station, where you will find Metrolink service and abundant parking. The station design mimics the distinctive arches of the historic San Fernando Mission. At about 1.7 miles, Truman Street separates from San Fernando Road; both the rail line and the rail trail parallel Truman Street as they continue southeast.

The Hubbard Avenue crossing is at 1.8 miles; the trail crosses the tracks to the northeast side and is now nicely landscaped, wedged between businesses and homes that line Truman and First Streets. There is trail access at

Lovely landscaping buffers the Mission City Trail from the active rail line that runs beside it.

Orange Grove Avenue, off First Street at 2.1 miles. A variety of plants provides a colorful textured backdrop for the wall that shields the right side of the route; a fence continues to provide separation between trail users and the active line on the left.

Cross Maclay Avenue at 2.6 miles, then Brand Avenue at 2.8 miles. The trail ends on Wolfskill Street at 3 miles; a little park at this point, dedicated to the memory of farm labor champion César Chávez, features a fountain, rose garden, benches, trash receptacles, and an interesting sculpture commemorating farm workers. Follow the bike route along First Street to another neighborhood park and ball fields, where you can rest and recuperate before returning as you came.

The city of Los Angeles plans to extend this route south of San Fernando to Branford Street by 2010.

34 CHANDLER BIKEWAY

This scenic median path cruises up the center of Burbank's Chandler Boulevard, providing easy pedestrian access to area neighborhoods and the North Hollywood Arts District.

Activities: 🏃 🚲 🛼 🏃 🏛

Location: Burbank, Los Angeles County

Length: 4 miles round-trip

Surface: Concrete

Wheelchair access: The trail is wheelchair accessible.

Difficulty: Easy

Food: There are no food outlets on the trail, but plenty of good eats in other areas of Burbank and North Hollywood. There is no water along the route.

Restrooms: There are no facilities on the rail trail.

Seasons: The trail can be used year-round.

Access and parking: To reach the Chandler Bikeway from Interstate 5 in Burbank, take the Burbank Boulevard exit. Head west on Burbank Boulevard for 0.2 mile to Victory Boulevard. Turn left (south) on Victory Boulevard and go 0.2 mile to Chandler Boulevard. Turn right on Chandler Boulevard; the trail begins 0.2 mile ahead at the intersection of Chandler and Mariposa Street.

To reach the western end point of the trail, follow Chandler Boulevard west for 2 miles to trail's end at Clybourn Avenue. There is on-street parking at both end points and along streets for the length of the rail trail.

Transportation: Burbank Local Transit offers shuttle services and transit links in the area; call (818) 246–4BLT or visit www.burbanktransit.com for details. Information about transit services in Los Angeles County may be obtained by dialing (800) COMMUTE in the Los Angeles calling area. The Los Angeles Metropolitan Transportation Authority Web site is www.mta.net.

Rentals: There are no rentals on the trail.

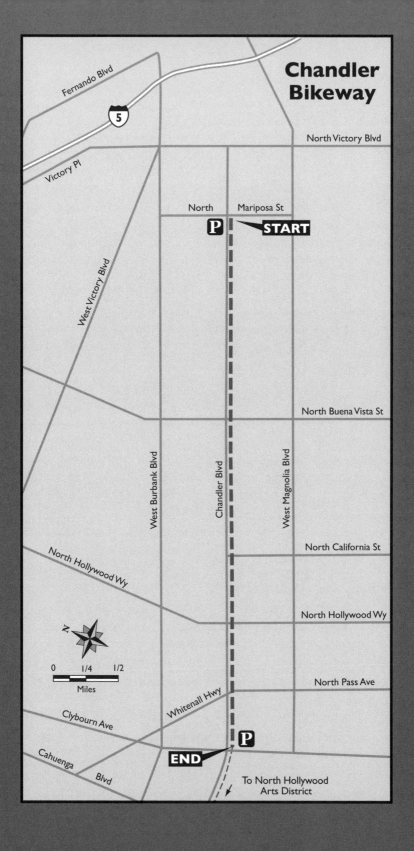

Contact: Joy Forbes, City of Burbank Planning and Transportation Division, (818) 238–5250; jforbes@ci.burbank.ca.us. The Web site is www.burbank ca.org/planning/chandler.htm, and includes links to newsletters logging development of the trail. You can also check out the Web site maintained by Friends of the Chandler Bikeway, at www.chandlerparkburbank.org/ friends.html, which includes links to railroad and bikeway history.

||||||||||||||||||||||||||||||||||||||||||||||||||||||||||||||||||||||||||||||||||||

The Chandler Bikeway splits Chandler Boulevard up the middle. While traffic occupies the roadways on either side of the rail trail, cyclists and walkers enjoy a meandering concrete pathway buffered by grass and flowers and shaded by trees, with benches for resting and enjoying views of the distant San Gabriel Mountains.

The trail is laid on the former bed of the Burbank branch of the Southern Pacific Railroad, a freight and passenger line. Construction on the abandoned right-of-way began in 2002; the trail opened in late summer 2004.

Beginning at the Mariposa Street end point, the route heads west through the median park, with Chandler Boulevard on either side and quaint homes fronting both the roadway and trail. It's a straight shot, impossible to lose track of (if you'll pardon the pun).

The first street crossing is at Keystone Street at 0.5 mile. Like all the intersections along the rail trail, this one is outfitted with benches and trashcans; the crossing is made via a stop sign. Next up is Buena Vista Street at 0.7 mile; this crossing is regulated by a stoplight.

Cross California Street; at this intersection you'll find a dedication plaque, along with benches, trash receptacles, and flowers and trees irrigated with recycled water. At 1.3 miles, a power station rises on the right (north) side of the route; at 1.4 miles, you'll reach Hollywood Way. This intersection is regulated by a stoplight and outfitted with a statue depicting a family enjoying the bike trail.

The next stop sign is at 1.7 miles at Pass Avenue, where the trail intersects a major power line easement. The median bikeway ends at Clybourn Avenue at the 2-mile mark.

Return as you came, enjoying views of the San Gabriel Mountains as you head back to the Mariposa trailhead.

If you'd like to extend your trip along Chandler Boulevard, continue west toward North Hollywood along the bike path that parallels the road-way and ventures into a more commercial and industrial setting. Cross Cahuenga Boulevard at 2.3 miles; the buildings backing onto the trail sport wonderful mural art—flowers, portraits, butterflies, and abstract images rendered on stucco in vivid color. At 2.8 miles, the route ends at Vineland Avenue, the boundary of the stimulating NoHo (North Hollywood) Arts District. After exploring the creative offerings, return as you came.

A cyclist enjoys the landscaped median of the Chandler Bikeway.

35 MOUNT LOWE RAILWAY TRAIL

This rail trail lies on the bed of one of the most famous and historic rail lines in the Los Angeles area. The Mount Lowe Railway, which featured a remarkable incline up Rubio Canyon to the Echo Mountain House, and a circular bridge that was world renowned as an engineering landmark, stopped transporting passengers in 1939, but the route continues to thrill modern visitors with its scenery and views.

Activities:

Note: Camping and backpacking opportunities exist along other routes in the Angeles National Forest. A Forest Adventure Pass, available for a small fee at sporting goods outlets throughout the Los Angeles area, is required.

Location: West of Pasadena in Los Angeles County, in the San Gabriel Mountains and the Angeles National Forest

Length: 4 miles on the railroad grade, but you must hike or bike up the very steep access road for 2.2 miles before you reach the rail trail. With the 1-mile out-and-back trip to the Echo Mountain ruins, the route totals 13.4 miles.

Surface: Ballast and dirt

Wheelchair access: The trail, given its steep grades and rough surface, is not suitable for wheelchairs.

Difficulty: Hard

Food: There are no food or water sources along the trail, nor are there any along the steep access road that leads to the trail. Be sure to pack in all you need. There are plenty of restaurants and grocery stores in Pasadena, Altadena, and the other cities at the foot of the mountains.

Restrooms: There are no restrooms at the trailhead, nor are there any along the route.

Seasons: The trail can be used year-round but may be muddy during and after winter rainstorms. The trail and access road also may be off-limits during periods of high fire danger.

Access and parking: There is no easy way to get to the Mount Lowe Rail-

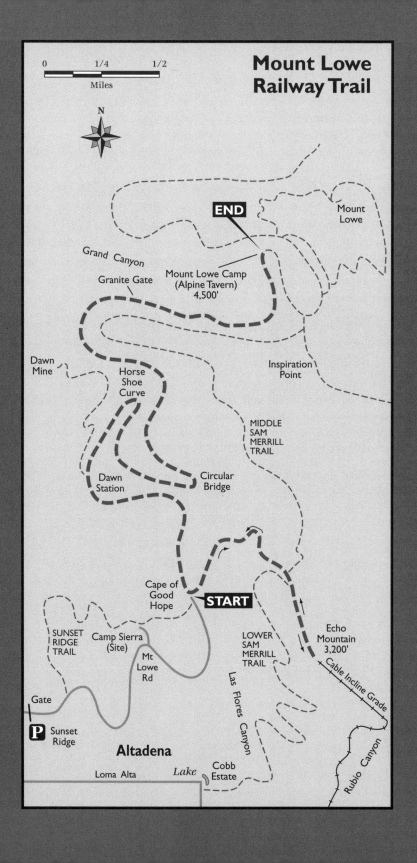

way Trail. Arguably the easiest, however, is to follow the paved access road up to the rail trail near its Echo Mountain end point.

To reach the access road and trailhead from Interstate 210 in Pasadena, take the Lake Avenue exit. Head north on Lake Avenue for 3.7 miles to Loma Alta Drive, which is at the base of the steep massif. Turn left (west) on Loma Alta Drive and go for 1.1 miles to Chaney Trail; a flashing yellow light marks the road. Turn right (north) on Chaney Trail and follow it for 1.4 miles, passing a display about the Forest Adventure Pass, to a gate. If the gate is open, you can proceed for another 1.1 miles to a saddle where you will find another gate and the beginning of the paved access road. There is limited roadside parking.

Transportation: There are no transit services directly to this trail, but public transportation is available to Pasadena. Transit services in Los Angeles County may be obtained by calling (800) COMMUTE in the Los Angeles calling area. The Los Angeles Metropolitan Transportation Authority Web site is www.mta.net; it offers information and trip planning services for Los Angeles County bus, rail, and other transit services.

Rentals: There are no rentals along the trail.

Contact: Los Angeles River Ranger District, Angeles National Forest, 12371 North Little Tujunga Canyon Road, San Fernando, CA 91324; (818) 899–1900.

||||||||||||||||||||||||||||||||||||||||||||||||||||||||||||||||||||||||||||||||||||||

Rising in stark contrast to all the other rail trails in Southern California, the Mount Lowe Railway Trail is fabulously wild. From an airy perch on this route, which winds through the tight, arid folds of the San Gabriel Mountains, you look down on the sprawling urbanity that makes the Los Angeles basin both famous and infamous.

On a clear day, the views from much of the railroad grade are, as you might expect, sublime, extending westward across the city to the Pacific Ocean. But even on hazy days you can enjoy vistas of the shimmering metropolis below, which is silver and gray and black like an orchestra in a pit, its cacophony muted to white noise by the time it reaches the heights.

From Echo Mountain, site of the ruins of the once grand Echo Mountain House, you can enjoy the same panorama that enticed folks to ride the railway more than a century ago.

The railway was remarkable for more than just its wonderful views. It, like the rail trail that now lies on its bed, featured breathtaking exposure, writhing like a sidewinder with a bellyache. It ran for 4 steep miles from the Echo Mountain House to the Alpine Tavern at the Mount Lowe Camp, but was fairly mellow compared to the incline railroad that climbed from Altadena to Echo Mountain via Rubio Canyon, ascending 1,500 feet via a 32 to 69 percent grade. Standing amid the foundations of this incline railway today invokes a feeling of incredulity—how could anyone ride up

A cyclist pedals up the Mount Lowe railroad grade.

(and then down) such a ferocious grade, much less build a railroad on it?

The Mount Lowe Railway and its accompanying incline railway were built in the early 1890s. The railroad was a tourist attraction for about forty years and was abandoned in 1940. But the route has never totally lost its appeal: It continues to attract recreationalists and is included on the National Register of Historic Places. Interpretive signs placed along the trail explain the railroad's complex and fascinating history.

Whether on foot, on wheels, or on horseback, you'll do most of the work just getting to the trail. You will climb more than 2,000 feet as you ascend from the trailhead to the Mount Lowe Camp, so plan on a full day, bring plenty of food and water, keep a reasonable pace, and enjoy.

From the trailhead, set out on the paved access road, which climbs past an interpretive sign with a map of the railroad. At 0.3 mile, pass the first intersection with the Sunset Ridge Trail; the second lies near the road's intersection with the rail trail.

The paved road is nipped into gullies and tucked behind ridges on the west face of the brush-covered mountainside. At about 1.5 miles, the road forks; stay right (east) on the main track, ignoring the road to the left (north), which leads to the site of Camp Sierra. Just beyond the intersection, at 1.7 miles, pass a gate at a switchback that swings the roadway north into the mountains.

At 2.2 miles, pass the second intersection with the Sunset Ridge Trail, which departs from the paved road to the left (west). Within 100 yards of this intersection, you will reach the Cape of Good Hope, where the portion of the rail trail leading to Echo Mountain breaks off to the right (east).

Although it's clear the rail trail continues straight ahead, take the time to visit the ruins of the Echo Mountain House. Turn right (east) onto the dirt track, which is lined with interpretive signs and narrows to single-track where it has been washed out. Railroad ties are embedded in the blond soil, and concrete foundations mark where trestles once spanned gullies that are slashed into the mountainside.

The trail leads gently downhill for 0.5 mile to the ruins, which command an awesome panorama of the Los Angeles basin. From a broad arcing staircase to a rusting bed frame, from potsherds to a large cistern to old track and other detritus of the railroad, the site is a history fanatic's dream come true. You can even shout into the Echo Phone and see if the mountains talk back to you. Interpretive signs include a discussion of the builders of the railroad and a map of the railway.

Once you've absorbed all you can, backtrack to the pavement at the Cape of Good Hope, passing the Sam Merrill Trail as you climb. The mileages that follow begin from the Echo Mountain House ruins.

Once on the paved road at 0.5 mile, turn right (north) and continue up the railroad grade, which turns to dirt about 100 yards beyond the Echo Mountain trail. As you climb to Dawn Station at 0.7 mile, pass three more interpretive signs, including one that notes that in the next 3.5 miles the railroad negotiated 127 curves. Benches shaded by a gazebo make this a perfect spot for rest and contemplation.

Continuing northward, the trail switchbacks through a major wash that is floored with concrete, then climbs to the upper end of the famed circular bridge, which lies on a switchback at the 1-mile mark.

The winding rail trail gains altitude gently as it meanders through shady gullies and across sun-washed faces, until it arcs onto the backside of the mountain at about 2 miles. Gone are views of the basin; now you skirt a steep-walled canyon—the "Grand Canyon of the Millard"—which wears a sparse cloak of desert scrub and trees, and offers views only of more mountains rising to the east. At 2.5 miles, pass through the portal of the famed Granite Gate, which was blasted through an outcrop of granite.

In late afternoon, when the sun settles behind the mountains to the west, this section of the track is washed in welcomed shade, making the remainder of the journey quite pleasant. At the 4-mile mark, you will arrive at the site of the Mount Lowe Alpine Tavern, which lies at the end of the line at a lofty 4,500 feet above sea level. The tavern suffered the same fate as the Echo Mountain House, burning to the ground in September 1936.

There are many options for exploration in the area of the Angeles National Forest served by the access road and the Mount Lowe Railway Trail, and you can use one of these other trails—such as the Sunset Ridge Trail—to return to the trailhead. If you return as you came, you'll have traveled a total of 13.4 miles.

36 PACIFIC ELECTRIC TRAIL (RANCHO CUCAMONGA)

This well-designed and landscaped trail cuts a linear greenscape through the peaceful neighborhoods of Rancho Cucamonga, creating opportunities for local residents and visitors alike to run, walk, and cycle in peace.

Activities:

Location: Rancho Cucamonga, San Bernardino County

Length: 5 miles one way

Surface: Asphalt with a parallel dirt path

Wheelchair access: The trail is wheelchair accessible.

Difficulty: Easy if taken in sections; moderate if done in its entirety

Food: There is no food available along the route, but there is plenty to eat in the commercial district along Baseline Road south of the trail.

Restrooms: There are public restrooms in Central Park and Ellena Park. You'll find water in parks along the route.

Seasons: The trail can be used year-round.

Access and parking: To reach the western end point on Grove Avenue from Interstate 10 in Rancho Cucamonga, take the Fourth Street exit and follow Fourth Street 0.2 mile to Grove Avenue. Turn right (north) on Grove and continue for 1.3 miles to Arrow Highway. The railroad grade intersects Grove beyond Arrow Highway at Avenida Vejar. There is on-street parking at this end point.

To reach the eastern end point at Etiwanda Avenue from Interstate 15, take the Baseline Road exit. Head west on Baseline Road for 0.3 mile to Etiwanda Avenue. Go right (north) on Etiwanda for 0.2 mile to the Etiwanda Station on the right (east), with both on-street parking and a small parking lot.

Transportation: Rancho Cucamonga and surrounding cities are served by Omnitrans, which can be reached at (800) 996–6428 or (909) 379–7100; the Web site is www.omnitrans.org. Los Angeles area public transportation is

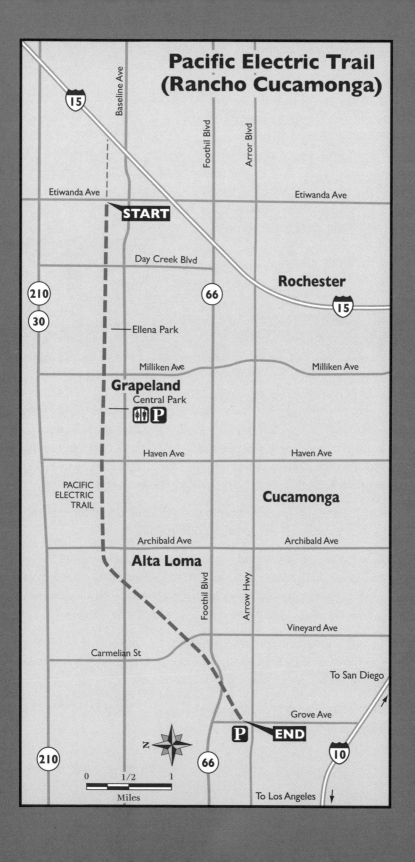

Etiwanda Station borders the Pacific Electric Trail in Rancho Cucamonga.

provided by the Metropolitan Transit Authority; (800) COMMUTE; www.mta
.net. Additional transportation information in San Bernardino County can
be obtained by contacting San Bernardino Associated Governments (SAN-
BAG) at (909) 884–8276; the address is 1170 West Third Street, Second Floor,
San Bernardino, CA 92410-1715. The Web site is www.sanbag.ca.gov.

Rentals: There are no rentals available along the trail. Check the local telephone directory for options in Rancho Cucamonga.

Contact: Planning Department, City of Rancho Cucamonga, 10500 Civic
Center   Drive, Rancho Cucamonga, CA 91730; (909) 477–2750; www
.ci.rancho-cucamonga.ca.us.The trail Web site is www.ci.rancho-cucamonga
.ca.us/govt/pet.htm.

For the trail segments in Fontana, contact the City of Fontana, 8353 Sierra
Avenue, Fontana, CA 92335; (909) 350–7600. Trail information is at www
.fontana.org/main/comm_conn/pac_trail.0505.htm.

You can also contact Justin Christopher of the Friends of the Pacific Electric Trail at justinaaronchristopher@yahoo.com.

The summer sun stains the pale stucco of Etiwanda Station pink as it sets in the west, and the Pacific Electric Trail runs in a clean white line toward the sinking orb. The trail is a neat, well-landscaped delight, offering a pleasant, safe romp through peaceful neighborhoods and passing through a dollop of wildland in a city park.

The trail lies on the abandoned railbed once used by the Pacific Electric Railway, one of the largest metropolitan rail service providers in the world during its heyday. The company provided transportation throughout the Los Angeles basin and into the Inland Empire, and a number of present-day rail trails have been built on its deserted grades. The Pacific Electric Railway became part of the Southern Pacific at the turn of the nineteenth century; it was from this larger company that the right-of-way for the Pacific Electric Trail was secured.

The stretch of trail that was completed as of summer 2007 in Rancho Cucamonga runs from Etiwanda Station on the east to Grove Avenue on the west. This is a sampling of a rail trail that, when completed, will be 21 miles long and stretch from Claremont to Rialto. Additional short trail segments in Upland and Fontana also were complete as of summer 2007; contact the Friends of the Pacific Electric Trail for more information.

Beginning at Etiwanda Station—fenced off in late summer 2007 but set to be restored—the trail heads about 0.3 mile east to I–15, providing access to the neighborhoods in the vicinity of the freeway. Heading west from Etiwanda, the route is set in a wide greenbelt, with parallel double-wide paved and unpaved paths nicely landscaped and bordered by well-maintained homes and sound walls. The route is lined with benches, lighting, and trash receptacles, all fashionably rendered.

At 0.2 mile, pass an access trail from one of the neighborhoods; continue straight on the obvious route. At about 0.3 mile, a bridge spans Victoria Park Lane. At 0.7 mile, the trail intersects Day Creek Boulevard; it veers left along the sidewalk to a traffic light, which is used to cross the busy roadway. A firehouse sits trailside on the other side of the street.

Continue west past the white fences that guard trail intersections, another straight shot between neighborhood homes, to a bridge that spans a small drainage ditch at 1.1 miles. Large power lines pass overhead from north to south. Beyond the lines, the houses border the greenbelt again.

At 1.2 miles, cross Rochester Avenue at a signal; at 1.7 miles, you'll reach Ellena Park, with a nice grassy area, picnic tables, water, restrooms, and a tot lot. Cross Kenyon Road and continue west.

At 1.9 miles, cross Milliken Avenue and enter Central Park. This huge open space has all the amenities, including water and restrooms, and also features an expanse of near-native landscape, desert scrub scented with sage, that stretches south of the trail toward Baseline Road. The park, with its ample parking and central location, is another good trailhead for rail trail users.

At the west end of Central Park at about 2.5 miles, cross a bridge over another canal and reenter the greenbelt, again bordered by homes. At about 3 miles, you reach Haven Avenue, with another signalized street crossing. It's more of the same ahead: The trail spans Hermosa Avenue and Ramona Avenue before the next major street crossing at Archibald Avenue at about 3.9 miles.

Beyond Archibald, the trail arcs southward, across busy Baseline Road, then cuts an angled swath through neighborhoods to the Vineyard Avenue crossing at about the 4.5-mile mark. The Foothill Boulevard crossing is 0.2 mile farther; trail's end at Grove Avenue is at about the 5-mile mark.

Return as you came—or, if you are lucky enough to visit after more of the trail has been completed, keep on heading west . . .

37 WHITTIER GREENWAY TRAIL

The Whittier Greenway Trail demonstrates how what once was derelict can be reborn. From the abandoned railroad grade that has been scrubbed into a classy paved path to the refurbished railroad bridges, this is a shining addition to the trail system in the Los Angeles basin.

Activities:

Location: Whittier, Los Angeles County

Length: 5 miles one way

Surface: Asphalt

Wheelchair access: The route is wheelchair accessible.

Difficulty: Moderate, due only to the path's length

Food: While there are no eateries located on the trail itself, nearby Whittier Boulevard offers a smattering of restaurants and markets. There is water at Palm Park.

Restrooms: There are restrooms at Palm Park, near the trail's northern end point.

Seasons: The trail can be used year-round.

Access and parking: The best trailhead is at Palm Park, which is at 5703 Palm Avenue; you'll find plenty of parking at this location. To reach Palm Park from Interstate 605 in Whittier, take the Whittier Boulevard exit. Head southwest on Whittier Boulevard for 0.3 mile to a left turn on Norwalk Boulevard. Go 0.4 mile on Norwalk Boulevard to Monte Vista Drive and turn right. Travel 0.2 mile on Monte Vista to Palm Avenue. Turn left (south) on Palm Avenue and go 0.2 mile to the park entrance on the right (northwest).

The trail's northern end point is at Pioneer Boulevard, near I–605. The southern end point is at Mills Avenue and Lambert Road. There is limited on-street parking at both end points. You can also access the route from a number of neighborhood streets.

Transportation: Information about transit services in Los Angeles County may be obtained by dialing (800) COMMUTE in the Los Angeles calling

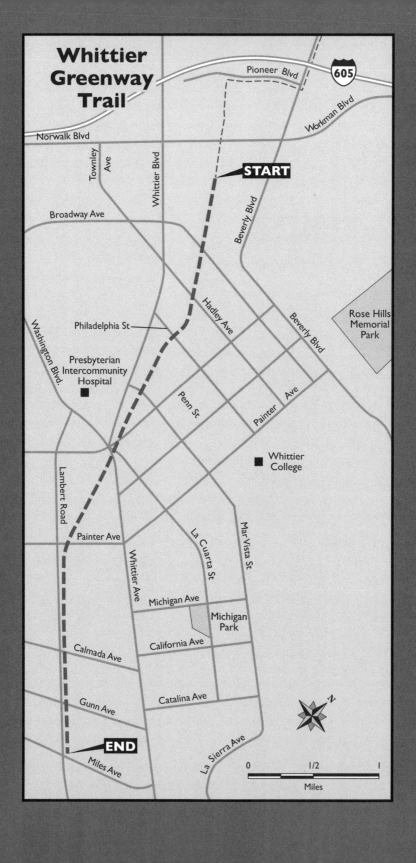

area. The Los Angeles Metropolitan Transportation Authority Web site is www.mta.net.

Rentals: There are no rentals on the trail.

Contact: Jim Kurkowski, Director of Parks, City of Whittier, (562) 464–3375; his e-mail address is jkurkowski@whittierch.org. You can also contact the city's Public Works Department at (562) 945–9003. The trail's Web site is www.whittierch.org/content/greenway.html.

||||||||||||||||||||||||||||||||||||||||||||||||||||||||||||||||||||||||||||||||||||||

It was a diamond in the rough when traveled in late summer 2007. But when the Whittier Greenway Trail is fully fleshed out, with mature landscaping and amenities in place, it will no doubt be one of the Los Angeles area's premier pedestrian thruways.

The trail, slated to be formally open in late 2007, runs along railroad right-of-way abandoned by Union Pacific and purchased by the city of Whittier in 2001. Not all the pieces were in place when I traveled the rail trail, but when finished, paved and unpaved pedestrian paths will run side by side for the length of the route, and various interpretive "stations"—Palm Station at Palm Park, Citrus Station at the old Sunkist packing plant, Sycamore Station, and Oak Station—will offer rest stops and educational opportunities along the way.

Jumping on the trail at Palm Park, which sports many amenities, among them picnic facilities, restrooms, lawns, a parcourse, and tennis and basketball courts, the grade heads both right and left. Going right (northwest), the route passes through the park, then across a railroad bridge over Norwalk Boulevard. Continue for about a half mile along the greenbelt between homes and past a schoolyard to the trail's northern end point among the residences at Pioneer Boulevard at about 0.75 mile.

Heading southeast from Palm Park, the trail crosses Palm Avenue almost immediately, then Howard Street, cruising through a well-shaded and well-kept neighborhood. All of the residential roads along this stretch are generally quiet, but crossings nonetheless require attention. The homes adjacent to the trail are screened by fences, some overgrown with flowering vines.

The Whittier Greenway includes passage over an original railroad bridge.

At about 0.5 mile, cross Broadway; a bit farther, cross Camilla Street. Beyond Camilla the trail takes on a more industrial and commercial aspect. The City of Whittier Corporate Yard is a fixture at the Hadley Street crossing at about the 1-mile mark. Continuing south, the route follows a sidewalk link along Gregory Avenue before returning to the separate railroad corridor. At about 1.5 miles, reach the Penn Street intersection, then cross Mar Vista Street. The route now parallels Whittier Boulevard, shielded by a wall of blooming oleander.

At about 2.5 miles, a historic railroad bridge spans the complex and busy intersection of Whittier Boulevard, Washington Boulevard, and Santa Fe Road. The route continues on the south side of the architecturally engaging bridge, passing through another neighborhood, to the Painter Avenue crossing at about 3.3 miles.

Beyond Painter, the trail parallels Lambert Road, maintaining its mixed residential and commercial flavor and fulfilling its role as a commuter route. You'll negotiate a number of street intersections as you continue—Laurel Avenue at 3.6 miles, Calmada Avenue at 4.1 miles, Gunn Avenue at 4.5 miles—before reaching the Greenway's southern end point on Mills Avenue at the 5-mile mark.

Plans call for the trail to be extended as a rail-with-trail along the active tracks that continue southeast from the Mills Avenue end point; contact the city of Whittier to check progress on the extension.

38 HERMOSA VALLEY GREENBELT TRAIL (VETERANS PARKWAY)

Meticulously landscaped and popular with local residents and visitors alike, this rail trail runs through a lovely strip of greenery that links two beachfront towns.

Activities:

Location: Manhattan Beach and Hermosa Beach, Los Angeles County

Length: 4 miles one way

Surface: Wood chips

Wheelchair access: Although the route is flat and has numerous access points, its wood chip surface would make it a challenge for wheelchair users.

Difficulty: Moderate, due to the trail's length and soft surface

Food: Restaurants are available very near the rail trail, but there are no food outlets directly on the trail.

Restrooms: There are no restrooms on the trail itself, but you may find them at Live Oak Park, located about 1.1 mile south of the trail's northern end point at Rosecrans Avenue.

Seasons: The trail can be used year-round, but it may be soft, and possibly muddy, during and after rainstorms.

Access and parking: To reach the northern trailhead from Interstate 405 in Manhattan Beach, take the Rosecrans Avenue exit. Head west on Rosecrans Avenue for 1.5 miles to a point just before its intersection with Sepulveda Boulevard. Turn left (south) into the large parking area that serves both the trailhead and the shopping center on Rosecrans Avenue. The lot stretches toward the trailhead, which is at the far south end, and is well signed.

There is no good parking at the rail trail's southern end point. To reach this end point from I–405, take the 190th Street exit and follow it west (it becomes Herondo Street) for 4.8 miles. The trail is on your right (north) at the intersection of Herondo Street and Valley Drive.

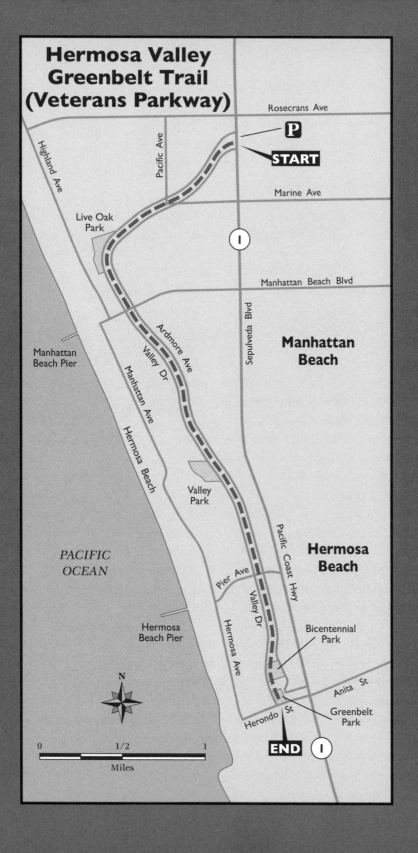

Transportation: Information about transit services in Los Angeles County may be obtained by calling (800) COMMUTE in the Los Angeles calling area. The Los Angeles Metropolitan Transportation Authority Web site is www.mta.net.

Rentals: There are no rentals along the route.

Contact: Mike Flaherty, Public Works Superintendent, City of Hermosa Beach, 1315 Valley Drive, Hermosa Beach, CA 90254; (310) 318–0214. The trail Web site is www.hbfop.org/parks/greenbelttrail.htm. The site is maintained by Hermosa Beach Friends of the Park. You can also visit www .ci.manhattan-beach.ca/index.aspx?page=379.

|||||||||||||||||||||||||||||||||||||||||||||||||||||||||||||||||||||||||||||||||||

A lthough never in sight, the Pacific Ocean's influence bathes the Hermosa Valley Greenbelt Trail. In summer, the fog rolls over it, smothering it in coolness. And the weak winter's sun seems just a bit brighter reflected off the surface of the water nearby. Regardless of the season, the rail trail is washed in the smell of salt carried by sea breezes.

The path is set in a gorgeously landscaped greenbelt that runs south from Manhattan Beach to Hermosa Beach between Valley Drive and Ardmore Avenue. The soft mottled browns of the wood chips, along with the generous greenery provided by evergreen shrubs and palm trees, conspire to create a comforting insulation from the roadways on either side of the rail trail. Not that this is needed: Both Manhattan Beach and Hermosa Beach present well-kept murals of pastel-colored homes along the trail, appropriate for a Southern California beach town.

The trail follows an abandoned Atchison, Topeka & Santa Fe line that once served the oil refineries in El Segundo, to the north of Manhattan Beach. This freight line was abandoned more than twenty years ago, and the land was purchased by the neighboring cities as open space, but because of political and monetary concerns, the rail trail wasn't built for several years after the abandonment. Local residents voted to tax themselves to pay for the construction of the greenbelt, and although you can still enjoy the shade of trees that were planted before the trail was formalized, the cities have updated the landscaping and added a second path that runs parallel to the main route. The trail is clearly a source of pride for the community, and rightfully so.

The route, called the Veterans Parkway in Manhattan Beach, begins at the south end of the Rosecrans parking lot, heading south under an overpass and into a wide swale lined with trees and low-growing flowering plants. It passes peacefully between the carefully tended yards of bordering homes. The dirt track runs alongside the wood-chipped path, and benches, trash cans, and water fountains are available along the route. Butterfly totems, placed in honor of the monarch butterflies that find habitat along the trail, offer an unusual visual amenity.

The Hermosa Valley Greenbelt is covered with wood chips and is beautifully landscaped.

Reach the first trail intersection at 0.4 mile, crossing 27th Street. Next comes the Pacific Avenue crossing at 0.6 mile, then, at about 1 mile, the 15th Street crossing. Live Oak Park, with its tot lot, ball fields, picnic facilities, and ample parking, is on the north side of Valley Drive.

The trail takes on a different demeanor at this point, passing through a business district. The crossing at Manhattan Beach Boulevard is complex; take care and use the crosswalks. If you have the time and inclination, a quick detour to the right (west) will take you to the beach.

A parcourse joins the greenbelt as you proceed. There is another busy intersection to negotiate at First Street, but the trail is peaceful and sheltered from the parallel roadways for the most part beyond that point, winding through quiet neighborhoods and sporting quaint little staircases built with railroad ties that offer access to local residents.

At the 2.3-mile mark, you will enter Hermosa Beach; just beyond, at Gould Avenue, pass Valley Park. The next major landmark is the Hermosa Valley High School and skate park, which is at about 3 miles. Palms have given way to eucalyptus by this point, with the shade a bit thinner but more fragrant.

The route dips down into a swale between Ardmore Avenue and Valley Drive again as it nears the Herondo Street end point at 4 miles. What appears to be a tiny parking lot at the end of the path is reserved for folks living in the adjacent residential complex. If you choose to park at this end, you'll have to do so on the street.

Unless you have arranged for a shuttle to pick you up and take you back to Manhattan Beach, head back the way you came.

39 ELECTRIC AVENUE MEDIAN PARK

If you believe in the value of the setting, you won't quibble with the brevity of the Electric Avenue Median Park rail trail. The path is ensconced in a beautifully maintained linear park and offers easy access to a spectacular Southern California beach.

Activities:

Location: Seal Beach, Orange County

Length: 1 mile one way

Surface: Concrete

Wheelchair access: The trail is accessible to wheelchair users.

Difficulty: Very easy

Food: There is no food available along the trail, but Seal Beach boasts a number of restaurants, many of which are near the route. There are several picnic benches along the route.

Restrooms: There are restrooms in the Mary Wilson Branch of the Orange County Library, which is about 0.1 mile south of the trail's northern end point at Marina Drive.

Seasons: The trail can be used year-round.

Access and parking: To reach the Electric Avenue Median Park from Interstate 405, take the Seal Beach Boulevard exit. Go west on Seal Beach Boulevard for 2.9 miles, crossing over the Pacific Coast Highway (California 1) to Electric Avenue. Parking is available along the street for the length of the route, and you can hop on it at any point. To reach the northern end point, follow Electric Avenue north for 1 mile to Marina Drive, and again, park along the street. Electric Avenue is one-way on either side of the median park.

Transportation: For transit information, call the Orange County Transportation Authority (OCTA) at (714) 636–RIDE (7433), or write OCTA, 550 South Main Street, P.O. Box 14184, Orange, CA 92863-1584. The Web site is www.octa.net. Transportation information is also available by calling (800)

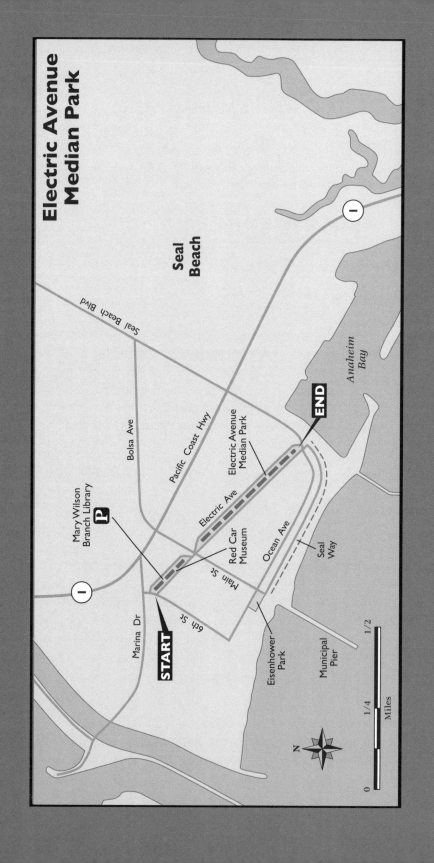

COMMUTE in the Los Angeles area. Transit information in Los Angeles is also available at www.mta.net.

Rentals: There are no rentals available along the trail.

Contact: City of Seal Beach, 211 Eighth Street, Seal Beach, CA 90740; (562) 431–2527.

‖‖

The Electric Avenue Median Park is exceptionally brief, but the setting is lovely, and it offers excellent coastal access to a wonderful Los Angles-area beach. The warm sands of Seal Beach are but a block to the west, reached via a paved path that breaks off from the trail's southern end point or via any of the streets that cross the route. On the beach, in addition to wonderful sunbathing and friendly wave sports, you'll find a playground and a public pier.

The trail is a clean strip of asphalt that winds through manicured grass beneath the filtering shade of sycamore and eucalyptus trees. Brickwork laid into the asphalt accents the trail's intersections with cross streets, as well as its two end points. In addition, a Red Line Car of the old Pacific Electric Railway, on whose bed the trail lies, now serves as the Red Car Museum, run by the Seal Beach Historical and Cultural Society. The red car is on the south side of the Mary Wilson Branch Library. Call the museum at (562) 683–1874 for its hours.

Walk the trail, visit the museum, go to the library and check out a good book to read on the beach, then finish the day with a meal in one of the local restaurants. Who could ask for anything more?

The trail is described beginning at the Marina Drive end point. Start at the brick roundabout; the wide concrete trail breaks off to the south and passes the library and Red Car Museum after 0.1 mile. Just beyond is the only major street intersection that you'll find along the trail—it's at Main Street and does require caution.

There are other streets to be crossed as you continue, but they are comparatively minor. The path meanders southward, edged in soft, verdant lawn and shaded by sheltering trees, with fine residences bordering the edges of Electric Avenue.

The trail ends at about the 1-mile mark at a covered picnic table. You can return as you came, but if you want to walk, skate, or ride to the beach, you can do so by continuing south, across Seal Beach Boulevard, to the paved path that skirts charming homes fronting the beach. The path arcs to the north and proceeds to Eisenhower Park and the municipal pier. You can follow Main Street east for a couple of blocks to return to Electric Avenue, or, again, return as you came.

40 JUANITA COOKE GREENBELT TRAIL

A broad swath of open space set among the residential areas of northern Orange County, the Juanita Cooke Greenbelt does double duty as a recreational trail and a regional commuter route. From the small lake at Laguna Lake Park near the trail's northern end point to the shady lane that skims busy Harbor Boulevard near its southern terminus, the trail presents a corridor that is ideal for easy mountain biking, hiking, and trail running.

Activities:

Location: Fullerton, Orange County

Length: 3.5 miles one way

Surface: Wood chips and dirt

Wheelchair access: Given the rough and sometimes soft surface, the trail is not suitable for wheelchairs.

Difficulty: Moderate

Food: There are no food outlets along the trail, but you will find grocery stores and restaurants in other areas of Fullerton.

Restrooms: There are restrooms at Laguna Lake Park, which is near the northern end point of the trail.

Seasons: The trail can be used year-round but may be muddy and very soft during and after rainstorms.

Access and parking: To reach the southern end point at the North Orange County Municipal Court Building, from California 91 (the Riverside Freeway), take the Harbor Boulevard exit. Head north on Harbor Boulevard for about 1.7 miles to North Berkeley Avenue. Turn left (west) on North Berkeley and go about 0.1 mile to the large, signed parking lot for the municipal building, which is on the corner as Berkeley bends northward. The Juanita Cooke Greenbelt Trail is the obvious path that heads northwest from the curve.

To reach Laguna Lake Park and the northern end point of the trail from the Riverside Freeway, take the Harbor Boulevard exit and head north on Harbor Boulevard for 3.8 miles to Hermosa Drive. Turn left (west) on West Hermosa Drive and go about 0.2 mile to Laguna Lake Park, which is on the south side of West Hermosa Drive. The trail crosses West Hermosa Drive near the park. There is streetside parking along this part of the park's boundary, and formal parking lots can be reached by circling the park on Lakeview Drive to the southwestern side of the lake.

Transportation: For transit information, call the Orange County Transportation Authority (OCTA) at (714) 636–RIDE (7433), or write OCTA, 550 South Main Street, P.O. Box 14184, Orange, CA 92868-1584. The Web site is www.octa.net. Transportation information is also available by calling (800) COMMUTE in the Los Angeles area. The Web site for Los Angeles County transit is www.mta.net.

Rentals: There are no rentals along the trail.

Contact: Community Services Department, City of Fullerton, 303 West Commonwealth Avenue, Fullerton, CA 92832-1710; (714) 738–6575; www .ci.fullerton.ca.us; (follow links to parks and recreation).

Thank the powers that be for the Juanita Cooke Greenbelt, and other greenbelts like it. In the midst of dense urban sprawl, where open spaces are swallowed by homes and businesses before people think twice, these strips of relatively undeveloped land are heartwarming and rejuvenating. The Juanita Cooke Greenbelt, shrouded in greenery and relatively insulated from the hectic highways and endless neighborhoods of Fullerton, offers hikers, mountain bikers, and equestrians a relatively long track upon which to forget they are in the midst of a modern metropolis.

The trail was built on a former Red Car Line run by the Pacific Electric Railway, which was a primary mover of people throughout the Los Angeles basin in the early years of the twentieth century. Today there are few signs along the trail that harken back to its origins, save where it crosses over the existing Union Pacific tracks, at about the midway point.

The trail begins in the welcome shade on the western side of the municipal court building. At about 0.2 mile, cross the first of many, mostly

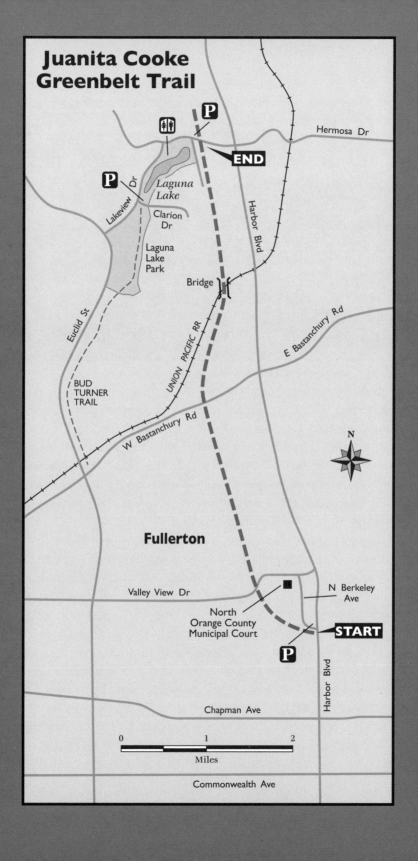

Juanita Cooke
Greenbelt Trail

Hermosa Dr

END

P

P

Laguna
Lake

Lakeview Dr

Clarion
Dr

Laguna
Lake
Park

Harbor Blvd

Euclid St

Bridge

E Bastanchury Rd

UNION PACIFIC RR

BUD
TURNER
TRAIL

W Bastanchury Rd

N

Fullerton

Valley View Dr

North
Orange County
Municipal Court

N Berkeley
Ave

START

P

Harbor Blvd

Chapman Ave

0   1   2

Miles

Commonwealth Ave

Laguna Lake Park is for the Bud Turner and Juanita Cooke Trails.

quiet, streets. Head up the little hill, passing a gate and trail sign and ignoring the single-track path that breaks off to the right (east).

At 0.5 mile, cross another residential street; the sign here indicates
you are on the bridle path. The route is obvious, passing through bowers of eucalyptus beneath which the flowering bougainvillea thrives, and
leading to an underpass, with trails from neighborhoods merging with the
railroad grade on either side of the structure.

Drop steeply to Bastanchury Road at Morelia Avenue at about 1 mile.
Carefully cross Bastanchury, using the signal, and follow the dirt path that
heads north alongside Morelia Avenue for about 0.3 mile to Laguna Road.
The rail trail proper resumes beyond the gate on the north side of Laguna
Road.

Gone is the eucalyptus, leaving this stretch of trail open to the desert
sun. At about 1.7 miles, the trail crosses a quaint trestle bridge. A single-
track path arcs right (northeast), down off the trail, to parallel the Union
Pacific line that runs below, quickly bending out of sight. The rail trail continues straight (north), across the bridge.

Shade and sun trade off as the trail proceeds through neighborhoods.
The next landmark is at 2.3 miles, where you will emerge at Laguna Lake
Park. Ducks swim in the lake's still green waters, and benches and picnic

tables invite trail travelers to sit and rest a spell. This is a nice turnaround point, although the trail does continue north from the park for a short distance.

To complete the route, cross West Hermosa Drive, which borders the park's northeastern edge, and follow the obvious railroad grade as it dips beneath an overpass. The rail trail has a decidedly urban conclusion, ending at 3.5 miles on a raised bed between stark apartment complexes at the lip of a cement canal.

41 SAN CLEMENTE BEACH TRAIL

From the stunning houses perched on cliffs above to the small crowds of surfers bobbing below and off-shore, this rail trail offers the best of both southern California's "scene" and scenery.

Activities:

Location: San Clemente, Orange County

Length: 2.3 miles one way

Surface: Asphalt, with a generous coating of sand in sections

Wheelchair access: The trail is paved and thus, in theory, wheelchair accessible. But given the rough surface and drifts of sand, only the hardiest should attempt it.

Difficulty: Easy

Food: You'll find restaurants and/or cafes at each end point as well as at the trail's midsection at the San Clemente municipal pier.

Restrooms: There are restrooms at each end point and also near the municipal pier.

Seasons: The trail can be used year-round

Access and parking: To reach the southern end point from Interstate 5 in San Clemente, take the Avenida Calafia exit toward San Clemente State Park. Go west toward the ocean on Avenida Calafia for 0.9 mile, passing the San Clemente State Park entrance, to Calafia Beach Park and the parking area.

To reach the northern end point at the Metrolink station, take the Avenida Pico exit off I–5. Go west on Avenida Pico for 0.8 mile to El Camino Real and turn right (north). Go 0.1 mile on El Camino Real and turn left into the Metrolink-San Clemente Station parking lot at 1850 Avenida Estacion (at the intersection of Calle Deshecha).

There are large parking lots at both end points, as well as at the municipal pier. Parking fees are levied.

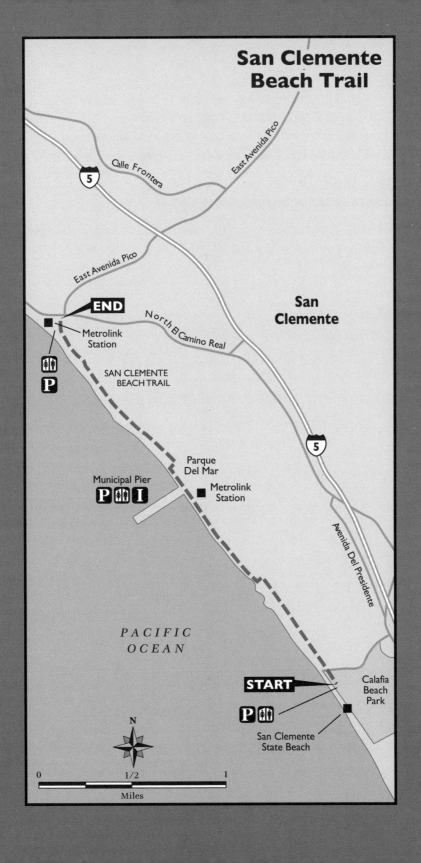

San Clemente Beach Trail

Calle Frontera

East Avenida Pico

East Avenida Pico

San Clemente

END

Metrolink Station

North El Camino Real

SAN CLEMENTE BEACH TRAIL

Parque Del Mar

Municipal Pier

Metrolink Station

Avenida Del Presidente

PACIFIC OCEAN

N

START

Calafia Beach Park

San Clemente State Beach

0   1/2   1

Miles

Transportation: For transit information, call the Orange County Transportation Authority (OCTA) at (714) 636–RIDE (7433) or write OCTA, 550 South Main Street, P.O. Box 14184, Orange, CA 92863-1584. The Web site is www .octa.net. Transportation information for Los Angeles can be obtained by calling (800) COMMUTE in the Los Angeles area or by visiting www.mta.net.

Rentals: There are no rentals available along the route.

Contact: The City of San Clemente Beaches, Parks, and Recreation Department can be reached by calling (949) 361–8264; the Web site is www.san-clemente.org.

R ecreation in southern California is all about the beaches. In San Clemente, along the spectacular rail trail that runs the length of the town's oceanfront, you can experience the best that sun, sand, and surf has to offer, from body surfing to bicycling, big views to burger joints, bikinis to beach umbrellas.

Technically a rail-with-trail, the San Clemente Beach Trail lies in the right-of-way of the active rail line used by commuter trains, including

Runners and other users enjoy great views from the elevated boardwalk on the San Clemente Beach rail trail.

Metrolink and Amtrak. As if the beach wasn't thrilling enough, the trail also offers up-close and loud views of passing trains, which are announced by flashing lights and gated access where the trail crosses the tracks.

The route, a segment of the California Coastal Trail, is described beginning at the southern end point at Calafia Beach, which is open from 6 A.M. to 10 P.M., dogs allowed on the beach (dogs on leashes are permitted on the trail), and signs admonish both trail and beach users to cross the Metrolink rails only at designated crossings. Not only is it dangerous to cross at random, but you can be fined if you get caught trespassing in the right-of-way. Cyclists must keep their speed below 10 mph and must walk their bikes through designated areas. Another note: Though the trail is paved, road cyclists may find it difficult to negotiate as the route takes a beating from wind, sand, and surf.

The trailhead is just inside the fence line that separates the beach from the parking lot. Head north (right) along the paved route, which is wedged between the tracks and the beachfront cliffs with their topping of spectacular (and enormous) homes.

At 0.1 mile, pass over a bridge and beach access for a neighborhood; a second bridge is at 0.2 mile. A fence intermittently separates the tracks from the trail; also intermittent are clusters of homes bordering the route on the right. On the beach you'll pass lifeguard towers, beach volleyball nets, and portable shelters beneath which sunbathers find shade.

The first railroad crossing is at 0.8 mile; if the lights are flashing and the gates are lowered, hold your ground, plug your ears, and watch the train go by. Beyond, the trail is on the beach side of the tracks, continuing northward and vaguely uphill, its surface covered with a thicker blanket of sand. Restrooms are located near this crossing.

Pass under a pedestrian bridge at about the 1-mile mark; a short distance beyond, the trail crosses a bridge and approaches the busy municipal pier. This stretch of trail is a "walk your bike" zone; cyclists must dismount and enjoy the activity on the beach and pier on foot. This is no hardship, given that the crowds of body surfers, picnickers, sunbathers, and fellow trail users dish up a heaping plate of color and joyful noise that's a pleasure to savor slowly. Restaurants, restrooms, maps, water, and other amenities can all be found at the pier's anchor at 1.2 miles. There's another railroad crossing here, offering access to the busy streets at the foot of the pier; again, if lights are flashing and gates are down, you must wait for a train to pass.

Back on the trail (cyclists can remount on the north side of the pier), pass a life-saving station at 1.4 miles and cross a boardwalk at 1.5 miles. Back on the inland side of the tracks, pass a beach access; at the next access path, the route switches upward onto an elevated boardwalk that offers a wonderful vantage point for viewing the beach, breakwater, and sea, as well as of the rail line directly below.

At 1.9 miles, you are back rail-side. Continue past another beach access at 2.1 miles to the North Beach trailhead and parking area at 2.3 miles. The trailhead features abundant parking, food, water, restrooms, and a Metrolink station.

Unless you've made other plans, return as you came.

42 INLAND RAIL TRAIL

This suburban rail trail, stretching from Escondido to Palomar College in San Marcos, provides safe passage to work and school for residents of both communities. Its length also makes it an ideal route for those seeking a good workout.

Activities:

Location: Escondido and San Marcos, San Diego County

Length: 6.1 miles one way

Surface: Concrete and asphalt

Wheelchair access: The trail is wheelchair accessible.

Difficulty: Moderate, due only to the trail's length

Food: Though there are no food outlets directly on the trail, plenty of restaurants and markets can be found in the host cities. There is no water along the route.

Restrooms: There are no public facilities along the route.

Seasons: The trail can be used year-round.

Access and parking: To reach Palomar College and the western end point of the trail from California Highway 78, take exit 118 for Las Posas Road. Head north on Las Posas; a sign directs you to Palomar College. Follow Las Posas for 0.3 mile and turn right (east) on Mission Road. There is no parking designated for the rail trail at this end point, but parking is available on the north side of Mission Road on the Palomar College campus.

The eastern end point of the trail is at the Escondido Transit Center, located on West Valley Parkway between North Tulip Street and North Quince Street in Escondido. To reach the transit center from Interstate 15, take the Valley Parkway exit and go 0.5 mile on West Valley Parkway to North Quince Street. Turn left on North Quince, then quickly left again onto westbound Valley Parkway; the transit center is on the left (north). The trailhead is at the back side of the terminal building at the Escondido Transit Center, behind the long-term parking area.

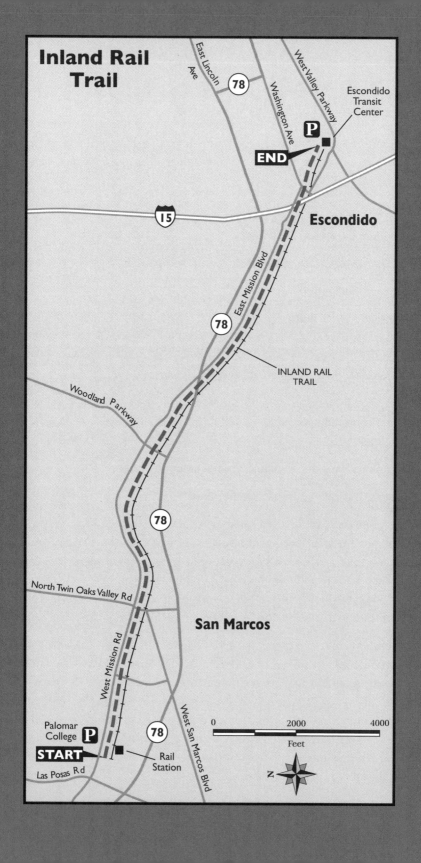

Inland Rail Trail

East Lincoln Ave

78

Washington Ave

West Valley Parkway

Escondido Transit Center

P

END

15

Escondido

East Mission Blvd

78

INLAND RAIL TRAIL

Woodland Parkway

78

North Twin Oaks Valley Rd

West Mission Rd

San Marcos

78

West San Marcos Blvd

Palomar College

P

START

Las Posas Rd

78

Rail Station

0   2000   4000

Feet

N

Transportation: The Metropolitan Transit System of San Diego provides a variety of transportation resources for San Diego County, including Escondido and San Marcos. The MTS can be reached by dialing 511 (north county) or (619) 233–3004 (south county). You also can get information from the Web site at www.sdcommute.com.

Rentals: There are no rental outlets along the trail, but the local telephone directory lists shops in both Escondido and San Marcos.

Contact: Ron Vinluan, park ranger with the city of San Marcos, (760) 744–9000 ext. 3535. The City of San Marcos Web siste is www.ci.san-marcos.ca.us.

The Escondido Public Works Department can be reached at (760) 839–4651. The Web site is www.ci.escondido.ca.us/depts./pw. The North County Transit District, which oversees the Sprinter line, can be reached at (760) 967–2001. The Web site is www.gonctd.com; follow links to the Sprinter pages.

||||||||||||||||||||||||||||||||||||||||||||||||||||||||||||||||||||||||||||||||||

B uilt alongside the active Sprinter rail line, the Inland Rail Trail will eventually connect coastal Oceanside with the inland towns of San Marcos and Escondido—a 23-mile run. As of summer 2007, only the segment from Palomar College in San Marcos to the Escondido Transit Center in Escondido was in place—about 6.1 miles one way—and it had yet to be opened to the public. I've described the trail as well as possible, given that constraint. Expect changes and improvements as time moves on.

The trail is described from the western end point at Palomar College in San Marcos to the eastern end point at the Escondido Transit Center. It is an eminently urban route, running through a primarily commercial landscape for its entire length. Offering access to shopping, work, and schools, it well serves the communities through which it passes.

The rail trail begins parallel to the Sprinter rail line and Mission Road; a tall black fence separates the trail from the tracks. Pass the Union Tribune building and the Palomar College rail station as you head east; at 0.3 mile, cross Aberdeen Avenue. The setting is commercial, and the trail is used by shoppers who carry bags as they walk the path.

At 0.6 mile, cross Knoll Road; at 0.8 mile, Marcos Street intersects the route. Pico Avenue is crossed at 1.1 miles; you'll see two sets of tracks in the rail bed adjacent to the trail at this point. At 1.4 miles, pass the San Marcos Boulevard rail stop and cross San Marcos Boulevard.

The trail and rail line diverge from Mission Road beyond the San Marcos Boulevard intersection, and at 1.8 miles, a bridge spans the tracks to deposit the trail on the south side of the rails. About 0.2 mile before the Woodland Parkway intersection, the route jumps back onto the north side of the active rail line via another bridge. The Woodland Parkway crossing is at about 2.8 miles.

The trail continues on the north side of the rail line, which between Mission Road and Ranchero Road is in the shadow of the CA 78 freeway. About 0.6 mile beyond the Woodland Parkway crossing, the trail crosses Rancheros Drive and the tracks to run along the south side of the Sprinter line. Pass under CA 78; a fence and trees separate the trail from the tracks. At 3.8 miles, cross Barham Drive and pass the Barham station, then pass Auto Park Way.

The trail is essentially a glorified sidewalk east of Auto Park Way, separated from the tracks by a chain-link fence. At the 4.6-mile mark, cross Enterprise Street, then Andreasen Drive at 5 miles; the trail veers right along Washington Avenue and passes under I–15.

Three tracks run alongside the rail trail as it cruises alongside Washington Avenue, then enters the North County Transit District yard. About 0.2 mile west of the Escondido Transit Center and the trail's eastern end point, cross a bridge; beyond, the trail parallels a canal before crossing a last bridge into the long-term parking area at the Escondido Transit Center at about 6.1 miles.

Unless you've arranged a ride back—or plan to hop on a bus or train—head back as you came.

43 FAY AVENUE BIKE PATH

Gazing out across the Pacific Ocean from the heights of the Fay Avenue Bike Path, you can't help but be struck by the gentle beauty of La Jolla. The easy trail, spectacular setting, and warm weather conspire to make this a wonderful, if brief, adventure.

Activities:

Location: La Jolla, San Diego County

Length: 1 mile one way

Surface: Asphalt and dirt

Wheelchair access: The trail is wheelchair accessible.

Difficulty: Very easy

Food: Although there is no food available on the trail itself, you'll pass a number of restaurants and a grocery store in downtown La Jolla as you drive to the trailhead.

Restrooms: There are no restrooms along the route.

Seasons: The trail can be used year-round.

Access and parking: To reach La Jolla from northbound Interstate 5, take the Ardath Road exit. Follow Ardath Road west for 1.2 miles to its intersection with Torrey Pines Road. Stay left (west) on Torrey Pines Road for 1 mile to Prospect Street. Turn right (west) on Prospect Street, which runs through the heart of downtown La Jolla, and continue for 0.6 mile to Fay Avenue. Turn left (south) on Fay Avenue and follow it to its end at Nautilus Street. There is ample parking in the La Jolla High School lot fronting Fay Avenue. The trailhead is on the south side of Nautilus Street opposite the stoplight at the end of Fay Avenue.

Transportation: The Metropolitan Transit System provides a variety of transportation services as well as links to other transportation authorities and services throughout San Diego County. The MTS can be reached by dialing 511 (north county) or (619) 233–3004 (south county). You also can get information about San Diego transportation services at www.sdcommute.com.

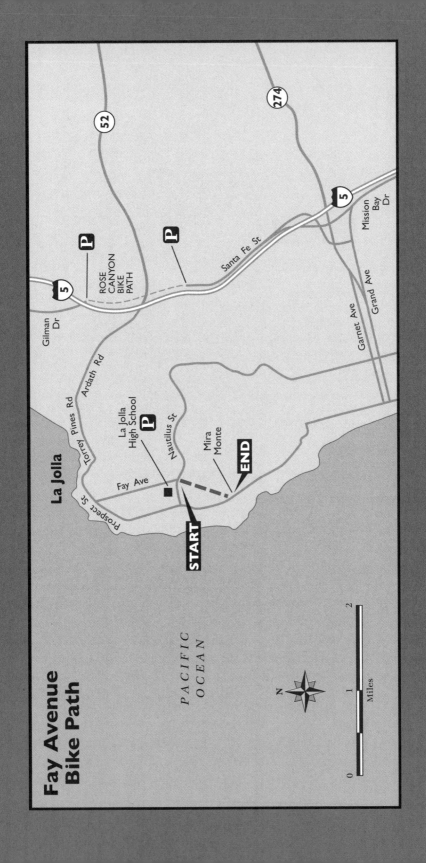

Rentals: There are no rental outlets near the trail.

Contact: Joel Rizzo, Bike Coordinator, City of San Diego, 1010 Second Avenue, Suite 800 MS609, San Diego, CA 92101; (619) 533–3110. At www .ridelink.org, a site sponsored by the San Diego Association of Governments (SANDAG), you can follow the links to an excellent map of San Diego bike routes, including Fay Avenue.

|||||||||||||||||||||||||||||||||||||||||||||||||||||||||||||||||||||||||||||||||||||

Quintessential southern California, spread before you in all its sun-bathed glory. Robin's-egg blue skies, melting into a glassy ocean a few shades darker and greener. Towering palms overlooking the beach-front. Immaculate homes with clean lines and broad expanses of glass creeping inland from the edge of the water. From the high points on the Fay Avenue Bike Path, these are the sights that you will enjoy.

The panorama, coupled with the extreme ease of this short route, make it the ideal choice for the visitor or resident who is short on time but has a hankering to get out. The rail trail is also perfect for families, a good number of which will be found on the path on any sunny weekend.

The path runs on the abandoned line of the San Diego, Pacific Beach, and La Jolla Railroad, a standard-gauge passenger line that was established in 1889 and abandoned in 1919. The trail was built in the late 1970s, and plans to extend the trail southward for another 1.2 miles are funded and ready for development.

Heading south from the Nautilus Street end point, you will first climb a short hill to where the paved trail breaks out from under the trees at about 0.1 mile. The climb crests with spectacular views. Looking west from here, and from along the trail for the next half mile or so, you will no doubt so enjoy the vistas to the west that you won't notice much else about the trail, which traverses a shrubby hillside above a row of nicely maintained homes.

The trail begins to head gently downhill to a bridge, which is crossed at 0.4 mile. The views are gone by the time you reach and cross Via Del Norte at 0.7 mile. Signs indicate that the bike path continues on Beaumont Avenue, but it's clear that the former railroad grade, and the rail trail, continue straight.

A father and son enjoy the Fay Avenue Bike Path in tandem.

The path proceeds southward until it drops behind a small park to the cul-de-sac at Mira Monte at 1 mile. While this is the formal end point, again, it is clear that the grade continues southward, passing through a parking lot, then across La Canada, following the power lines to La Jolla Hermosa Avenue at 1.3 miles. Bike route signs indicate you can continue south along La Jolla Hermosa, but this is a good turnaround point—as is the Mira Monte cul-de-sac. Whichever you choose, return along the same route.

44 MARTIN LUTHER KING PROMENADE

Promenade on this rail trail, which follows the existing railroad tracks along Harbor Boulevard in downtown San Diego, and you'll have easy access to some of the best this delightful city has to offer: wonderful shopping, delightful restaurants, the historic Gaslamp district, maritime exhibits, bayside parks, and more.

Activities:

Location: San Diego, San Diego County

Length: 1.5 miles

Surface: Concrete and asphalt

Wheelchair access: The entire trail is wheelchair accessible.

Difficulty: Very easy, given the trail's short length.

Food: There is a plethora of restaurants in the downtown San Diego area, as well as a number of other cultural amenities, including theaters, museums, and shopping.

Restrooms: There are no public restrooms along the trail.

Seasons: The trail can be used year-round.

Access and parking: The trail can be reached via a number of streets in downtown San Diego. In addition to parking in commercial lots, ample on-street parking is available.

The downtown area is crisscrossed by one-way streets, so it is helpful to have a good map. There are a number of exits off Interstate 5 feeding into the downtown area. Take any of these and head south to Harbor Drive. Eighth Street is south of the heart of town, but you can pick up the trail anywhere along Harbor Drive.

Transportation: The Metropolitan Transit System provides a variety of transportation services, as well as links to other transportation authorities and services throughout San Diego County. The MTS can be reached by dialing 511 (north county) or (619) 233–3004 (south county). You also

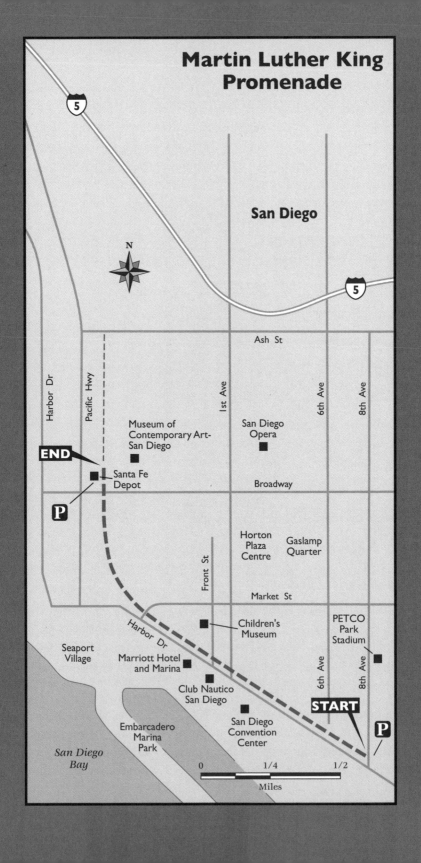

can get information about San Diego transportation services at www.sd commute.com.

Rentals: There are no bike or skate rental outfits located on the trail in the downtown area.

Contact: For the section of trail in downtown San Diego, contact the Port of San Diego, P.O. Box 120488, San Diego, CA 92112; (619) 686–6200, www .portofsandiego.org. You can also contact Joel Rizzo, Bike Coordinator, City of San Diego, 1010 Second Avenue, Suite 800 MS609, San Diego, CA 92101; (619) 533–3110.

S an Diego is visually and culturally rich. The King Promenade rail trail reaches into the core of this wealth, offering access to the city's convention center, Embarcadero, shopping and Gaslamp districts, PETCO Park, and piers.

Calling the trail a promenade is very appropriate. While you can bike or skate on the path, the downtown section truly lends itself to a slow stroll, a leisurely pace at which you can chat with a companion and take in the sights.

The path is beautifully landscaped, bordered by charming fences and old-fashioned lampposts. The towers of the surrounding city sparkle in the nearly omnipresent sunshine, the stimulating architecture offering shade and pleasure to the viewer.

The trail follows the right-of-way of existing tracks for the Coaster, San Diego's commuter train, and the San Diego Trolley. Given the popularity of these lines, you are bound to see a number of trains pass as you promenade.

Only the downtown section of the trail is described in detail here, but a paved trail continues north from Santa Fe Depot. What it loses in visual charm as it heads toward Mission Bay it gains in utility, offering safe off-street passage for commuters and area residents.

The path's Eighth Street end point has a rough, almost industrial feel. You are right alongside the railroad tracks, just south of the center of the city, where warehouses and low-rise buildings dominate the landscape. You'll see PETCO Park at this end point as well.

A trolley rolls down the tracks beside the Martin Luther King Promenade.

The path quickly becomes more urbane as it heads northwest along Harbor Drive. By the 0.5-mile mark, the buildings have become cleaner and architecturally complex, and patches of lawn, plots of flowers, and shady palm trees border the concrete walkway. At Fifth Avenue, you can detour to the north into the Gaslamp Quarter National Historic District, with its wonderful restaurants and shops. The Gaslamp district borders Horton Plaza as well, where you'll find yet more to tempt your tummy and your pocketbook. To the south of Harbor Drive at Fifth Avenue, you can walk to Marina Park.

After passing Fifth Avenue, the San Diego Convention Center dominates the left (southwest) side of the trail, with its accompaniment of hotels. At about the 1-mile mark, where the rail trail bends north away from the convention center at a San Diego Trolley station, you reach Kettner Boulevard, which offers access to an additional pair of cultural attractions: Seaport Village and Embarcadero Marina Park lie to the left (southwest).

The path crosses Kettner Boulevard to the west and continues north to the Santa Fe Depot, which is on the left (west) side of the trail at 1.5 miles. San Diego's Museum of Contemporary Art is on the right (east). Continuing north toward Ash Street, you can take a side trip west to the Maritime Museum and the Star of India, as well as other piers along Harbor Drive.

If you wish to continue past the end of the rail trail, explore the route beyond Ash Street (the limit of the scenic center of San Diego), or travel north on the paved path to Mission Bay.

45 BAYSHORE BIKEWAY (SILVER STRAND)

The Silver Strand, a ribbon of sand and surf arcing into the Pacific Ocean at the southwestern tip of the United States—and the bikeway that runs along it—offers fascinating views of Coronado Bridge, the skyline of San Diego, and, of course, the endless Pacific.

Activities:

Location: San Diego and Coronado, San Diego County

Length: 9 miles one way

Surface: Concrete and asphalt

Wheelchair access: The entire trail is wheelchair accessible.

Difficulty: Hard. Walking or skating the trail—especially out and back—is an all-day proposition. Cyclists will find the route described here easy or moderate, depending on their fitness level. Arranging a shuttle or tackling shorter sections of the trail reduces its difficulty.

Food: There are grocery stores and restaurants in Coronado at the north end of the trail and in Imperial Beach at the south end, but there is nothing in between. Water is available at either end point and at Silver Strand State Beach.

Restrooms: There are public restrooms at the Coronado ferry complex and at Tidelands Park. You can also use restrooms, as well as other facilities, at the Silver Strand State Beach, located at the trail's halfway point. There are no public restrooms at the Imperial Beach end point.

Seasons: The trail can be used year-round. Use caution and common sense if venturing onto the exposed path during a winter storm, as there is no shelter from potentially furious winds and vigorous downpours.

Access and parking: To reach the Coronado ferry complex from Interstate 5 in San Diego, take the California 75 exit, and go west, over the lovely bridge, to Coronado. Follow the highway, which becomes Fourth Street, to Orange Avenue, and turn right (east). Follow Orange Avenue, to First Street, which is on the waterfront. The ferry complex is in the shopping center to the right (south) of the intersection of Orange Avenue and First Street. There is ample parking available along the street.

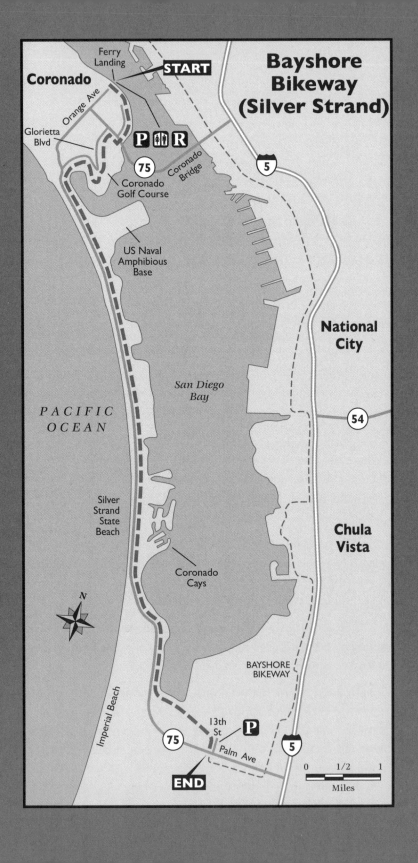

To reach the Imperial Beach end point from I–5 in Chula Vista, take CA 75/Palm Avenue east to 13th Street. Turn right (north) on 13th Street to the trailhead, which is at the end of the road. Parking is available at the trailhead.

Transportation: The Metropolitan Transit System provides a variety of transportation services, as well as links to other transportation authorities and services throughout San Diego County. The MTS can be reached by dialing 511 (north county) or (619) 233–3004 (south county). You also can get information about San Diego transportation services via the Internet by visiting www.sdcommute.com.

Rentals: Bicycles are available at Holland's Bicycles in the Coronado ferry complex. The phone number is (619) 435–7180. The Web site is www.hollands bicycles.com.

Contact: Joel Rizzo, Bike Coordinator, City of San Diego, 1010 Second Avenue, Suite 800 MS609, San Diego, CA 92101; (619) 533–3110. At www .ridelink.org, you can follow the links to an excellent map of San Diego bike routes, including the Bayshore Bikeway. At www.efgh.com/bike/bayshore .htm, you will find a trail fact sheet.

A more lovely stretch of seaside trail would be difficult to find anywhere in southern California. Miles and miles of the Bayshore Bikeway lie on the narrow spit of land that connects Coronado with Imperial Beach, bordered on the west by the Pacific Ocean, and on the east by San Diego Bay, which separates you from the continent proper. When you travel on this path, you travel on the very edge of America.

The Silver Strand segment is but one link in the San Diego area's premier bike tour. To complete a 26-mile circumnavigation of San Diego Bay, the Bayshore Bikeway continues from the south end of the Silver Strand at Imperial Beach, north through Chula Vista and National City, to the ferry landing in downtown San Diego. The route incorporates separate bike paths, bike lanes along existing roadways, and, of course, the rail trail along the Silver Strand, but will include additional railroad right-of-way in its alignment on the mainland side of the bay. Construction on the new rail trail portion of the route was slated for 2008. The San Diego Region Bike Map is a good source for the route.

The tidal areas and dunes on the San Diego Bay side of the spit, along with the fragile environments and species that they support, are partially protected within the confines of the California Least Tern Preserve. On the ocean side, the Silver Strand State Beach offers duneland perches from which you can watch the sun set into the Pacific, staining sky, sea, and sand vivid shades of orange and pink.

The culture and history of the area are rich and multifaceted. There is the military: Coronado is home to the North Island Naval Air Station and the U.S. Naval Amphibious Base, and the beach just south of the city is littered with the shells of military aircraft. There is the cultural: Coronado is alive with restaurants, theaters, shopping, and art galleries. There is the natural beauty: the stunning views of the San Diego skyline, the state beach, the least tern preserve, and San Diego Bay.

And, of course, there is the railroad: The rail trail runs on a line originally built by the Coronado Railroad Company, which was merged into several other San Diego–based railroad companies before finally being incorporated into the Southern Pacific rail empire. The right-of-way was abandoned by Southern Pacific in 1977 and is now the bed of the rail trail.

The trail begins along the eastern shoreline of the island at the ferry terminal and shopping mall. It meanders south past the storefronts, leaving the bustle behind after less than a quarter mile.

At 0.5 mile, cruise through Tidelands Park, which offers picnic tables, a tot lot, restrooms, and large expanses of lawn upon which you can lie back and enjoy the scenery. Continuing south, a switchback arcs under the Coronado Bridge, then the trail parallels a fence that screens it from the Coronado Golf Course.

At 1.2 miles, the trail turns left (west) and runs alongside Glorietta Boulevard. Cross Glorietta at Fifth Street and continue westward, circling around the golf course and tennis courts to Pomona Avenue. Use the crosswalk to get across the street; the trail continues 100 yards west of the intersection.

The route skirts the Glorietta Marina and by the 2-mile mark is on the strand, with CA 75 a near neighbor. Large hotels screen the views to the west, but they are almost as fun to look at as the ocean. Almost.

Pass the U.S. Naval Amphibious Base at about 2.5 miles. Both trail and highway are now bordered by dunes and water. On the left (east) is the bay, on the right (west) is the beach, which serves here as a graveyard for naval equipment and is posted off-limits. At 2.8 miles, pass a Silver Strand sign and overlook; pause to take in the views, then continue south on the trail.

You may feel constrained by the signs warning you to stay off the beach on the Pacific side and the fence that guards the bay side. The restrictions serve their purposes. While it is apparent the graveyard is private property, the purpose of the fence is less obvious; it was erected to protect the habitat of the California least tern. Another overlook is at the 3.5-mile mark, and a dirt path now parallels the paved route.

At 4 miles, pass the Fiddlers Cove Marina and the Silver Strand residential community. The path continues southward, wedged between the dunes and the now fence-free bay shore, to Silver Strand State Beach at 5.2 miles. Here, you will find restrooms, picnic sites, and camping opportunities, as well as unrestricted access to the beach and views of an endless horizon.

From the rail trail, however, the ocean and the islands that sit offshore flicker in and out of view between the dunes. Looking across the bay, the mountains rising east of San Diego sculpt a striking skyline, especially when they glow with the fading light of a setting sun.

The trail continues south to pass the Coronado Cays at 6.2 miles. About a mile beyond the Cays, you will lose sight of the ocean and the

The Silver Strand offers views of the Pacific Ocean and the Coronado Bridge.

islands as the rail trail slowly bends eastward around the south end of the bay. Salt marsh sweeps in from the bay toward the trail.

At about 8 miles, the trail borders the parking area for the South Bay Marine Biology Study Area. A half mile beyond, the route pulls away from the highway as it arcs eastward, and some of the rails that used to carry trains appear alongside the trail. The path weaves around residences and businesses that border the bay as it enters the city of Imperial Beach. The trail leaves the railroad grade behind at an abandoned trestle that lunges east into the wetland. It ends in the cul-de-sac at the end of 13th Street. If you've arranged for a shuttle, this is the end of the line. Otherwise, return as you came.

More Rail Trails

O DUARTE BIKE TRAIL

Running along the base of the San Gabriel Mountains, the Duarte Bike Trail ties the east end of this small city to the west end via a lovely suburban trail. The path provides safe, off-street access to the playground, tennis and basketball courts, and greens of Royal Oaks Park. The trail sits on an abandoned stretch of the Red Car passenger line.

Activities:

Location: City of Duarte, Los Angeles County

Length: 1.6 miles one way

Surface: Asphalt and concrete

Wheelchair access: The trail is wheelchair accessible for its entire length.

Difficulty: Easy

Food: There are no outlets for food along the trail, but you will find a smorgasbord of choices within surrounding communities.

Restrooms: There are restrooms at Royal Oaks Park, but none along the rest of the trail.

Seasons: The trail can be used year-round.

Access and parking: To reach the eastern end point at Royal Oaks Park, take Interstate 210 to the interchange with Interstate 605. Go north on I–605 until it ends on Mount Olive Drive. Follow Mount Olive Drive north for 0.3 mile, crossing Huntington Drive, to Royal Oaks Drive. Go right (east) on Royal Oaks Drive for 0.4 mile to Royal Oaks Park. The small but adequate parking area is located just beyond (east of) Vineyard Avenue.

There is limited on-street parking at the trail's western end point at Buena Vista Street. To reach this end point, follow the directions above, but turn left (west) on Royal Oaks Drive and follow it to Buena Vista Street.

Walkers and a cyclist on the suburban Duarte Bike Trail

Transportation: Duarte Mini Transit offers public transportation along the route. Call (626) 357–7931 for more information.

Rentals: There are no rentals available along the trail.

Contact: Donna Georgino, Duarte Parks and Recreation Department, 1600 East Huntington Drive, Duarte, CA 91010; (626) 357–6118 ext. 204.

CULVER CITY MEDIAN BIKEWAY

The Culver City rail trail runs through a nicely landscaped median park where broad umbrellas of mature palm trees drop pools of shade on patches of lawn and park benches. The trail is mostly frequented by local residents but is long enough to give runners or walkers a good workout. The asphalt main line is shadowed by a dirt walkway, both laid on the bed of a former Red Car route. You can also continue north from trail's end into Veterans Memorial Park and beyond.

Activities:

Location: Culver City, Los Angeles County

Length: 2 miles one way

Surface: Asphalt

Wheelchair access: The trail is entirely wheelchair accessible.

Difficulty: Easy

Food: There are small markets and restaurants on Culver Boulevard near the trail, as well as in other areas of Culver City.

Restrooms: There are no restrooms along the trail.

Seasons: The trail can be used year-round.

Access and parking: To reach the Culver City Median Bikeway from Interstate 405 in Culver City, exit at Sawtelle Boulevard or Sepulveda Boulevard. Follow either Sawtelle Boulevard or Sepulveda Boulevard south to Culver Boulevard. The trail runs down the center of Culver Boulevard, so it can't be missed. The best parking is at the western end point of the trail at Panama Street and McConnell Avenue. This trailhead can be reached by driving right (southwest) along Culver Boulevard to McConnell Avenue, then turning left (southwest) onto Panama Street, which parallels the rail trail. There is abundant on-street parking along Panama Street.

The Culver City Median Bikeway divides opposing lanes of traffic.

There is limited on-street parking at the eastern end point of the trail, which is at Elenda Street.

Transportation: Transit services in Los Angeles County may be obtained by calling (800) COMMUTE in the Los Angeles calling area. The Los Angeles Metropolitan Transportation Authority Web site is www.mta.net; you can get additional information at this site for rail, bus, and other transit services. You can reach the Culver City Bus at (310) 253–6500; www.culvercity.org/bus.

Rentals: Wheel World Cycles is located less than a mile northwest of the trail at the intersection of Sepulveda Boulevard and Washington Boulevard. Contact Wheel World Cycles at 4051 Sepulveda Boulevard, Culver City, CA 90230; (310) 473–3417. The Web site is www.wheelworld.com.

Contact: Michelle Mowery, Bicycle Coordinator for the City of Los Angeles, can be reached by calling (213) 972–4962. Her e-mail address is michelle .mowery@lacity.com. The L.A. Department of Transporation Bicycle Services Web site is at www.bicyclela.org.

WATTS TOWERS CRESCENT GREENWAY

This extremely short rail trail—you can see from one end to the other—parallels an existing rail line in the vicinity of the Watts Towers Art Center, home of the striking and unique twin sculptures known as the Watts Towers. Primarily a utilitarian path used by local residents, the palm-lined rail trail is a winding band of concrete wedged between Willowbrook and the active Metro Blue Line tracks.

Activities:

Location: The Watts section of Los Angeles, Los Angeles County

Length: 0.2 mile one way

Surface: Concrete

Wheelchair access: The trail is wheelchair accessible for its entire length.

Difficulty: Easy

Food: There are no restaurants or food markets along the route, but these can be found elsewhere in Watts and adjacent neighborhoods.

Restrooms: There are no restrooms along the trail.

Seasons: The trail can be used year-round.

Access and parking: To reach the Watts Towers Crescent Greenway from the intersection of Interstates 110 and 105 in Lost Angeles, go east on I–105 for 2.2 miles to Wilmington Avenue. Go left (north) on Wilmington Avenue for 1 mile to 108th Avenue. Turn left (west) on 108th Avenue for 0.2 mile to Willowbrook. Go right (north) on Willowbrook for 0.1 mile to the trailhead. There is no formal parking area, but there is on-street parking available.

Transportation: Transit information for Watts can be obtained by calling (800) COMMUTE in the Los Angeles calling area. The Los Angeles Metropolitan Transportation Authority Web site is www.mta.net.

Rentals: There are no rentals available along the route.

Contact: Metropolitan Transportation Authority, P.O. Box 194, Los Angeles, CA 90053-0194; (213) 244–6456.

R LONG BEACH GREENBELT

It could take less than fifteen minutes to walk the Long Beach Greenbelt and back, but if you do it that fast, you'll have missed the point. Plopped in the midst of suburban Long Beach, this rail trail, laid on the abandoned right-of-way of the Pacific Electric Railway, encapsulates the goal of any land preservation movement: to preserve (or re-create) a natural environment that will nurture the human spirit. The dirt path is surrounded by more than forty species of native plants, an eyedropper-full of a landscape that once was ubiquitous in the Los Angeles basin. A couple of blocks northwest of the route, local residents have created a community garden in the rail corridor, yet another nice amenity in this suburban enclave.

Activities:

Location: Long Beach, Los Angeles County

Length: 0.4 mile round-trip

Surface: Dirt

Wheelchair access: The trail is not wheelchair accessible.

Difficulty: Very easy

Food: No food or water is available along the trail.

Restrooms: There are no facilities on the route.

Seasons: Year-round, though the path may be muddy in the rain.

Access and parking: To reach the greenbelt from the Pacific Coast Highway (California Highway 1) in Long Beach, go west on Seventh Street for about 0.5 mile to Bennett Avenue. Turn right (north) on Bennett and go 0.1 mile to Eighth Street. Turn left; the trailhead is 0.1 mile ahead at the intersection of Termino Avenue and Eighth Street. There is on-street parking at the Eighth Street and Termino Avenue intersection, as well as on other neighborhood streets. There is no parking at the Seventh Street end point.

The trailhead is about 2.5 miles from Interstate 405 in Long Beach, via California 22 and East Seventh Street.

Transportation: Long Beach Transit provides bus service to this area; call (526) 591–2301 or visit www.lbtransit.com for more information. Information about transit services in Los Angeles County may be obtained by dialing (800) COMMUTE in the Los Angeles calling area. The Los Angeles Metropolitan Transportation Authority Web site is www.mta.net.

Rentals: There are no rentals on the trail.

Contact: Los Cerritos Wetlands Stewards Inc. maintains the greenbelt, as well as a Web site that describes this and other preservation projects in Southern California. For more information, visit www.lcwstewards.org/lcws/projects/greenbelt.htm or e-mail info@lcwstewards.org.

Long Beach Parks, Recreation, and Marine is located at 2760 Studebaker Road, Long Beach, CA 900815-1697; (562) 570–3100; www.ci.long-beach.ca.us/park/.

HOOVER STREET TRAIL

Three transportation corridors run along Hoover Street between Bolsa Avenue and the Garden Grove Freeway: the four-lane street itself, the tracks of an active railroad, and the paved rail trail. The route is used primarily by local residents and commuters.

Activities:

Location: Westminster, Orange County

Length: 1.3 miles of the 2-mile trail (one-way) is on the railroad grade.

Surface: Asphalt

Wheelchair access: The trail is wheelchair accessible.

Difficulty: Easy

Food: There are no restaurants located along the route, but a neighborhood grocery store is on the corner of Trask Avenue and Hoover Street. Restaurants and supermarkets can be found elsewhere in Westminster.

Restrooms: There are no restrooms at either trailhead, nor are there any along the trail.

Seasons: The trail can be used year-round.

Access and parking: To reach the Bolsa Avenue trailhead from Interstate 405 in Westminster, take the Bolsa Avenue exit. Head east on Bolsa Avenue for 0.4 mile to Hoover Street. The trail is obvious, running between the street and the active Union Pacific Railroad line. The second end point, at Garden Grove Boulevard, is most easily reached by following Hoover Street north to the trail's end. There are no formal parking areas at either end of the trail, and only limited parking along the street.

Transportation: For transit information, call the Orange County Transportation Authority (OCTA) at (714) 636–RIDE (7433), or write OCTA, 550 South Main Street, P.O. Box 14184, Orange, CA 92863-1584. The Web site is www.octa.net. Transit information for Los Angeles is available at (800) COMMUTE or www.mta.net.

The Hoover Street Trail is a perfect example of an urban rail-trail.

Rentals: No rentals are available along the route.

Contact: City of Westminster, 8200 Westminster Boulevard, Westminster, CA 92683-3395; (714) 898–3311 ext. 217.

PACIFIC ELECTRIC BICYCLE TRAIL (SANTA ANA)

A neighborhood trail of the first order, Santa Ana's Pacific Electric Bicycle Trail links well-kept middle-class neighborhoods on either side of tree-lined Maple Street. Following the abandoned right-of-way of the Pacific Electric Railway Company, the trail links with the Alton Avenue Bike Trail (see Trail U), rendering it not only ideal for locals but good for a workout, too.

Activities: 🚶 🚲 🛼

Location: City of Santa Ana, Orange County

Length: 2.1 miles one way

Surface: Asphalt

Wheelchair access: The trail is wheelchair accessible for its entire length.

Difficulty: Easy

Food: There are no restaurants or grocery stores along the trail, but such amenities are available elsewhere in Santa Ana. Verdant strips of grass and occasional benches offer trail users the chance to picnic.

Restrooms: There are no restrooms at either end point or along the trail.

Seasons: The trail can be used year-round.

Access and parking: To reach the northern end point from Interstate 5, take the Fourth Street exit in Santa Ana. Follow Fourth Street west to Grand Avenue and go left (south) on Grand Avenue to East First Street. Turn right (west) on East First Street and follow it to Maple Street, which is on the left (south) side of the road. Go south on Maple to East Chestnut Avenue; the rail trail starts at this intersection.

To reach the southern end point on East Adams Street, you can either follow Maple and then Rousselle Street south along the route to the

The Pacific Electric Bicycle Trail runs through a pleasant Santa Ana neighborhood.

southern end point, or go left 1 block to Orange Avenue, which also goes south all the way to East Adams Street.

There is parking along the streets at both end points.

Transportation: For transit information, call the Orange County Transportation Authority (OCTA) at (714) 636–RIDE (7433), or write OCTA, 550 South Main Street, P.O. Box 14184, Orange, CA 92863-1584. The Web site is www.octa.net. Transportation service information can also be obtained by calling (800) COMMUTE from the Los Angeles calling area. The Web site is www.mta.net.

Rentals: There are no rental shops along the route.

Contact: Ron Ono, Design Manager, Parks, Recreation and Community Services, City of Santa Ana, P.O. Box 1988, Santa Ana, CA 92702-1988; (714) 571–4200.

U ALTON AVENUE BIKE TRAIL

Running alongside an active Southern Pacific railroad line, this trail primarily serves the recreational needs of local residents, who can stretch their limbs on the route, and commuters, who can use it as an alternative to traveling by car through this section of Santa Ana. At its eastern end point, it links to the more scenic Pacific Electric Bicycle Trail (Trail T), described in the previous section.

Activities:

Location: City of Santa Ana, Orange County

Length: 1.8 miles one way

Surface: Asphalt

Wheelchair access: The entire length of the trail is wheelchair accessible.

Difficulty: Easy

Food: There are no restaurants, grocery stores, or picnic sites along the trail. There are, however, abundant gastronomic outlets in other areas of Santa Ana and neighboring cities.

Restrooms: There are no restrooms located at either trailhead or along the trail.

Seasons: The trail can be used year-round.

Access and parking: To access the trail from Interstate 405 in Santa Ana, take the South Bristol Street exit. Head north for 1.1 mile on South Bristol to Alton Avenue. You can turn right (east) on Alton Avenue and park along the street, or continue west along Alton Avenue to the Susan Street end point and start there.

Parking for this trail is limited. None is available at the Flower Street end point. There is limited parking along the street at the Susan Street end point and at points along the trail.

Transportation: For transit information, call the Orange County Transportation Authority (OCTA) at (714) 636–RIDE (7433), or write OCTA, 550 South Main Street, P.O. Box 14184, Orange, CA 92863-1584. The Web site is www.octa.net. For transit information in Los Angeles, call (800) COMMUTE or visit www.mta.net.

Rentals: There are no rentals available along the trail.

Contact: Paul Johnson, Senior Park Supervisor, City of Santa Ana, Park, Recreation and Community Services, P.O. Box 1988-M-23, Santa Ana, CA 92702-1988; (714) 571–4211.

V TUSTIN BRANCH TRAIL

The Tustin Branch Trail consists of three distinct sections, each link having its own unique feel. The Newport Avenue section is basically a glorified sidewalk, offering pleasant pedestrian access to local businesses. Along Esplanade Avenue the route is more suburban in nature, passing through a quiet residential neighborhood. The Wanda Road link also leads through a residential area, but with a busy four-lane road running alongside. All sections lie on the abandoned bed of the Pacific Electric Railway.

Activities:

Location: Tustin and Villa Park, Orange County

Length: 2.5 miles total, broken into three disconnected sections. The Newport Avenue section is 1 mile long, the Esplanade Avenue section is 1 mile long, and the Wanda Road section is 0.5 mile long.

Surface: Asphalt and crushed stone

Wheelchair access: The Newport Avenue and Wanda Road sections of the trail are paved and easily accessible to those using wheelchairs. The Esplanade Avenue section is nicely surfaced with crushed stone and may be passable for hardy wheelchair users.

Difficulty: Easy

Food: There is a variety of food outlets located along the Newport Avenue section of the trail. Both the Esplanade Avenue and Wanda Road sections are in residential areas and offer no trailside eateries, but the towns of Tustin and Villa Park host restaurants and grocery stores.

Restrooms: There are no public restrooms located along any of the sections of the trail.

Seasons: The trail can be used year-round.

Access and parking: To reach the Newport Avenue section of the trail from Interstate 5 in Tustin, take the Newport Avenue exit and head northeast on Newport Avenue. The trail runs along the northwest side of the road between El Camino Real and Irvine Boulevard.

To reach the Esplanade Avenue section of the trail, continue north on Newport Avenue to 17th Street, which is about 2.3 miles from I–5. Turn left (west) on 17th Street and go 0.6 mile to the Esplanade section of the rail trail, which parallels Esplanade Avenue on its east side.

To reach Wanda Road from I–5 in Tustin, take California 55 (the Costa Mesa Freeway) north through the city of Orange to the Katella Avenue exit. Go right (east) on East Katella Avenue to Wanda Road and turn left (south). The trail begins at Lincoln Street and goes south to East Collins Avenue.

There are no formal parking areas for any sections of the trail. However, there are parking lots for shopping centers along the Newport Avenue section of the trail. Limited on-street parking is available along Esplanade Avenue. There is no parking along Wanda Road.

The Esplanade Avenue section of the Tustin Branch Trail is bordered by a high fence overgrown with bougainvillea.

Transportation: For transit information, call the Orange County Transportation Authority (OCTA) at (714) 636–RIDE (7433), or write OCTA, 550 South Main Street, P.O. Box 14184, Orange, CA 92863-1584. The Web site is www.octa.net. Transit information for Los Angeles is available at (800) COMMUTE; the Web site is www.mta.net.

Rentals: There are no rentals available along this rail trail.

Contact: Trails Planner, Harbors, Beaches, and Parks, Public Facilities and Resources Department, County of Orange, P.O. Box 4048, Santa Ana, CA 92702-4048; (714) 834–3137.

W BUD TURNER TRAIL

The Bud Turner Trail is hitched to the Juanita Cooke Greenbelt (Trail 40) at pretty Laguna Lake Park, circling the northern edge of the lake and a riding ring for equestrians. When it departs the park and the former Red Car Line bed upon which it lies, it narrows to little more than a strip of dirt alongside a busy suburban thoroughfare.

Activities:

Location: City of Fullerton, Orange County

Length: 1.7 miles one way

Surface: Dirt

Wheelchair access: There is limited access for wheelchairs around the north and east shores of Laguna Lake.

Difficulty: Easy

Food: There are no restaurants or grocery stores along the trail, but if you pack a lunch, you can picnic by the lakeshore. Restaurants and grocery stores are abundant in Fullerton.

Restrooms: There are restrooms available near the dam at Laguna Lake Park.

Seasons: The trail can be used year-round, but it may be muddy during and immediately after rain.

Access and parking: To reach the Laguna Lake Park end point from California 91 (the Riverside Freeway) in Fullerton, take the Euclid Street exit and head north on Euclid Street for about 4 miles to Lakeview Drive. Turn right (east) on Lakeview Drive and go 0.5 mile to Hermosa Drive. Turn right (east) on Hermosa Drive and go 0.1 mile to Lakeside Drive; the northwest entrance to Laguna Lake Park is at this intersection. There is parking along the street. There is no parking or easy trail access at the Euclid and Bastanchury intersection.

Transportation: For transit information, call the Orange County Transportation Authority (OCTA) at (714) 636–RIDE (7433), or write OCTA, 550 South Main Street, P.O. Box 14184, Orange, CA 92863-1584. The Web site is www.octa.net. Los Angeles area transit information may be obtained at (800) COMMUTE or at www.mta.net.

Rentals: There are no rental shops located along the route.

Contact: Community Services Department, City of Fullerton, 303 West Commonwealth Avenue, Fullerton, CA 92832-1710; (714) 738–6575, www.ci.fullerton.ca.us.

ATCHISON, TOPEKA & SANTA FE TRAIL

The AT&SF Trail has surprising appeal for a route that runs adjacent to active railroad tracks and beneath massive power lines, adding a whole new dimension to the concept of "utility corridor." Also known as the Walnut Trail, it primarily serves local residents, offering a nice stretch of open space upon which to ride a bike, walk, or run. Two small parks bordering the rail trail allow neighbors to stretch out on the grass and let their children run free.

Activities:

Location: Irvine, Orange County

Length: 3 miles one way

Surface: Asphalt

Wheelchair access: The trail is wheelchair accessible.

Difficulty: Easy

Food: There are no restaurants or grocery stores located along the route, but if you pack a lunch or snack, you can picnic in Flagstone Park or Hoepner Park. You can find restaurants and grocery stores at other locations in the city of Irvine.

Restrooms: There are no restrooms along the trail.

Seasons: The trail can be used year-round.

Access and parking: To reach the Sand Canyon Avenue trailhead from Interstate 5, take the Sand Canyon Avenue exit. Go west on Sand Canyon Avenue for 0.5 mile, across the Orange County Transportation Authority (OCTA) Metrolink railroad tracks, to the rail trail, which is on the right (west) and is signed Walnut Trail. There is no parking at the Sand Canyon Avenue end point, but you might find on-street parking along Oak Canyon Road, which is about 100 yards west of the trail.

To reach the Harvard Avenue end point from I–5, take the Culver Drive exit. Take Culver Drive west for 0.5 mile to Walnut Avenue. Turn right (north) on Walnut and go 0.5 mile to Harvard Avenue. Go left (west) on Harvard

The AT&SF Trail winds along a greenbelt in Orange County.

for 0.5 mile, crossing the OCTA Metrolink tracks, to the trail, which is also signed Walnut Trail at this end point. There is limited on-street parking here and on nearby neighborhood streets.

Transportation: For transit information, call the Orange County Transportation Authority (OCTA) at (714) 636–RIDE (7433), or write OCTA, 550 South Main Street, P.O. Box 14184, Orange, CA 92863-1584. The Web site is www.octa.net. Transit information for Los Angeles is available at (800) COMMUTE; the Web site is www.mta.net.

Rentals: There are no rentals available along the trail.

Contact: Trails Planner, Harbors, Beaches, and Parks, Public Facilities and Resources Department, County of Orange, P.O. Box 4048, Santa Ana, CA 92702-4048; (714) 834–3137. The city of Irvine maintains the bikeway.

COASTAL RAIL TRAIL (OCEANSIDE/ CARLSBAD/SOLANA BEACH)

Efforts to create a rail trail that runs the length of California's scenic southern coastline involve the preservation and development of disconnected links like those in Oceanside, Carlsbad, and Solana Beach. These brief patches of rail trail will one day be part of a much larger whole—the 42-mile Coastal Rail Trail, which will run adjacent to the active tracks of the Los Angeles–San Diego rail corridor, used by Amtrak, Metrolink, and Coaster commuter trains. Meantime, the links in Oceanside, Carlsbad, and Solana Beach offer locals and visitors access to neighborhoods, businesses, and beaches, and a glimpse of what will come.

The section of trail in Oceanside, paved and double-wide, runs between the fenced-off active rail line and Myers Street, with modest homes on the ocean-side of the path. The Carlsbad link begins in a commercial district and ends among residences. The neat, well-landscaped Solana Beach rail trail follows the scenic Coast Highway through the oceanfront town.

Activities:

Location: Oceanside, Carlsbad, and Solana Beach in San Diego County

Length: 0.5 mile in Oceanside, 0.7 mile in Carlsbad, and 1.7 miles in Solana Beach. The Oceanside and Carlsbad sections can be linked by 1.5 miles of travel along historic U.S. Highway 101.

Surface: Asphalt, concrete

Wheelchair access: All sections of trail are wheelchair accessible.

Difficulty: Easy if each path is taken separately; hard if the Oceanside and Carlsbad sections are linked via the highway

Food: The Solana Beach trail segment offers easy access to eateries along the Coast Highway and to the markets of the Cedros Design District. The link through Carlsbad is near downtown restaurants and shopping. There is no water along the trail segments.

Restrooms: There are no restrooms along the Oceanside and Carlsbad links. Restrooms are available at the Solana Beach Amtrak station, just east of the tracks on Cedros Avenue.

Seasons: The trail can be used year-round

Access and parking: The section of trail in Oceanside runs from the intersection of Morse Street and South Myers Street to the intersection of Vista Way and Broadway. To reach the Morse/Myers intersection from the Coast Highway (US 101), turn west on Cassidy Street and follow it across the railroad tracks to Myers. Turn right on Myers and follow it to the trailhead, which is along the street above Buccaneer Park. There is on-street parking here.

To reach the northern end point of the trail section in Carlsbad from the Coast Highway, turn left (east) on Carlsbad Village Drive. Go a couple of blocks east to State Street; a public parking sign indicates a lot is to the right (south) on State Street. There is also a blue-and-gold Coastal Rail Trail sign. Oak Avenue and the trailhead are just south of the parking lot.

To reach the southern end point, continue down the Coast Highway to Tamarack Avenue and turn left (east) on Tamarack. There is no parking at the Tamarack end point.

Both the northern and southern trailheads for the Solana Beach link border US 101. There is no formal trailhead or parking at the northern end point, which borders Cardiff-by-the-Sea and the San Elijo Lagoon. A bike lane, however, leads along the highway to the beachfront north of the trailhead, where you'll find parking.

The southern end point is at Via de la Valle, at the border between Solana Beach and Del Mar. There is on-street parking available east on Via de la Valle, and on Cedros Avenue, which runs parallel to the rail trail on the east side of the active rail line. The Via de la Valle end point is 0.8 mile west of Interstate 5.

Transportation: The Metropolitan Transit System of San Diego provides a variety of transportation resources for San Diego County, including

Oceanside, Carlsbad, and Solana Beach. The MTS can be reached by dialing 511 (north county) or (619) 233–3004 (south county). You also can get information from the Web site at www.sdcommute.com.

There is a Metrolink station just north of the northern end point of the Carlsbad Coastal Rail Trail segment, north of Carlsbad Village Drive between State and Washington Streets.

The North County Transit District Web site is www.gonctd.com. The phone number is (760) 967–2001.

Rail transportation via Amtrak and the Coaster is available in Solana Beach; the Solana Beach Amtrak Station is at 105 South Cedros Avenue, Solana Beach, CA 92075, adjacent to the rail trail.

Rentals: There are no rentals available along the trail segments. However, shops are located in all three cities; consult the local telephone directories for more information.

Contact: For information on the Oceanside section of the trail, contact Nathan Mertz, Parks Development Coordinator for the Oceanside Public Works Department, 300 North Coast Highway, Oceanside, CA 92054; (760) 435–5619.

For more information on the Carlsbad portion of the trail, contact the City of Carlsbad Recreation Department at (760) 434–2826. The address is 1200 Carlsbad Village Drive, Carlsbad, CA 92008. City trail information is at ci.carlsbad.ca.us/trails. The Carlsbad Convention and Visitor Bureau is located in the old Santa Fe railroad depot at the corner of State Street and Carlsbad Village Drive. The address is 400 Carlsbad Village Drive, Carlsbad, CA 92008; the phone number is (760) 434–6093 or (800) CARLSBAD; the Web site is www.carlsbadca.org.

For more information on the Solana Beach link, contact the city of Solana Beach at 635 South US Highway 101, Solana Beach, CA 92075. The phone number is (858) 720–2400. The project manager, Dan Goldberg, can be reached at (858) 720–2470. More information about the trail is at www .ci.solana-beach.ca.us/contentpage.asp?ContentID=169.

Z | ROSE CANYON BICYCLE PATH

Tucked in scenic Rose Canyon, and wedged between Interstate 5 and the active Coaster railroad line, the Rose Canyon Bike Path is a brief but exhilarating rail trail. Views from the scrubby canyon are pleasant, of scrub-covered canyon walls and up the sycamore-lined stream that spills out of San Clemente Canyon. It is primarily a commuter route.

Activities: 🚶 🏃 🚴 🛼

Location: San Diego, San Diego County

Length: 1.3 miles one way

Surface: Asphalt

Wheelchair access: The trail is wheelchair accessible. Those using wheelchairs should use the southern access point at the end of Santa Fe Street.

Difficulty: Moderate

Food: There are no food outlets along the trail.

Restrooms: No restrooms are available along the trail.

Seasons: The trail can be used year-round.

Access and parking: To reach the southern end point on Santa Fe Street from northbound I–5 in San Diego, take the Balboa Avenue/Garnet Avenue exit. Head left (west) on Garnet Avenue to Mission Bay Drive and turn right (north). Follow Mission Bay Drive to Damon Avenue and turn right (east) on Damon. Follow Damon Avenue for 0.3 mile to Santa Fe Street and turn left (north). Follow Santa Fe Street north to its end in a cul-de-sac.

To reach the Santa Fe end point from southbound I–5, take the Balboa Avenue/Garnet Avenue exit. This puts you right on Mission Bay Drive. Turn left (east) onto Damon Avenue, then follow the directions above to reach the trailhead.

To reach the northern end point from either northbound or southbound I–5, take the La Jolla Colony exit. Go west on Gilman Drive for about 0.1

The Rose Canyon Bicycle Path parallels an active train track.

mile to a left-hand turn into the Park-and-Ride lot, which is on the left (south) side of Gilman Drive.

There is ample parking at both end points.

Transportation: The Metropolitan Transit System provides a variety of transportation services, as well as links to other transportation authorities and services throughout San Diego County. The MTS can be reached by dialing (800) 266–6883 (north county) or (619) 233–3004 (south county). You also can get information about San Diego transportation services via the Internet by visiting www.sandag.cog.ca.us/sdmts.

Rentals: There are no rentals available near the trail.

Contact: Joel Rizzo, Bike Coordinator, City of San Diego, 1010 Second Avenue, Suite 800 MS609, San Diego, CA 92101; (619) 533–3110. At www.ridelink.org you can follow the links to an excellent map of bike routes in San Diego, including Rose Canyon.

Index

About the Author

Tracy Salcedo-Chourré has written more than a dozen guidebooks to destinations in Colorado and California, including *Hiking Lassen Volcanic National Park, Exploring California's Missions and Presidios, Exploring Point Reyes National Seashore and the Golden Gate National Recreation Area* and the *Best Easy Day Hikes* guides to Denver, Boulder, Aspen, and Lake Tahoe, among others.

She is also an editor and newspaper columnist, works in her local public schools, and volunteers with her sons' soccer teams—and still finds time to hike, cycle, swim, and ski. She lives with her husband, three sons, and a small menagerie of pets in California's Wine Country.

You can learn more about her by visiting her Web page at the Falcon-Guides site, www.falcon.com/user/172. Her other guidebooks are available online through FalconGuides and The Globe Pequot Press, at various outdoor shops, and through local and national booksellers.